Language, Structure and Reproduction

Paul Atkinson

LANGUAGE, STRUCTURE and REPRODUCTION

An introduction to the sociology of Basil Bernstein

Methuen . London

First published in 1985 by
Methuen & Co. Ltd
11 New Fetter Lane,
London EC4P 4EE

Published in the USA by
Methuen & Co.
in association with Methuen, Inc.
29 West 35th Street,
New York, NY 10001

Photoset by
Rowland Phototypesetting Ltd
Bury St Edmunds, Suffolk

Printed in Great Britain by
Richard Clay (The Chaucer Press)
Ltd, Bungay, Suffolk

British Library
Cataloguing in
Publication Data

Atkinson, Paul
Language, structure, reproduction: an introduction to the sociology of Basil Bernstein.
1. Bernstein, Basil
2. Learning, Psychology of
3. Children, Language
I. Title
370.15'2 LB1139.L3
ISBN 0-416-35600-1
ISBN 0-416-35610-9 Pbk

This book is dedicated to my parents,
Margaret and Cyril Atkinson

Contents

Acknowledgements

For their support and encouragement in preparing this book I am grateful to Basil Bernstein and Brian Davies. They have both read and commented on draft versions. Sara Delamont has, as always, been the perfect supporter, colleague and critic. Deirdre Burton offered words of wisdom when they were most needed. If I have not always acted on the advice offered, that reflects my stubborn nature, not a lack of gratitude.

In preparing this book I have consulted a large number of sources, only a fraction of which appear in the text: the bibliographical work would not have been possible without the aid of a personal grant from the British Academy and the help of colleagues in the library at University College, Cardiff. In particular I should like to thank Hilary Calwell, Tom Dawkes, Andrew Green, Thelma Probert, Nancy Smith and Nick Smith.

Martin Read provided invaluable support in the preparation of various drafts of this book.

Finally, my thanks to all at Berni's for keeping body and soul together.

1 *Introduction to a split subject*

Basil Bernstein is, in one sense, an author who needs no 'introduction'. He is one of the best known and most influential of British sociologists. His work is known throughout the world by sociologists, linguists and educationalists. His writings have been widely reported, reproduced, anthologized and debated. His ideas have been the subject of interest and dispute for many years, and generations of students have been acquainted with at least some version of them. Bernstein's name appears time and time again in textbooks on education and language. Yet this wide dissemination provides the rationale for my own 'introduction' in this book. For, influential though Bernstein's work has been, its influence has often been quite contrary to the spirit of his own intentions. The debate and controversy surrounding his ideas have often been conducted on the basis of thoroughgoing misunderstandings of Bernstein. All too often, therefore, partial and inadequate interpretations of Bernstein are enshrined in the textbooks and other secondary sources, and it is often these misconceptions that are handed on as received wisdom to students and practitioners.

Further, Bernstein's work is often dealt with in the secondary literature in a fragmented way. The totality and coherence of his *oeuvre* is rarely, if ever, given adequate consideration. Bernstein is, of course, best known for his theoretical and empirical work on language, and the relationships between language, social class and educational attainment (though even this shorthand reference is misleading). This is the aspect of his output that has been most widely adapted, adopted or attacked by others. For many this is all that is known of Bernstein. Indeed, on occasions when I have mentioned the preparation of this book with colleagues, many have assumed that I was planning a book exclusively concerned with perspectives on language. For those who have been exposed to vulgarized and garbled versions of the work, 'Bernstein' may be all but synonymous with theories of 'linguistic deficit' as explanation of 'educational failure'. As we shall see, it was Bernstein's good fortune to become such a well-known and widely quoted author: it was his misfortune that such popularity was often founded upon misinterpretations and misrepresentations of his own position. Like many such figures, Bernstein found his fame (or notoriety) partly because his own original and complex ideas appeared to translate readily into catch-phrase and cliché.

As Sinclair Rogers has perceptively noted, there are 'apocryphal' Bernsteins: 'The religious fervour with which the work of Bernstein is associated has tended to lead to a generation of newly trained teachers with a veneration of his work hardly matched by their understanding of it' (1976, p.20). This apocryphal author has been responsible for the creation of one of the most potent myths of modern educational theory, constructing and confirming deeply held popular beliefs concerning social class, language and educability. Rogers again summarizes this apocryphal theory:

> There are WC [working class] and MC [middle class] children coming from their respective backgrounds. The WC children have restricted language, the MC children do not. Children are generally proficient in one 'language' only and are thus relatively unable to switch codes.
>
> School uses, society requires, the MC language so that WC children who cannot change their ways of speaking do less well at school and in society. This is self-evident. WC language also involves a different (shallower?) kind of thinking thus making it even more difficult for a WC child to be successful in a mainly MC world. (ibid., p.20)

This is certainly close to views of Bernstein on language held by teachers (cf. Gordon, 1978a, 1978b; Creber, 1972) and by academic critics (see Rosen, 1973 for an oft-cited example). It would be hard to discern behind such stereotypes the work of a sophisticated sociologist attempting to develop a complex argument concerning cultural transmission, the division of labour, changes in the moral order, power and discourse – indeed, the major themes of the sociological tradition.

While it is undeniable that Bernstein's work on language constitutes a major part of his total work, it is by no means the whole of it. It is the inspiration and foundation for a much more general and far-reaching programme of sociology. His other contributions – most notably on the social organization of school curricula – combine with the original focus on language *per se* to make up an impressively sustained and consistent treatment of major themes of sociological enquiry. Indeed, Bernstein's steady output of papers over the years has been quite remarkable for a single-minded preoccupation with the same set of themes. Those themes were established in essence quite early in Bernstein's career, and he has concerned himself with writing variations and elaborations on those themes. The work has progressed, the ideas have increased in complexity and generality, and the layers of interpretation have multiplied. But while the theory has become more dense, it has not departed from the original inspirations.

Unlike many other commentators, then, in this book I shall try to assess the whole of the work, and deal systematically with it in a cohesive manner. The emphasis throughout will be on Bernstein the sociologist; not just as a sociologist of language or sociologist of education; much less as a sociolinguist *manqué*, as many of his interpreters and detractors imply. In doing so I shall redress what I see as imbalances in former treatments of Bernstein, and provide a more appropriate conceptual framework for such an appreciation.

I shall propose a particular interpretation of Bernstein, and a good deal of this book will be devoted to outlining, justifying and commenting on that view. While introducing Bernstein's sociology to the reader, then, the book will simultaneously construct its own version of that sociology. It is a construction towards which Bernstein himself has expressed some sympathy, but it is my construction and not his. I shall not attempt to recapitulate all of Bernstein's formulations of his ideas, nor all of the empirical work he has been associated with. By the same token it will not consist of a series of 'translations' of Bernstein's papers into simpler, more everyday language, eked out with homespun examples and simple-minded prescriptions for policy and practice. This 'introduction' will not be a crib in that sense. Of course, I hope to help the reader to make sense of Bernstein, but comprehension must come through an appreciation of the complexities of his thought, not through oversimplification. This book aims to be comprehensive, in the sense that it gives due attention to all facets of Bernstein's work; it does not aim to be comprehensive in terms of offering a critical exegesis of every single one of his own publications, or those of his colleagues and collaborators, or those of his critics and commentators. The sheer volume of work which draws on and refers to Bernstein makes that quite impossible.[1]

This book is not a hagiography. My admiration of Bernstein is considerable, but it is by no means unreserved. In proposing a general framework for understanding Bernstein and his contribution to sociology, I am not thereby proposing it as an approach (much less the only approach) to sociology in general. I am not seeking sociological converts on Bernstein's behalf. And while attempting to shed light on his work, I am not preoccupied with portraying him in the best possible light. (I have no doubt, however, that despite this disclaimer my own intentions will be as open to misinterpretation and misrepresentation as Bernstein's have been.)

Like many other readers I first encountered Bernstein when I was an undergraduate. I came across his work while I was grappling with an optional course in linguistics as part of a degree in social anthropology. At the time I was by no means convinced of the detail of many of Bernstein's arguments. (In retrospect, I realize how thoroughly I had failed to grasp them anyway.) But at the same time I felt that whatever my reservations and problems of understanding, Bernstein was addressing something of profound significance. What was more, he seemed to be 'on to something' which related fundamentally to the dominant themes and perspectives of anthropology, as I understood the discipline then, and as I do now. I was dimly aware that I was dealing with ideas that went far beyond the specific topic of social class correlates of educational success and failure. The work I read hinted at much broader themes – of ritual and control, culture and experience, the division of labour and its reproduction. A sense of Bernstein's actual and potential importance remained with me, and when I had the opportunity I resolved to undertake doctoral work on a topic related to Bernstein's sociology of language. Various circumstances (the usual mixture of accidents and decisions) led me away from that resolve, but over the years I have retained a strong interest in and admiration for Bernstein's work, which has continued to develop since I first encountered it in the late 1960s.

Having for years mulled over my response to Bernstein's original and provocative ideas, and having taught aspects of his work to successive cohorts of sociology students, I decided to essay a brief paper on what I saw as the most apposite approach to Bernstein's sociology (Atkinson, 1981). That paper received a good deal of sympathetic response, which prompted me to try to develop it at greater length. One short essay was quite insufficient to do justice to the many facets and ramifications of Bernstein's thought. Hence this book, where I hope to do them greater justice, although I am all too aware that much of the work demands even more extensive treatment.

In that original paper I outlined a view which is the recurring motif for this book. I suggested that Bernstein is to be seen as one of the very few original British contributors to the tradition of thought in the 'human sciences' known as *structuralism*. This view is developed in the chapters that follow, as will be some of the actual and potential links between Bernstein and other protagonists in the structuralist movement. He is too often portrayed as an idiosyncratic figure, staking a solitary claim to his chosen field. It is true that his style of thought is not one which has been at all characteristic of British traditions in the social sciences (although it is perhaps significant for my own interests that structuralism did take root in some sectors of British social anthropology, and was developed by some of its leading British figures). On the other hand, Bernstein's preoccupations and his distinctive treatment of them are quite in keeping with the spirit of European structuralism.

The structuralist movement has gained considerable currency in various quarters in the social sciences and humanities, and its influence has been felt in the development of so-called 'post-structuralist' thought – most notably in theories of literary criticism. In presenting my appreciation of Bernstein I shall necessarily touch on several aspects of structuralist thought – or at least some of its preoccupations and leading figures. I shall have neither the space, capacity nor inclination to develop an exhaustive account of structuralism as such. I shall be content to indicate how its concerns are those of Bernstein too, and that the conceptual frameworks and problematics furnish the key to much of Bernstein's own sociological enterprise.[2]

The reader may wonder why such an exercise be thought necessary. Why should it be useful or important to provide a framework for understanding Bernstein at all? Surely, it might be objected, he is quite capable of doing that for himself. Of course, in one sense he is, and he has done so on several occasions. On the other hand, while Bernstein has on numerous occasions provided statements of his current thinking, and the Introductions to the three volumes of *Class, Codes and Control* – referred to hereafter as *CCC*, vols 1 to 3 – as well as the retrospective 'Postscript' to the first of those provide retrospective views, he has never produced a single synoptic view of his work as a whole. That in itself would present little problem were it not for the fact that many of his readers profess to find his ideas difficult, obscure and elusive. And a thorough appreciation of Bernstein's work – as opposed to one or other of the vulgarized versions – does require the reader to grapple with some rather abstruse and slippery notions.

There are accessible secondary sources, but for the most part they deal with partial and restricted readings of Bernstein's publications. Most notably, a good deal of the commentary and critique concentrates on Bernstein as a student of language: there has been a consistent tendency to treat him as a sociolinguist – often as a sociolinguist *manqué*. There is no doubt good reason for such partial readings. Bernstein's preoccupation with language has been an abiding theme. The early and middle periods of his career to date were marked by widespread dissemination and discussion of his work on language. For many readers, therefore, Bernstein was, and remains, an author who writes about 'language'. Since his research and language became involved in a highly contentious area of debate in educational theory and practice, that side to his sociology has always received particular attention. This is, regrettably, reflected in the recent survey of 'recent' British sociology by Eldridge (1980): the discussion of Bernstein is anything but recent. But Eldridge is by no means alone in these failings.

While language is central, on the other hand, that does not make Bernstein a sociolinguist *tout court*. Language is but one of the substantive topics with which he has dealt, and while it is central to the entire analytic programme, it does not exhaust it. In itself, language is not *the* theme or substance. Rather, as I hope to demonstrate in the remainder of this book, language is but one aspect of a much more general, and fundamental, concern. Underlying the treatment of language (and the more general sociology of schooling) is Bernstein's working and re-working of major recurrent themes of sociological theory. These themes comprise a sociology which goes well beyond the confines even of the 'sociology of education' as it is conventionally portrayed. The scope and generality of Bernstein's perspective is amply demonstrated in one of his most recent papers (Bernstein, 1981), where the structuralism is also most readily apparent. This summary statement of Bernstein's theories reveals them to be concerned with a general theory of structuration and reproduction.

Again, it is the case that Bernstein has normally been treated within the confines of that branch of empirical sociology. That is not in itself surprising: the substantive occasion of his writing has normally been of direct relevance to socialization and schooling. It would, however, be misleading to assume that Bernstein is so easily confined to that empirical field, however broad and important its subject matter. It is a matter of regret that we all too readily compartmentalize our intellectual domains in that way (a topic we shall have to return to, in a different guise, later), so that authors like Bernstein are pigeon-holed. The generality of his work, as well as its internal coherence and continuity, is thus lost to view: now he is seen as a sociolinguist, now as a theorist of curriculum and school organization, now as a critic of educational policy and practice. Rarely is he seen as one of the most original and creative of modern British sociologists – a reputation I believe he richly deserves.

Bernstein, then, is continually working the same themes into intricate patterns and motifs. Unfortunately for the general reader this work rarely – if ever – quite takes on the appearance of completion. Often the fabric turns out to be the labour of a Penelope: the threads are undone only to be re-worked into ever more intricate designs. Sometimes the patterns that Bernstein weaves become so intricate that the original figures are all but lost to view: like an ornate Saxon design, the elements are elaborated and turned back on themselves. It is as if the formal design takes over, and becomes almost as valued as the original representation. Bernstein has on occasion offered his reader programmatic statements of a particular stage of his thinking, but has never seemed altogether at ease with the task of explaining, simplifying or justifying his train of thought. (I refer here to published work: I do not include the courses of lectures delivered at the Institute of Education, London.) Nor has he himself made a sustained attempt to display the relationships between his own work and that of other authors or traditions of sociological thought, other than Durkheim, Marx and Mead, acknowledged sources of inspiration. This is not in itself a weakness on Bernstein's part, but it has not aided the sympathetic treatment of his thought by commentators, teachers and students.

The apparent lack of 'closure' is in many ways indicative of the strength and fecundity of Bernstein's enterprise. He himself has declared that he is more interested in the heuristic and dynamic value of his ideas than in their specification in anything resembling a definitive or final version. It does mean that the reader must be alert to the fact that Bernstein's work has never been static. While there has been considerable continuity in terms of themes and theories, there has always been a continuous process of change, development and modification. I do my best to display this, but I am not concerned with the detailed rehearsal of the development of particular ideas. Indeed, I have avoided a chronological presentation of the work. This is a deliberate ploy in an attempt to break with the received wisdom. The reader should therefore be aware that my attempted characterization of Bernstein's various positions cannot possibly do justice to the process of development, and the nuances of the different versions he has essayed. Furthermore, the space available in this brief introduction means that I have recapitulated one weakness of other secondary literature, in that the empirical work conducted under Bernstein's direction at the Sociological Research Unit in the

Institute of Education has not been dealt with systematically. For references to this body of literature, see the bibliographical note on Bernstein and the SRU on page 187.

It might be objected that no book of this sort is necessary, since Bernstein's work is 'old hat'. Some colleagues with whom I have discussed the preparation of this book have indeed voiced some such view. (Though, interestingly, they have almost without exception assumed that I was to be concerned only with the theme of language.) On the other hand, there are plentiful indications that the work is indeed of current interest. While it is not in itself a guarantee, a search of the relevant citations and abstracts indexes demonstrates that numerous authors have drawn and continue to draw on Bernstein's ideas. The same is indicated by a perusal of relevant textbooks – especially in the sociology of education. Bernstein remains a dominant figure. Moreover, he himself continues to produce original work. Any perception that Bernstein is 'played out' reflects on the perceiver rather than on the currency and status of Bernstein himself.

I have not attempted a systematic review of the empirical evidence for and against theories of socialization, class or ethnicity, linguistic development, cognitive abilities and educational attainment. Again, the literature here is vast, but it is not for that reason alone that it is under-played here. This reflects my intention to concentrate on Bernstein's general sociological framework rather than the detailed analysis of language use in different social contexts by members of different social categories and classes. The cost of this is that detailed empirical research evidence for and against Bernstein's views is absent here, and a comprehensive review of that material is yet to be written. I hope that in the end my rationale will become clear in the course of the book itself, but some preliminary remarks are in order.

For many people who are directly or indirectly acquainted with Bernstein, his name is associated entirely with the debates concerning 'linguistic deficit' as an explanation for the relative educational failure of lower-class and ethnic minority pupils. His theory of language – the identification of 'elaborated' and 'restricted' codes – was a major feature of highly contentious disputes in academic circles. The work was taken up with enthusiasm in many quarters, and was equally the object of attack and supposed refutation.

Bernstein suffered that rather particular fate, of generating a potent idea which was almost too 'successful' in the market-place of ideas. His insights were melted down into a debased coinage of platitude and cliché. Semi-scholars of all persuasions seized upon Bernstein and assimilated his ideas to support or detract from existing theories, prejudices, policies and programmes. Bernstein himself has ruefully noted the contrasting reactions he experienced:

> To begin with, the left wing saw the work as another powerful indictment of the class system. In the end, the left wing, especially the new left, saw the work as yet another stereotype of the working class from a middle-class perspective. . . . The right wing, on the other hand, felt I had given some justification to the curious idea that 'high culture' was not for the working class, or that the thesis offered an approach to their assimilation into the existing middle class. Both left wing and right wing were convinced that the basic model was that of deficit. (1974a, *CCC* 1, pp.18–19)

The language theories and their empirical research became widely diffused in Britain, North America and the rest of the world (though often in second-hand versions). The use of Bernstein as a 'taken-for-granted reference' in textbooks and research reports on child development, educational attainment, sociolinguistics and the like fostered an uncritical reception of some versions of the work, and critical – but equally poorly informed – rebuttals. The language theories receive some attention, as does their reception in some quarters. It would be unduly perverse to ignore them altogether. Chapter 6 in particular is devoted to a discussion of Bernstein and the linguists. There the purpose is not to attempt a comprehensive review of Bernstein's critics and champions. Rather, selected reference is made to some of the best-known and contentious issues to serve as a counterpoint to the *sociology*, and to highlight how sympathetic readers among the linguists have themselves appreciated the nature of his structuralist semiotics. But for reasons I hope to make clear, an undue emphasis upon the 'linguistic' strand of the work is likely to recapitulate major misunderstandings of the work as a whole.

Indeed, in the course of preparing this book I have been tempted on more than one occasion to go to the other extreme, and argue that the language theme is all but irrelevant to the main thrust of the sociology. In the event I have not gone that far. It would be absurd to do so: language, though perhaps not linguistics, is a key component of Bernstein's sociology and is central to the structuralist tradition in which he is located. In any event, it is vitally important to go well beyond the debates concerning language 'deficit' and 'difference' in the context of educability. There are several relevant secondary sources and the reader will be referred to them, although it must always be borne in mind that this secondary literature is very patchy in quality.

This is not intended to be a 'life and works' sort of introduction, and the biographical is kept to an absolute minimum. Bernstein himself has drawn attention to the intersections of his own career, his experience of socialization and the sources of his theory, in the introductory essays to the volumes of collected papers (*Class, Codes and Control*).

Some of his earliest experiences reported there project many of the themes of his later sociology. After the Second World War, before he went up to the London School of Economics, Bernstein was a resident worker in the Bernhard Baron Settlement, in Stepney, where he was involved in running boys' clubs, and was also introduced to family casework. As he himself acknowledges: 'This experience in more ways than one had a deep influence upon my life. It focused and made explicit an interest I always seemed to have had in the structure and process of cultural transmission' (1974a, p.2).

There was, for example, 'discontinuity and sometimes conflict' between senior staff and the club members. In part these discontinuities were centred on religious values. The Settlement drew on Reform Judaism, while the community it served was Orthodox.

> Thus the Settlement introduced me to the interrelationships between social class and religious belief within the context of an apparently distinct and homogeneous cultural group. I was both fascinated and disturbed by the *process* of transmission of the Settlement's values and standards of conduct. (1974a, *CCC* 1, p.3, emphasis in original)

In this Bernstein would be by no means the first social theorist to have drawn on his experience of Jewish identity. The experience of being simultaneously 'insider' and 'outsider', 'member' and 'stranger' is one which has often nurtured the sensibilities of scholars in the human disciplines. It gives rise to the heightened perception of symbolic boundaries and membranes which create the universe of the 'we' relationships of inclusion and exclusion; and, as Bernstein indicates in his autobiographical remarks, it makes one sensitive to the lines of internal stress and cleavage.

The *transmission* (or not) of values between generations, the monitoring and *control* of conduct, the symbolic partition of the *sacred* from the *profane*, and the *ritualization* of everyday matters: these are the content of such early experiences, and they recur as themes in Bernstein's sociology. The role of personal experience in the genesis and elaboration of sociological theory is not something we are always conscious of. Yet its influences can be profound. In Bernstein's case, it is something which in part he has brought to consciousness, and those biographical features go some way to explaining his repeated return to those selfsame themes.

This aspect of the biography is well known, as is the other which Bernstein himself recounts. After graduation and teacher-training, he worked at the City Day College from 1954 to 1960. He has written about his experiences with day-release students from the Post Office and other industries. Here again we encounter problems of 'discontinuity', heightened perhaps by the irony of attempting to teach on the topic of the internal combustion engine while being unable to drive and ignorant of the workings of cars.

It was during this period that Bernstein became interested in specific aspects of the symbolic order. Writing of his exploratory teaching of poetry, he tells us that

> we experimented, putting together often weird or bizarre, sometimes unexpectedly beautiful series of lines, and exploring the symbolic nature of the space. I became fascinated by condensation; by the implicit. In my teaching I covered a range of contents and contexts, and yet, despite the variations, I felt that here was a speech form predicated upon the implicit. (1974, p.6)

This practical experience of educational work, with its implications of class differences, the exploration of domains of condensed and implicit orders of meaning, and the problematic status of educational contents (curriculum) provided further grist to Bernstein's imaginative mill. To these ingredients add the observation that the young workers had failed in, or had been failed by, the system of formal, compulsory education.

Bernstein's early academic career coincided with a number of other major British sociologists who were educated at the LSE after the war and turned their attention to education and social inequality. Halsey (1982) has written about that generation of post-war sociology students at the LSE who had become part of the academic 'establishment' by the mid-1960s. He describes their academic and personal concerns primarily in terms of British provincialism and their proletarian or 'marginal' origins: 'All, as Wyndham Lewis would have put it in those days, were "branded on the tongue". Short of strenuously sustained efforts of elocution their class and province would henceforth claim ownership of them' (p.154).

It is tempting to attribute Bernstein's sensitivity to language and cultural reproduction to such markers of social class and caste. This would be congruent with Karabel and Halsey's suggestion that Bernstein's distinctive contribution derives from such a particularly British experience of class and its manifestations:

> Indeed, it is difficult to imagine that a series of explorations as bold and innovative as Bernstein's studies in the sociology of language could have developed in a society lacking the sharpness of British class relations and the overtones of the accompanying linguistic distinctions. (Karabel and Halsey, 1977, p.63, n.84)

Karabel and Halsey in fact suggest that the work is so very British that it is an 'open question' whether Bernstein's work could be generalized to other industrial societies or whether it reflects only the 'peculiarities of British society'.

Any such emphases on the 'Britishness' of Bernstein are only partly justified, however. While Bernstein's preoccupations and perspectives may have *derived* from such biographical and intellectual sources, it is quite misleading to attribute to him the same provincialism and allegiance to the British Labour movement Halsey himself has celebrated autobiographically in the Reith lectures (Halsey, 1978). Far from remaining constrained within the sort of blinkered tradition described by Anderson (1969) as typical of the social sciences in Britain, Bernstein has consistently looked towards European – especially French – theoretical positions. He has drawn inspiration not from British provincialism but from French structuralism; it is that which provides the counterpoint to Marx rather than British Fabianism. The sociology has also been taken up by scholars from many other countries, and expressed in many languages: Karabel and Halsey are quite wrong to imply that it is of local interest only. Its generalizability is not an 'open question'; the ideas are contested, but that is quite a different matter.[3]

Bernstein's thinking was influenced profoundly by his acquaintance with various philosophical and anthropological authors on language and symbolism – including Cassirer and Whorf. To this was added the work of the Russian psychologists Vygotsky and Luria. These provided a general framework on the regulative and constitutive nature of linguistic categories. These were combined with his absorption with the sociology of Durkheim, in providing the foundations for a neo-Kantian concern with the cultural and linguistic frameworks that shape and regulate our experience of the world, and the transmission of such experience through symbolic forms.

The specifically linguistic thrust was deepened by a two-year stay in the Department of Phonetics at University College, London. There the work of Frieda Goldman-Eisler made a considerable impact, and it was at this stage, in the early 1960s, that the distinctive papers on language, perception and social class were first formulated in any detail. They were preceded by the earliest pieces, published in 1959 and 1960. Had Bernstein's ideas found more enthusiastic support among his fellow sociologists, and had the support from the linguists not been forthcoming, the whole shape of his subsequent work would doubtless have been considerably different. There is equally no doubt, however, that the main themes had already been established implicitly before Bernstein undertook formal 'research' among the phoneticians.

The consolidation and development of the research was established from 1963, with the foundation of the Sociological Research Unit at the London University Institute of Education, to which Bernstein was appointed Senior Lecturer in the Sociology of Education. Throughout the rest of the 1960s the SRU under Bernstein's direction undertook major research projects relating to his general theory, while Bernstein himself continued to publish papers which developed the conceptual apparatus of his work. I do not attempt the massive task of exposition and critique of all the empirical research projects that were done, much of which appeared in the series of monographs 'Primary Socialization, Language and Education' (see the bibliographical note on page 184). I shall, however, attempt to refer to them as they relate to the particular sociological arguments outlined. It is noticeable that many of the secondary sources expressing criticism of Bernstein tend to neglect the scope of those empirical research projects, and hence to overlook the dialectic between theory and research in the development of the sociology. For while the main themes are derivable from the theoretical and biographical antecedents, I do not intend to convey the impression that his ideas sprang fully armed from a programme of theory and introspection.

As indicated already, the research on language is by no means the whole story, and more general work on the sociology of schools, with special reference to the sociology of school knowledge, emerged from the early 1960s onwards. There was no 'epistemological break': the various strands were logically interrelated and they progressed *pari passu*. Introducing the third volume of collected papers, the author remarks on the relative neglect of these later themes: 'Much of the criticism of the sociolinguistic thesis fails to take into account the essays in this book. Yet it is the case that the series started *at the same time* as the major SRU research in 1964' (1977a, p. 1; emphasis in original). Indeed, as he goes on to remark, the 'sociolinguistic' work featured little in his courses of lectures at the Institute; these were devoted to the more overtly sociological themes of his 'theory of educational transmissions'.

The work is marked by a high degree of internal coherence, in terms of themes and treatments. It has also been marked by considerable change and development, and the entire series of essays provides an unusually clear insight into the growth of one sociologist's thinking over the years.

It is possible to identify a number of stages or phases in that process of growth. The following brief summary of those phases is intended as no more than a rough-and-ready guide to the relative chronology; it does not suggest any special theoretical or methodological shifts and boundaries. I have also indicated some of the papers which are key benchmarks in the corpus. A much more extensive bibliography of Bernstein's papers is to be found at the end of the book. A comprehensive listing of all the publications is a daunting task. Some papers appear in different versions in different places, while others have been reprinted and anthologized on numerous occasions. I have not made a sustained attempt to list every single location.

Likewise, no attempt is made to review and comment on each and every one of the publications. Although at times I follow a chronological approach, at other points I abandon that. I am not intent on documenting all the minor variations between the various publications. Even some apparently major discrepancies are played down in my account. Whereas much of the secondary literature dwells on inconsistencies, I find myself more keen to alert the reader – especially the reader who is new to Bernstein – to those fundamental issues which have continued to exercise his imagination. It may be that in doing so I have been unduly charitable. If that is so, then I can plead that there are plenty of less charitable authors all too eager to proclaim the fallibility and incoherence of Bernstein. Any creative author struggling to find a voice for complex and often elusive ideas is likely to be guilty of inconsistency. Indeed, it takes a fairly pusillanimous interpreter to view such inconsistency as a matter of 'guilt' at all.

It is unfortunately the case that misleadingly crude and mistaken views on Bernstein are still held by teachers, students and practitioners in education, health occupations and similar fields. Often enough in thoroughly well-meaning ways, they draw on taken-for-granted stereotypical views in order to account for 'inequalities' in education, problems in 'communication' between professionals and clients, and so on.

It is therefore Bernstein's fate to have become a 'split subject' in the discourse of linguistics and education. In addition to the historical author of the papers, lectures and seminars, there is a

Bernstein's sociology: a relative chronology

Language	*Schools and Knowledge Transmission*	*Key/Illustrative Papers*
Earliest papers on language, perception and social class. First formulation of 'public' and 'formal' language.		'A public language: some sociological implications of a linguistic form', 1959
Reformation in terms of 'codes': empirical specification of linguistic realization of codes.	Early papers on changes in the moral order, pupil involvement and ritual in schools.	'Linguistic codes, hesitation phenomena and intelligence', 1962
		'Open schools – open society?', 1967
Establishment of Sociological Research Unit.		
	Transitional paper on the curriculum.	'On the curriculum', 1969
Research projects on various aspects of the theory: uses of language in primary socialization; social control in school, and in mother–child interaction.		'Social class differences in the relevance of language to socialization', 1969
	Major papers on curriculum and pedagogy.	'On the classification and framing of educational knowledge', 1971
		'Class and pedagogies: visible and invisible', 1975
	Most recent papers on codes, modalities and pedagogic discourse.	'Codes, modalities and the process of cultural reproduction – a model', 1981

doppel-gänger. This mythological figure is the imputed author of diverse theories and pronouncements; these latter are all more or less transformed versions of the originals, as they have entered into the discourse of textbooks, bibliographies and so on. These versions and the Bernstein they imply are then invoked as mythological charters or demons. The mythical 'Bernstein' has thus become a straw man, or a token in the complex ploys and counterploys of academic squabbling, and ideological disputation.

We need, then, to take stock of Bernstein's contributions to sociology in an attempt to rescue the work from the accretions of repeated readings and misreadings. To that end, therefore, a good deal of what follows will consist of exposition. I hope to go some way towards 'setting the record straight' as to what is and what is not contained within Bernstein. If I do not review all the authors and positions critical of Bernstein, that is not a reflection of unconscious bias on my part; or at least it is not only that. Rather, it reflects my main desire to establish the main elements and continuities in the sociology itself. For readers who are already thoroughly familiar with Bernstein's output some of this exercise may seem tedious. I apologize to them and hope that they may nevertheless find something fresh here. For those as yet unacquainted with Bernstein, I hope to provide an accessible introduction and to persuade them of the fascination and fecundity of his sociology. We are not constrained to agree with each and every aspect of his work in order to appreciate its scope and complexity.

Notes

1 This can be illustrated from the on-line search of citations I commissioned in preparing this book. Even when allowance is made for some rogue references to other authors (including composer–conductors and investigative journalists) the search threw up well over 1000 journal citations. I do not pretend to have consulted them all. The bibliographical work was supported by a personal grant from the British Academy. Annotated bibliographies and research notes deriving from this project will become available as working papers of the Sociological Research Unit, Department of Sociology, University College, Cardiff.

2 The structuralism of Bernstein has recently been incorporated into textbooks. In one (Gibson, 1984) the author rightly sees him as a major figure in that tradition – indeed he is the only author dealt with at any length. In the other (Sarup, 1983) Bernstein is dealt with in a cursory and strangely dismissive fashion. Neither author is sympathetic to Bernstein's structuralism or interested in demonstrating its links with the broader sociological tradition.

3 One of the notable things is the extent to which debate, exploration and exemplification of Bernstein's notions of language are to be found in different cultures and languages. It is by no means the case that there is agreement as to the theories and the relevant evidence, any more than there has been in Britain. It is, however, striking that Bernstein's theories, or versions of them, are 'thinkable' in many national contexts. In addition to the extensive literature in Britain and North America, relevant studies and interpretations or critiques have been produced in: France (e.g. Cherkaoui, 1974; Bisseret, 1975; Esperet, 1976; Marcellesi, 1976); Germany (e.g. Ebel, 1972; Hess-Luttich, 1974; Klann, 1975; Quasthoff, 1975; Bertram, 1977; Schmidt, Lamm and Trommsdorff, 1978; Schlumbohm, 1979); Poland (e.g. Kloskowska, 1973; Bokszanski, 1978; Borzym, 1981); Hungary (e.g. Pap and Pleh, 1972, 1974); Holland (e.g. Hagen, 1976); Belgium (e.g. Van den Broek, 1977); Norway (e.g. Nafstad and Blakar, 1975; Nafstad, 1977); Israel (e.g. Peleg and Adler, 1977; Weller and Levi, 1981; Cais, 1982); Chile (e.g. Brunner, 1978); Brazil (e.g. Grinberglewin, 1979); Japan (e.g. Nakano, 1974); Australia (e.g. Poole, 1976, 1977, 1978a, 1978b, 1979a, 1979b; Evans and Poole, 1975; Robinson, 1978).

Bernstein's theories of educational knowledge and cultural transmission have likewise been widely taken up. His sociology is far more cosmopolitan than Karabel and Halsey's 'local' emphasis would suggest.

2 *A structuralist anthropology of schooling*

A conventional starting point for most discussions of Bernstein's work is the earliest formulation of his theories concerning language: these, equally conventionally, are treated as accounts of 'educability' and differential success in the school system on the part of contrasting social classes or ethnic groups. The theories are thus assimilated to the abiding preoccupations of British educational research and practice, on the effects of early socialization, class membership and life chances; they are equally assimilable to American concerns with cultural pluralism. That approach, while preserving some of the chronological features of Bernstein's emerging perspectives, has its dangers. It invites the trap of assigning priority to the language research, while treating the rest of the sociology as subsidiary to or derivative from it. Bernstein himself has protested against such a view, which does violence to the overall unity and true chronology of his undertaking. Introducing the collected papers on 'educational transmissions' (1977a, pp. 1 ff.), he complains that much of the criticism of the sociology of language fails to take account of his papers on schools and school knowledge (grouped as 'changes in the moral basis of schools' and 'changes in the coding of educational transmissions'). Yet, as he points out, the major research in both areas started simultaneously, in 1964.

I begin, therefore, not with 'language', but with an account of Bernstein's observations on rituals of schooling and the 'moral basis' of schools as institutions and agencies of cultural transmission. Quantitatively, the papers I begin with do not comprise a major part of the corpus. Indeed, Bernstein is somewhat apologetic about them, describing the analyses contained in them as 'no more than sketches', and admitting to being 'acutely conscious of how slight are the early pieces' (1977a, p. 3). Yet they raise and exemplify – albeit in embryo form – the main themes and approaches of all the other papers. Moreover, they do so in ways which allow us to focus quite specifically on Bernstein's *sociological* approach. (Bernstein's own introduction to these papers in volume 3 of *Class, Codes and Control* is illuminating of the sociological inspirations and conceptual links.) Initially, therefore, attention to these papers removes the blinkers imposed by an unduly restricted or selective perspective – from the standpoint of sociolinguistics, curriculum theory or whatever. We can concentrate on the sociology itself. Having done so, we shall then be much better placed to return to the major substantive areas of Bernstein's interest, and examine them from an informed point of view.

Bernstein's comments on schooling represent an embryonic anthropology of schools as agencies of reproduction. Here, as ever, Bernstein's inspiration stems primarily from the Durkheimian tradition. Indeed, Bernstein himself has repeatedly acknowledged the profundity of that influence: 'I have yet to find *any* social theorist whose ideas are such a source (at least to me) of understanding of what the term *social* entails' (1977a, p. 17). His is not a slavish copying of Durkheim; as Macrae writes (1974) in introducing the first volume of *Class, Codes and Control*, 'its concerns, but not its procedures, are Durkheimian' (p. xiv). Bernstein's sociology is thus Durkheimian in spirit, and draws on many of Durkheim's themes, but is by no means a literal reworking. In his own autobiographical notes, Bernstein has outlined the early impact of Durkheim on his development as a sociologist. Writing of his undergraduate studies at the LSE he tells us:

> I read Durkheim and although I did not understand him it all seemed to happen. I did not care that he was a naughty functionalist with an over-socialized concept of man, that he neglected the institutional structure and the sub-strata of con-

> flicting interests, that his model of man contained only two terms, beliefs and sentiments. In a curious way I did not care too much about the success of his various analyses. It was about the social bond and the structuring of experience. (1974a, p. 3)

This brief comment is, incidentally, revealing of more than the influence of Durkheim *per se*. It also illustrates how Bernstein has been concerned primarily with the heuristic value and inspiration that ideas afford, rather than with the orthodoxies of theoretical exegesis.

This is, of course, not the only source of Bernstein's ideas: among many others, Marx and Mead are selected from the progenitors of sociology for special mention, and among contemporary colleagues, the linguistics of Halliday and the anthropology of Mary Douglas have been major inputs. Their contributions will be explored later. Yet Durkheim is clearly the 'true north' to which his thought is aligned, and to which it naturally returns.

In this trilogy of papers (1966a; 1967a; Bernstein, Elvin and Peters, 1966) Bernstein is, as he himself expresses it, concerned with changes in the moral order of schools as institutions and as transmitters of systems of meaning, value and instrumentality. A number of features of these papers is characteristic of the vast majority of Bernstein's publications, and it may be as well to alert the reader to them at the outset.

In the first place, the papers are expressed at a high level of generality and abstraction. The detailed contents of institutions are glossed over. The day-to-day running of any particular school or classroom is a part of Bernstein's own taken-for-granted background, and the reader is left likewise to fill in such empirical content for him or herself. Such concrete detail that is offered appears in the guise of brief exemplification – often, indeed, in the form of a 'throw-away' line.

Secondly, the *forms* which Bernstein documents can be realized, empirically, in diverse ways. Bernstein attempts to generate a model of sufficient generality to apply to (say) all secondary state schools. Ultimately, in fact, applicability to all education or socialization agencies is aimed at. But this is not meant to imply that the model is intended to serve as a description of any single institution: nor does it imply that the concrete manifestations in all such institutions will have the same appearance. One can, for example, talk of 'rituals' of social control without believing that all such rituals are identical, even though they may conform to the same general pattern.

Thirdly, a good deal of the argument is expressed in terms of apparently probabilistic propositions. That is, Bernstein is happy to express himself suggesting 'tendencies' and 'likelihoods'. He does not formulate models which precisely predict under what circumstances events or changes *will* arise. He often is to be found saying that such-and-such 'may' be the case, or 'may' arise in response to changing circumstances. This too is thoroughly characteristic of his more general style. Although more tightly formulated propositions and hypotheses are often derivable from such statements, Bernstein is as often as not content to leave his own argument suggestive rather than definitive: this can give rise to irritation, incomprehension and frustration on the part of commentators. And, in fairness to at least some of the detractors, it sometimes proves difficult to establish what empirically testable (in the widest sense) propositions might actually follow. Some of the statements are so gnomic that they all but defy further exploration or exemplification.

These general features of the papers should not be treated as major stumbling-blocks, however. A more sympathetic and constructive starting-point is to see them as reflections of Bernstein's enthusiasm for *generating* theory, and correspondingly less interest in the detailed operationalization and testing of all its aspects. This should not be overstated, however: the Sociological Research Unit, under his direction, conducted a good deal of empirical work on implications of the theoretical programme.

In Bernstein's own spirit, then, let us examine the general features of his papers on the moral order of the school, rather than subjecting them to line-by-line scrutiny. Along the way we shall be able to digress to amplify on theoretical antecedents and links.

In essence, the papers outline the basis for profound changes in the organizational and sentimental order of the contemporary school. Whether or not they document widespread changes in actual day-to-day conduct of schools and classrooms, they attempt to summarize and characterize substantial shifts in ideologies and belief-systems relating to the proper nature of schooling – its patterns of social relations and the organization of its contents. They also suggest formal analytic tools for the analysis of staff and pupil roles or identities within such changing institutions.

The papers – 'Open schools – open society?' (1967a, *CCC* 3) in particular – are informed by a Durkheimian focus on changes in the basis of the social order. They draw primarily on the distinction between mechanical and organic solidarity. This distinction is fundamental equally to Durkheim's and to Bernstein's views on the division of labour and its corresponding effect on social institutions and individual persons. While familiar enough territory, the Durkheimian background is so fundamental that it must be sketched in here.

The distinction in Durkheim is based upon a model of social complexity and differentiation. Mechanical solidarity is said to characterize a society where there is a high degree of uniformity and consensus. Values and sentiments are shared and adhered to. Solidarity in such a context rests upon the association between functionally equivalent social units. Organic solidarity, on the other hand, is the outcome of diversity. Characteristic, for instance, of modern industrial society is the increasing specialization of functions embodied in the division of labour. Solidarity thus rests on the complementary distribution of social functions, and thus upon the functional interdependence of its constituent units. Under conditions of a highly specific, complex and diverse division of labour, there is progressively greater scope for the development of individual differentiation among persons and institutions. Individuation entails a corresponding decrease in consensual value systems and sentiments.

Durkheim's distinction between mechanical and organic solidarity is often used to characterize a supposed difference between 'simple' undifferentiated societies and the densely complex and variegated 'modern' industrial society. In Bernstein's hands, the distinction refers not to an absolute difference (simple/complex or undifferentiated/differentiated) but to different *principles of differentiation* which have very different consequences for the social placement of individuals. Hence it is important to remember that when Bernstein writes of a school exhibiting mechanical solidarity he is not referring to an institution which is internally homogeneous or undifferentiated. On the contrary, as we shall see, for Bernstein it implies very clear internal cleavages and variations: what is at stake are the principles on which such differences rest and the relations in time and space of the segments.

Bernstein's re-working of the Durkheimian principles of solidarity differs from the original in one particular. Durkheim used them to characterize whole societies, but – as Bisseret (1979, p. 103) emphasizes – for Bernstein it is a matter of differing principles *within* the same society. For Bisseret this is a stumbling-block, yet Bernstein's is by no means an unusual juxtaposition of such contrasting modes of organization. It is remarkably close to the difference proposed by Burns and Stalker (1961) between 'mechanistic' and 'organismic' orders in formal organizations – a distinction which, as Hickson (1966–7) shows, finds parallels in many similar studies (cf. Weeks, 1973).

Bernstein argues that, in principle, contemporary state schools are in a process of change and transition – from social arrangements founded upon and manifest in mechanical solidarity to those associated with organic solidarity. Let us enumerate briefly those features of school organization which Bernstein seeks to capture. Under the 'old' order, teacher and pupil roles are relatively fixed and determinate. Pupils, for example, are categorized, grouped and processed in terms of a few generic categories: age, sex and ability are major dimensions of such schemes. Units of social organization are arranged in such a way as to maximize internal homogeneity, and the attributes used to classify pupils (and teachers) are regarded as fixed and stable. 'Ability' for example will be treated as a more or less stable attribute, used to classify pupils in the same way across years and across school subjects. Pupils would thus be allocated to forms or streams on the basis of such measured ability: there would be little mobility between streams, and pupils in a given stream or form would remain together for substantial amounts of their school work. Under such conditions, pupils are placed within the school on the basis of what pass for *ascribed* roles or characteristics.

As schools shift in organization and ideology towards principles of organic solidarity, on the other hand, the emphasis moves towards the establishment of *achieved* roles for pupils. 'Ability', for instance, will no longer be thought of as a fixed and generic attribute. Rather, ability will be portrayed as a process, which is realized in the context of learning, and of interaction between teachers and taught. Hence ability may be thought to be manifested differently in different pedagogic contexts: pupils may be placed in sets for different school subjects, for instance. They are less likely to be placed in fixed structural units which uniquely define the individual pupil's position within the school. Pupils' roles are therefore more flexible – or at any rate potentially so. School careers are achieved in terms of individual biographies, rather than ascribed in terms of predetermined structural attributes or classes (in the most general sense of that term).

A parallel shift is suggested for teachers' roles in school. Under conditions of 'mechanical' solidarity, the social arrangements of the staff tend to follow disciplinary or subject lines. Subject departments tend to define the teacher's role: here again we find it is a matter of ascription and professional attributes which are socially defined as relatively fixed. But the order changeth. The teacher's role, Bernstein suggests, is increasingly fragmented: classroom teaching of school subjects is supplemented by wider pastoral and careers duties. And as the range of school subjects taught also becomes increasingly diverse, so the division of labour within the teaching staff becomes more complex, diffuse and fragmented. Here, too, then, the person's role or biography is one which is to be made actively or *accomplished* rather than being given.

These shifts are paralleled by changes in pedagogy, curriculum and social control. The teacher ceases to operate solely as the provider of standard routines and solutions, and becomes the creator of problems for the pupils to solve. Pedagogy thus stresses pupil-discovery and self-discovery. The *means* of learning are valued, as much as or more than its ends.

The curriculum is no longer conceived of as a series of more or less self-contained units ('subjects'). Rather, subjects are treated as subordinate to general principles or ideas. There is a new principle of integration at work here: organic solidarity and curriculum developments weaken the boundaries which insulated teachers into departments, and school knowledge into disciplines.

Social control in the school is mobilized in much more personalized or individualized ways in the newer 'organic' schooling: teachers and pupils confront one another as individuals, not simply as the interchangeable members of different social categories. Such a growth of individuation corresponds to a weakening of the consensual regulation of conduct.

Without pausing for the moment to consider whether Bernstein's remarks are justified, or looking at evidence from other authors which bears on such changes in organization and sentimental order, let us consider what themes or elements are already available to us in this précis of the argument.

A social arrangement which Bernstein would characterize as displaying mechanical solidarity has the following characteristics. It is segmented: that is, members are arranged in relatively insulated, self-contained units. Its members' roles are thus ascribed in terms of a small number of primitive categories. Within such a system, the scope for achieving uniquely individual biographies or careers (in organizational terms) is curtailed. Likewise, mechanisms of social control are couched in terms of shared values and group loyalties which exist independently of individual dispositions. Organic solidarity, on the other hand, is manifested through an increasingly individualized mode, and a weakening of the boundaries which formerly defined structural segments.

The notion of *boundary*, and the relative strength of boundaries is a major theme in the 'Open schools' paper, and it is fundamental to much of the Bernstein corpus. 'Boundary' refers to the social arrangements and practices whereby social groupings or domains of knowledge and experience are kept separate. Boundary here is not first and foremost a material manifestation (though it may be marked in concrete ways): it is primarily a symbolic issue.

Symbolic boundaries are often placed round domains which have that special significance conventionally referred to as the 'sacred'. The sacred is carefully bounded in time and space, and personal access to sacred domains is achieved by the carefully managed penetration of such boundaries or thresholds (normally involving what anthropologists refer to as 'liminal' rituals: cf. e.g. Van Gennep, 1960; Leach, 1976). Such boundaries and their ritualized manifestations thus serve to demarcate and separate the respective spheres of the sacred and the profane.

Bernstein explicitly draws on such anthropological connotations of 'boundary'. Within the old order of the segmented, mechanical forms, domains of knowledge are treated analogously to the 'sacred', and – like most such sacred areas – are treated as rather dangerous:

> Knowledge . . . is dangerous, it cannot be exchanged like money, it must be confined to special well-chosen persons and even divorced from practical concerns. The forms of knowledge must always be well insulated from each other: there must be no sparking across the forms with unpredictable outcomes. Specialization makes knowledge safe and protects the vital principles of social order. (1967a, p.74)

Here the relationship between teacher and taught is strictly hierarchical and the teacher's authority and control are hieratic.

The newer arrangements, on the other hand, are marked by significant weakening of these symbolic boundaries. There is a mixing of categories: elements of the curriculum mingle, teachers and pupils participate in heterogeneous groupings. Most significantly, perhaps, the value system of the school is rendered more ambiguous, and the symbolic membranes insulating it from extra-mural influences are correspondingly weakened. The distinction between the sacred and the profane is blurred or removed altogether.

It is at this point that one of the acknowledged contemporary influences is apparent. The theme of boundary, while derived from Durkheim, has been given particular prominence by contemporary structural anthropologists – in the English-speaking world by Mary Douglas. Her monograph on the dialectically linked categories of 'purity' and 'danger' is precisely concerned with the symbolic and ritual ways in which our experience of the world is classified and categorized, and how the purity of those classes is maintained. 'Dirt' and 'pollution' – Douglas's starting-point – are values attached to 'matter out of place', which thus contravenes the logic of natural classes of cultural convention. Her analysis of the logic underlying the dietary taboos enshrined in the 'Abominations of Leviticus' is a classic and typically elegant exemplar of this particular approach (Douglas, 1966). Leach, another exponent of the approach to anthropological enquiry, summarizes one aspect of it in this way:

> There is always some uncertainty about just where the edge of Category A turns into the edge of Category not-A. Whenever we make category distinctions within a unified field, either spatial or temporal, it is the boundaries that matter; we concentrate our attention on the differences not the similarities, and this makes us feel that the markers of such boundaries are of special value, 'sacred', 'taboo'. (Leach, 1976, p.35)

We shall have occasion to return in more detail to the parallels and influences between Bernstein and Douglas. The lesson to be drawn out at this early stage is to note the parallel development between Bernstein's thought and that of modern British structuralist anthropology (of which Douglas and Leach are leading proponents). Indeed, Bernstein's espousal of the Durkheimian spirit has led him to produce, in his papers on the moral order of schools, a schematic structural anthropology of such institutions: it is one which precious few authors have subsequently taken up and developed (but see Kapferer 1981 and Walker 1983 for anthropological deployment of Bernstein's perspectives).

This anthropological flavour is intensified in Bernstein's essay on 'ritual' in education (Bernstein, Elvin and Peters, 1966, *CCC* 1). Characteristically, this paper is not an ethnographic account of school rituals: indeed, little empirical support or exemplification is provided. What he does provide us with is a highly suggestive if schematic outline of the topic. As with the paper I have referred to above, its importance lies in its display of Bernstein's most general themes and perspectives.

The models of schools invoked by Bernstein are now familiar in outline. He contrasts two forms or structures: the 'stratified' and the 'differentiated'. The stratified order corresponds with what we have just seen characterized in terms of mechanical solidarity. There is an explicit social organization based on strong divisions and determinate pupil attributes. The differentiated model corresponds to the principle of organic solidarity. Here the emphasis is on the process of achieved roles or identities. For purposes of explanation here I shall refer to contrasting modes of organization *between* schools, but these principles can also refer to differences *within* schools as well.

The strong boundaries of the stratified school are marked by highly developed rituals. Bernstein distinguishes between two varieties of such ritual – 'consensual' and 'differentiating'. Consensual rituals bind the school into a single collectivity. They rest on 'consensual lineaments of dress, the imagery of signs, totems, scrolls and plaques for the revivifying of special, historical contexts and other symbolic features' (Bernstein, Elvin and Peters, 1966, *CCC* 3, p. 55). The rituals of social control – of punishment and reward – are important components of this expressive domain.

Differentiating rituals, on the other hand, separate and demarcate the various groups and segments within the school (such as those based on ability, gender or age). They foster loyalty within such a segment and a degree of social distance from other equivalent segments. In this way, then, are the units of a segmental, mechanical solidarity created and re-created through symbolic forms. Within the differentiated school, social control is likely to be based upon individualized and interpersonal relations, rather than the collective acquiescence to a consensually ritualized system of common values. There is, Bernstein suggests, a fundamental difference in the way these contrasting modes of social control are realized and expressed. Within the stratified school the ritual expression of order and control is based upon highly condensed symbolic 'messages'. The expression and exploration of individualized orders of meaning is subordinated to the ritual enactment of shared understandings. In the differentiated school, on the other hand, the corresponding stress is on the statement of personal meanings and motives. As Bernstein and his colleagues summarize the crucial difference between these contrasting orders:

> If the basis for social control through ritual is extra-verbal or indirect, impersonal and non-rational, then the basis for social control where ritual is weakened is likely to be personal, verbally explicit and rational. (Bernstein, Elvin and Peters, 1966, *CCC* 3, p.62)

Bernstein characterizes the interpersonal control of the differentiated school as 'therapeutic' – in terms which are reminiscent of Durkheim's description of 'restitutive' law under conditions of organic solidarity, as opposed to 'repressive' social control of mechanical forms. Within the stratified school, control and retribution rest upon sentiments of *guilt*; within the differentiated school the corresponding sentiment is that of *shame*.

Bernstein focuses upon ritual therefore not in order to revel in the peculiarities of particular observances and practices. His is not an exercise in folklore, although in a different context he acknowledges among early influences the opportunity to review *The Lore and Language of Children* (Peter and Iona Opie, 1959). Ritual is simultaneously a marker of structural features of school organization, and a component of that selfsame structure. Moreover the rituals (or their absence) are a powerful analytic lever on principles of authority, power, control and meaning. The underlying themes of the ritual paper are encapsulated as an interest in 'the procedures which are used to maintain continuity, order and boundary and which control ambivalence towards the social order' (Bernstein, Elvin and Peters, 1966, *CCC* 3, p. 54).

It is important to grasp at this early stage that while Bernstein expresses himself in terms of dichotomous categories, this is for purposes of analytic simplification in the first instance. The categories are not intended to represent self-contained entities, nor is the model a static one. It is apparent, indeed, that the analysis is intended to capture a process of transformation and change. The analysis is also intended to portray the mechanisms whereby particular social forms are reproduced.

In the two essays already referred to Bernstein is clearly striving to find devices, concepts and frameworks which can be used to link a wide range of analytic and institutional levels. In doing so he draws directly upon major themes in the history of sociological thought. We can begin to discern that Bernstein, far from being an idiosyncratic social thinker, is located directly in that tradition of which Durkheim was the forebear.

Within the contemporary sociology of education (as in other domains of sociological enquiry) there is a tendency to dichotomize schools of theory and research into 'macro' and 'micro' sociologies. Common representations of these schools or meta-schools of sociology often portray the 'macro' as concerned primarily with structural patterns and continuities, conceptualized at the societal/system level (e.g. in terms of the state, social class, education systems, modes of production). The 'micro' sociologies, on the other hand, are portrayed as embodying a concern for social action, and as emphasizing interactions between individual social actors (in terms of their perspectives, motives, rules, strategies and the like). (For a recent collection of papers reviewing this area, see Knorr-Cetina and Cicourel, 1981; see also Hammersley, 1984, for a recent discussion of the 'micro–macro' debate in educational sociology.) There are repeated calls in the literature for the reconciliation of such perspectives and a *rapprochement* between their respective advocates. On balance, such calls tend to come from those sympathetic to a supposedly 'macro' perspective, who encourage practitioners of the opposed tendency to tailor their work to facilitate this conceptual 'fit'.

Now, it might be thought that Bernstein epitomized an essentially 'macro' point of view. It is undoubtedly true that in Bernstein's general approach there is little or no concern for the perspectives, strategies and actions of individual social actors in actual social settings. As will be elaborated on later, it is characteristic of the work (and the tradition within which I locate it) that the human subject is absent from its conceptual repertoire. On the other hand, it is clear that Bernstein's analysis ranges over the entire *scale* of magnitude and generality of social forms and institutions. While grounded in a broad view of the division of labour, the models Bernstein develops allow for the exploration of interpersonal relations of pedagogy and social control at classroom level, the school as a social institution, forms of message or communication within the school, relationships between schools and labour markets, and so on.

While radically different from the humanist, individualistic bent of much so-called micro-sociology, therefore, Bernstein's general anthropology or meta-theory cuts across simplistic distinctions between small-scale and societal scope of analysis. Indeed, it is central to Bernstein's entire programme that the analysis should provide conceptual links between apparently diverse institutional levels and contexts. Such theoretical constructs as 'code' (a recurrent theme in the sociology) are significant precisely because they accomplish such analytic work (cf. Bernstein, 1981).

One of the difficulties which students and readers of Bernstein's papers seem often to encounter is occasioned by the fact that the conceptual frameworks appear (and indeed are) highly abstract. Their generality is gained at some cost. There is a relative lack of clear empirical demonstration or exemplification, and the reader who is unwilling or unable to enter into a sympathetic interpretation of the essentially suggestive and heuristic concepts is likely to feel frustrated. While Bernstein's work does have clear empirical reference, it is not empirical sociology as that which has conventionally been practised in Britain and North America, say.

Before continuing to a more general view of Bernstein's themes and purposes, let us turn to a brief look at the third of the trilogy of papers on schools and the moral order: 'Sources of consensus and disaffection in education' (1966a, *CCC* 3, pp.37–53). Here Bernstein addresses the general topic of the culture of the school, how that culture is transmitted, its consequences for pupil roles – especially for pupils' degree of involvement in the school and its culture – and different types of family settings in relation to perceptions of that school culture.

In keeping with his penchant for formal conceptual frameworks, Bernstein suggests that the investigation of school culture and its transmission should encompass four major factors affecting pupils' lives: the family setting; the age group or friendship patterns; the school itself; the pupil's perception of his or her likely occupational fate. Further, he suggests, the model should be general enough to hold good for *any* particular school type. Bernstein identifies two orders or 'complexes' of behaviour being transmitted within the school: the expressive order (concerned with conduct and character) and the instrumental order (concerned with formal learning of school knowledge and skills). In terms similar (though not identical) to the essay on ritual Bernstein suggests that the instrumental order tends to be divisive: it divides pupils and staff into different segments. The expressive order, on the other hand, aims to transmit a moral order which is held equally and consensually: 'It tends to bind the whole school together as a distinct moral collectivity' (1966a, *CCC* 3, pp.38–9).

There may be tensions between the expressive and the instrumental – between the consensual and the fissiparous. The greater the school's emphasis upon the instrumental order, the more difficult it may become for the expressive order to link the pupils in a cohesive fashion:

> It is quite likely that some pupils who are only weakly involved in the instrumental order will be less receptive to the moral order transmitted through the expressive order. In this situation, the children may turn to an expressive order which is pupil-based, and anti-school. It is also likely that a strong involvement in the instrumental order may lead, under certain conditions, to a weakening of the pupil's involvement in the expressive order and the values it transmits. (1966a, *CCC* 3, p.39)

There are, he posits, certain strains imposed upon both orders. The instrumental order may be subject to rapid change, reflecting new technical and curricular demands and the changing division of labour. Likewise, in a complex and pluralistic society consensus over the expressive order cannot be assumed. In a comment later developed more fully in the 'ritual' paper, Bernstein comments that under these latter circumstances, it will become increasingly difficult for the school to transmit cohesive behaviours.

Families and pupils are then typed in relation to their perceptions of the *ends* of the instrumental and expressive orders, and of the *means* of their transmission. Families may thus accept both means and ends, accept the means and reject the ends, accept the ends and reject the means, or may reject both means and ends. The typology is open to the complication that instrumental and expressive orders may be treated separately and could in principle vary independently. Likewise for pupils: the pupil's role may vary from complete involvement (accepting both means and ends for both instrumental and expressive orders), through intermediate categories of 'detachment', 'deferment', 'estrangement' to 'alienation', where means and ends of both orders are rejected.

The precise details and possible implications of these typologies need not detain us here: King (1971) and Delamont (1976) explore the class and gender implications of the model. But Bernstein's general conclusion is instructive:

> This analysis . . . points to the critical importance of both the organizational structure of the school *and* the principles of transmission. In other words, *how* the expressive order is transmitted, *how* the instrumental order is transmitted, *what* is

> transmitted by both, what the official and unofficial goals are, of both orders, will structure the role positions of teachers and pupils, affect the nature of teacher and pupil relationships and their respective friendship and pressure groups and affect the pupil's relationship to his family and community. (1966a, *CCC* 3, p.48: emphases in original)

The important aspects here, then, are – first – the establishment of essentially *sociological* categories for understanding the respective positions of pupils and families in relation to the school. The categories are used to express purely formal relationships, and are not intended to characterize psychological states of individual members. Secondly, such an analysis allows for a degree of autonomy for the school itself: the school operates as an agency of transmission independently of the family, the class system, occupational outcomes and the like:

> What the school does, its rituals, its ceremonies, its authority relations, its stratification, its procedures for learning, its incentives, rewards and punishments, its very image of conduct, character and manner, can modify or change the pupil's role as this has been initially shaped by the family. (1966a, *CCC* 3, pp.48–9)

Here one can clearly discern one of Bernstein's most distinctive characteristics. Little time is devoted to the 'ethnographic' or the descriptive exploration of any particular institution or social form. In the discussion of family types and pupil roles, brief sketches or pen-portraits are appended to each, but they are sufficient only to indicate to the engaged reader the sort of thing Bernstein has in mind. What we are offered is a typical *tour de force* in the construction of formal typologies, whereby possible relationships are indicated between school organization, the content of schooling, types of family (or family orientation) and pupil roles.

It is again characteristic of this display of virtuosity that all the links and relationships are not spelled out in detail. The same is true between papers as it is within individual essays. The same, or similar distinctions are drawn, and models constructed in different contexts. They are not always to be read as if they expressed direct equivalence, but should be appreciated as expressions of homology or parallelism in the formal models.

In other words, what is important in grasping Bernstein's dichotomous distinctions is that they all conform to the following general form:

$$a : b :: x : y$$

which is to be read as 'a is to b as x is to y'. In this way one can see what I take to be a very important truth about the entire corpus of Bernstein's work. That is: the subject matter of his essays is the nature of formal or structural relationships between cultural units and/or institutions, and the organization of his theses is itself ordered in terms of such a set of structural relationships. In that sense, the writing is self-referential.

I shall be going on to elaborate on these very general observations, in an attempt to explicate the nature of Bernstein's structuralist programme. But we already have to hand some of the basic thematic building-blocks, and we can begin at this stage to sketch out some of the homologies that are implied in the papers already discussed. A summary statement of them will provide a springboard for a more detailed consideration of the structuralist sociology of cultural transmissions, expressed largely through the formulation of 'codes'. The homologies are summarized in tabular form below.

Bernstein's sociology: themes and variations

Social integration	mechanical	organic
Division of labour	segmental/ stratified	complex/ differentiated
Boundary maintenance	strong	weak
Social roles	ascribed	achieved
Ritual/expressive order	strong	weak
Cultural categories	pure	mixed
Social control	collective values/ punishment, 'guilt'	individualized/ therapeutic, 'shame'
Message types	condensed, implicit in ritualized collective forms	explicated, individual motives

This summary representation is not intended to be an exhaustive listing. The categories represented here are not exclusive, nor is their ordering strongly implicative. They represent a series of linked 'transformations' of fundamental oppositions. Bernstein has clearly derived from his application of the Durkheimian foundations a richly variegated anthropology or sociology of cultural transmissions. This rests on the complex interrelationships between a series of structural principles.

The list presented here provides an initial characterization of Bernstein's structuralism. The development and implications of that position will be outlined in the rest of this book.

We should note, before going into detail about the structuralist programme, that this approach is entirely in keeping with the spirit of Durkheimian sociology or anthropology. Indeed, I wish to argue that in his enthusiastic espousal of the then rather unfashionable Durkheim, Bernstein in fact started to develop his own native version of the European structuralist movement – associated in particular with the 'human sciences' in France, of which Durkheim himself was a progenitor.

3 *Structure and community*

There is a tendency among sociolinguists to be pretty dismissive of Bernstein's earliest papers on language. They tend to emphasize discontinuities in the development of the thought, rather than searching for thematic coherence. The earliest essays are thus portrayed as superseded and discredited, even in Bernstein's frame of reference. (Of course, for some critics, the whole *oeuvre* is suspect.) Gordon's remarks, for instance are typical of those which play up 'frequent changes in terminology, largely unacknowledged shifts in focus, ambiguities and obscurities and, most confusing of all, at least two outright contradictions' (Gordon, 1981, p.66). Stubbs provides a characteristic portrayal of the discontinuities; commenting on what he finds difficult in interpreting Bernstein, he says:

> Bernstein has complicated this problem, for he has recently republished a collection of his papers (*CCC* 1) which span the years 1958 to 1973 and contain many contradictory statements. He has also recently published experimental papers (*CCC* 2) based on his early and now outdated theoretical position. He admits (*CCC* 2) that this experimental work is based on a 'much coarser theoretical position' than he now holds. (Stubbs, 1983, p.48)

Stubbs goes on to remark that the difficulties of interpretation are compounded by the fact that the version of Bernstein's work on language which is most widely known is the 'out-of-date version' (p.49). In fact, the real problem is not that Bernstein is known through out-of-date versions, but that many interpretations of his work, old and recent, derive from inappropriate readings.

Now it is perfectly true that there are major changes in the work. Indeed, considering the time-span of its development and its general scope, it would be remarkable if it were otherwise. Unacknowledged ambiguities and shifts are certainly problematic, and I have no desire to gloss over such problems here. On the other hand, some authors have been quite exaggeratedly concerned – even a little hysterical – about this. Jackson (1974) expresses an anguished sense of betrayal in what he claims is a fundamental shift in the programme:

> One is entitled . . . to ask what public notice has been taken, by Bernstein himself and by his colleagues and collaborators, of this reversal of position. The answer is, as far as I know, that no notice has been taken at all. The theory has continued to be respectfully quoted, as a continuously developing thing, without anybody noticing that it has in effect been retracted, and the opposite theory substituted. This phenomenon may be unique in the history of science.

The absurd hyperbole of that last sentence is indicative of the extent to which the internal differences are exaggerated by unsympathetic critics, at the expense of an exploration of the continuities.

I recognize, as I have said, that the theories have undergone real changes: it is the nature and direction of those changes that confirm Bernstein's project as essentially structuralist in outlook. He has gradually worked his way from his original sources and inspirations (drawing on one collection of sociological, psychological and linguistic traditions) to a much more sophisticated paradigm, and a much more general theory of cultural reproduction. Nevertheless, many of the more general ideas are identifiable in embryo in the earliest papers.

The original presentation of the language thesis rests on the distinction between *formal* and *public* language-use. This dichotomy is proposed in a pair of early papers (1958 and 1959a) while others (e.g. 1959b, 1960a) exemplify the general orientation.

Authors who concentrate on a purely linguistic (sociolinguistic or psycholinguistic) perspective present these early essays as primarily (or solely) concerned with the specification of two contrasting dialects or sociolects (that is, language varieties associated with specific social groups or strata). Gordon (1981) for example begins his commentary on Bernstein with a summary of 'public language' and 'formal language' precisely because, he contends, they furnish the most explicit statement of the two language types in the entire corpus:

> Some may feel that it is unreasonable to quote a list that Bernstein compiled over twenty years ago, especially as the theory has undergone modifications since then. The reason for quoting these lists is that they constitute the fullest set of superficially plausible recognition criteria for his two dichotomous types of language presented anywhere in his sociolinguistic writings. (p.70)

To some extent this is fair comment: the subsequent developments do not go on to furnish ever more explicit or definitive linguistic characteristics and criteria. On the other hand, it rather misses the point (and in this Gordon is in company, if not always good company). For Bernstein's purpose, even in the earliest papers, was not principally to describe two such sociolects. For that reason subsequent commentaries on 'dialect' and education (e.g. Trudgill, 1975), while important correctives to popular misreadings of Bernstein, are not in themselves relevant to his own sociological interests.

If Bernstein had had such a motive then it is hard to see why in the 1958 paper the characteristics of 'public language' are tucked away in a footnote (1958, *CCC* 1, pp.38–9). The footnote is expanded in the subsequent essay, to be sure, but a return to the original versions of these formulations shows that they were far from being purely linguistic exercises. On the contrary, Bernstein's interest lies in expressing not simply issues of language variation, but orientations to means, ends and objects, relationships between objects, the creation and re-creation of identities, and modes of social control. These are addressed through the medium of language use, but the latter is not the exclusive concern.

The guiding preoccupation appears at the outset to be how persons acquire and manipulate certain *structural* understandings and relationships. These are expressed in highly abstract and formal ways:

> It is contended that members of the unskilled and semi-skilled strata, relative to the middle classes, do not merely place different significances upon different classes of objects, but that their perception is of a qualitatively different order. (1958, *CCC* 1, p.24)

Bernstein outlines two sorts of sensitivity to objects. First, there is sensitivity to the 'structure' of objects, which is dependent upon the ability to respond to an object within a context of a 'matrix of relationships' with other objects. Secondly, 'sensitivity to content' refers to a person's responses to the 'boundaries' of an object. He goes on to suggest that key differences between social strata include different sensitivities to structure and content.

The aspects of *public* language which Bernstein lists are therefore selected in relation to this particular sociological-cum-anthropological thesis. In no way intended as an exhaustive characterization of language-types, the features of public language and its formal counterpart are intended to relate to the particular constellation of functions and values of structure and social control Bernstein addresses. They relate to the ways in which structured and structuring relationships are established *vis-à-vis* the meaning of objects and the motives of persons.

What then are the proposed features of the 'public' use of language, and how do they relate to the fundamental concerns of the ordering of experience and modes of social order? They have been reproduced and discussed frequently, but I present them here yet again, as their implications do seem to me to be of fundamental importance, though in ways not always apparent through many of those other discussions. The language features are summarized first, and their implications are then discussed briefly.

Public

1 Short, grammatically simple, often unfinished sentences, a poor syntactical construction with a verbal form stressing the active mood.
2 Simple and repetitive use of conjunctions (so, then, and, because).
3 Frequent use of short commands and questions.
4 Rigid and limited use of adjectives and adverbs.
5 Infrequent use of impersonal pronouns as subjects (one, it).
6 Statements formulated as implicit questions which set up a sympathetic circularity, e.g., 'Just fancy!', 'It's only natural, isn't it?', 'I wouldn't have believed it'.
7 A statement of fact is often used both as a reason and a conclusion, or, more accurately, the reason and conclusion are confounded to produce a categoric statement, e.g. 'Do as I tell you', 'Hold on tight', 'You're not going out', 'Lay off that'.
8 Individual selection from a group of idiomatic phrases will frequently be found.
9 Symbolism is of a low order of generality.
10 The individual qualification is implicit in the sentence structure, therefore it is a language of implicit meaning. *It is believed that this fact determines the form of the language.*

Formal

1 Accurate, grammatical order and syntax regulate what is said.
2 Logical modifications and stress are mediated through a grammatically complex sentence construction, especially through the use of conjunctions and relative clauses.
3 Frequent use of prepositions which indicate logical relationships as well as prepositions which indicate temporal and spatial contiguity.
4 Frequent use of impersonal pronouns (it, one).
5 A discriminative selection from a range of adjectives and adverbs.
6 Individual qualification is verbally mediated through the structure and relationships within and between sentences. That is, it is explicit.

7 Expressive symbolism conditioned by this linguistic form distributes affectual support rather than logical meaning to what is said.

8 A language use which points to the possibilities inherent in a complex conceptual hierarchy for the organizing of experience.

A key difference lies in the capacity afforded for the manifestation and qualification of individual, personal meanings and motives: 'A critical difference between the two speech forms is that whereas in a *formal* language subjective intent may be verbally elaborated and made explicit, this process is not facilitated in a *public* language' (1959a, *CCC* 1, p.47). This is related directly to patterns of authority and control, with special reference to primary socialization within the family.

Public language use, with its lack of verbal elaboration and explication of meaning and motive, is characteristic of a situation where authority is implicit in ascribed roles or positions within the family: here the statuses and roles themselves are, of course, explicit. Such a highly segregated family system will not provide an environment where the sensitive exploration and elaboration of personal intentions is encouraged. Formal language, on the other hand, arises in family settings where complex logical relations are articulated, and personal intentions and sensibilities are explored.

The specific link with social class arises here, as Bernstein suggests that such family types, and their associated modes of language use, are characteristic of different social strata. It is the working-class family which gives rise to an emphasis upon public language, within a system of determinate statuses. The middle-class family, on the other hand, socializes the child into a 'more formally articulated structure', within which there is an early emphasis on the individual qualification of meaning: 'The child is born into an environment where he is seen and responded to as an individual with his own rights, that is he has a specific social status' (1958, *CCC* 1, p.27). This is reflected in Bernstein's proposed criterion of public language: the selection from a limited stock of idiomatic expressions. The repetitious use of language drawn from a restricted pool in this way is very well suited to the affirmation and re-confirmation of pre-existing, shared meanings and orientations. They need not necessarily be socially recognized (or stigmatized) as cliché, but like clichés they do not promote novelty or individuation of expression (cf. Zijderfeld, 1979). This is paralleled by the implications of 'sympathetic circularity'. In this usage, items such as tag-questions are deployed so as to solicit the agreement of the listener to the speaker's meaning. Implicitly, it is argued, such idiomatic expression tends to impose a form of closure on the dialogue. While agreement is solicited – and indeed presupposed – there is little incentive or opportunity expressed for the exploration of individual differences between interlocutors. Public language is therefore a form of language use characteristic of social solidarity, shared meanings, and common values (cf. Brown and Gilman, 1960). By the same token, it is not a use of language which promotes individuation and novelty.

It is important to note that this argument does not, of itself, propose a strict linguistic determinism. As Bernstein himself remarks, the use of language provides:

> important means of initiating, synthesizing, and reinforcing ways of thinking, feeling and behaviour which are functionally related to the social group. It does not, of itself, prevent the expression of specific ideas or confine the individual to a given level of conceptualization, but certain ideas and generalizations are facilitated rather than others. (1959a, *CCC* 1, p.43)

The differences that are proposed between public and formal language use are therefore related to differences in potential, facility and adaptation. In and of themselves, they do not determine absolutely users' capacities for thought and expression.

The expression of authority and identity, and their relation to family socialization are detectable in one further criterion of public language. That is, the feature whereby 'reason and conclusion are confounded' in the construction of a categoric statement (often realized as an imperative). Bernstein's examples indicate what he has in mind here: 'Do as I tell you'; 'Hold on tight'; 'You're not going out'. They carry the implication: 'Because I say so'. Such categorical statements will tend to preclude disagreement or negotiation, just as sympathetic circularity tends to solicit shared perspectives. Each is an idiom of closed rather than open discourse (though this terminology is perhaps somewhat anachronistic when applied to Bernstein's early papers, as here).

Bernstein does not appear in this context to be concerned with a detailed specification of social class *per se*. It is a pervasive feature of this and his subsequent work that theories or measures of class are not discussed extensively, and this has long been a complaint on the part of some critics. His work has, over the years, been squeezed between class-theorists on the one hand and the linguists on the other; they have, of course, been joined by snipers of other persuasions as well. One thing is clear, however: Bernstein is not dealing with the sort of measures of social class that were being utilized by his contemporaries in the late 1950s. This does *not* reflect a cavalier disregard for the theorization of social class, but reflects a very different approach, not only to the division of labour, but to the nature of sociological theory in general.

One of the interesting differences between Bernstein and the British sociologists who were his contemporaries in the late 1950s resides in the importance Bernstein attaches to females in his analyses. Most measures and studies of social class have concentrated primarily – even exclusively – on the categorization of males by occupation, qualifications, income etc., and of families or households by the occupational grading of the male 'head of the household'. In Bernstein's formulation, however, wives are crucial:

> The basic requirements for the group termed 'middle class and associative levels' will be a family where the father is more likely to have received grammar school education, or some form of further education or certificated training for a skill, *or one in which the mother is more likely to have received something more than elementary schooling, or before marriage to have followed an occupation superior to that of the father, or a non-manual occupation.* (1958, *CCC* 1, pp.24–5, my emphasis)

Although it is not commented on in great detail, it is apparent that the role of the *mother* is seen as central to the process of socialization, and its different class forms. As we shall see, this goes rather further than the traditional emphasis on the role of the mother in early socialization. The mother is seen as crucial to the processes of cultural and social reproduction, and hence in the nature and replication of class itself.

Bernstein places great emphasis on the role of a child's parents in the middle-class family, whose scrutiny of the child is seen almost in terms of 'work': 'the scrupulous observation of the child by the parents so that the very fine stages of development and the emergence of new patterns of behaviour are the object of attention and comment' (1958, *CCC* 1, p.27). The middle-class mother plays a major role here, therefore. In the early papers the full implications are not worked out, but in later essays it is claimed that the modern middle-class (or 'new middle-class') mother is central to the work of cultural transmission; she is a carrier of symbolic property from one generation to the next. In the references to the mother's occupation/educational attainment, and the subsequent empirical emphasis on mother–child communication, this theme is identifiable from the outset of Bernstein's work, and is a constant theme throughout its maturation. In the later papers of the 1970s the significance of the 'new middle class' resides largely in the 'professionalization' of parenthood and the special tasks of the mother in that work.

Bernstein is not very specific about the 'working class' with whom public language use is identified. He writes that: 'The term "working class" includes all members of the semi-skilled and unskilled group except the type of family structure indicated as the base line for the middle-class and associative levels' (1958, *CCC* 1, p.25). The base line to which he refers is the 'transitional family structure which modifies social perception and orients it to sensitivity to the structure of objects' (*CCC* 1, p.25). Despite the generality of this category of 'working class', however, it is I think clearly perceptible that a rather particular view of the working class is drawn on, however implicitly.

We should, for instance, refer to the works cited in the bibliographies appended to Bernstein's papers. (It has been Bernstein's practice to append his sources without necessarily referring to them specifically in the text of a paper.) The 1958 paper ('Some sociological determinants of perception') is revealing from this point of view. A number of classic urban 'community' studies and similar accounts are referred to (Dennis, Henriques and Slaughter, 1956; Shaw and McKay, 1942; Thrasher, 1927; Warner *et al.*, 1944; Whyte, 1943; Wirth, 1929 and 1956; Zorbaugh, 1944). Studies deriving from the Chicago school of urban ethnography are conspicuous here.

The implications Bernstein drew from these studies are not detailed, but it is arguable that he was influenced by the *gemeinschaftlich* view of such social settings. Indeed, he makes brief reference to this, in discussing the politics and ethics of language change, such as might be implied by the substitution of 'formal' for 'public':

> To simply substitute a *formal* language . . . is to cut off the individual from his traditional relationships and perhaps alienate him from them. This is the old polarity of *Gemeinschaft* and *Gesellschaft* in another guise. The problem would seem to be to preserve *public* language usage but also to create for the individual the possibility of utilizing a *formal* language. (1959a, *CCC* 1, p.54)

This polarity, and Bernstein's expression of 'the problem' is in fact thoroughly reminiscent of a dominant theme in the urban sociology of Chicago. That is, a concern with the safeguarding of 'traditional' values, through 'primary groups' in the face of social change and the 'transplantation' of old-world cultures into the North American metropolis.

The Chicago tradition – in common with similar varieties of community study – promoted the view of 'natural areas' in the city, and drew on the 'social worlds' perspective to describe them as relatively self-contained geographical and social milieux, and symbolic universes in their own right (Faris, 1970). These, then, are the relatively self-contained working-class 'communities' which exerted (and continue to exert) such a powerful influence on sociological imagery and argument (cf. Lofland, 1975).[1]

The nomenclature and imagery of the following passage are surely revealing. Disclaiming the view that public language use in any way implies the existence of a uniform language, he writes: 'The vocabulary of the Elephant and Castle is different from the Angel, Islington; is different from the Gorbals; and is different from Tiger Bay' (1959a, *CCC* 1, p.43). Conjured up are images of the classic 'traditional' community. The working-class, public language user is a person of group loyalty and allegiance: individual identity is subordinated to shared, collective values. The 'sympathetic circularity' of which Bernstein writes not only throws its embrace around interlocutors, but casts a symbolic membrane about the entire 'community'.

As with other characterizations of such communities, Bernstein writes of the 'protective' character of differences in language use:

> Another important protective function of the *public* language is that other forms of language-use (e.g. *formal* language) will not be directly comprehensible but will be mediated through the *public* language. In other words, a formal language will be translated into the *public* language and thus an alternative orientation, which would lead the individual beyond the confines, affective and cognitive, of the *public* language, is neutralized. (1959a, *CCC* 1, p.48)

Note that Bernstein is here talking of the assumptions and orientations which inform the contextual use and understanding of the language; he is not implying that users speak mutually unintelligible 'different languages'.

We have already encountered the Durkheimian analogue of the *Gemeinschaft* view of social solidarity: that is, the mechanical solidarity. The contrast that Bernstein draws between the public and formal modes of language use directly parallels the mechanical and organic orders. Organic solidarity rests on differentiation of function and increases in the individualization of identities. Formal language use, with its emphasis upon individual qualification of meaning and motive, is the symbolic counterpart of such an organizational mode. Of course the Durkheimian threads we have seen already were derived from chronologically later essays, and that mode of analysis becomes increasingly prominent as the work progresses. It is, however, discernible at the very outset.

It is, perhaps, ironic that subsequent critics should have seen in Bernstein a commentator unsympathetic to the working class he describes. It is equally arguable that the sociological sources which seem to have informed his thinking in the late 1950s portrayed an unwarrantably romantic version of 'the community'. It is noteworthy that Bernstein cites Hoggart (1957) who, while distancing himself from cosy associations of the word 'community' itself, did much to promote a fashionably *gemein-*

schaftlich view of the working classes. There is more than a hint of *nostalgie de la boue*. Hoggart's working-class members have a strong sense of group, which they express proverbially: 'Y've got to share and share alike'; 'y've got to 'elp one another out'; 'y've got to 'elp lame dogs'; 'we must all pull together'; 'it's sink or swim together' (1958, p.82).

Bernstein and Hoggart too were mindful of various harsher aspects of working-class sentiments. Bernstein portrays public language use among the working class as a 'tough' language:

> Tender feelings which are personal and highly individual will not only be difficult to express in this linguistic form, but it is likely that the objects which arouse tender feelings will be given tough terms – particularly those referring to girl-friends, love, death and disappointments. (1959a, *CCC* 1, p.48)

Hoggart draws attention to what he classes the 'strain of coarseness and insensitivity running through working-class life'.

> Thus, working class speech and manners in conversation are more abrupt, less provided with emollient phrases than those of other groups: their arguments are often conducted in so rude a way that a stranger might well think that after this, at the worst, fighting would follow, and at the best a permanent ending of relations. I find that even now, if I am not to be misunderstood, I have to modify a habit of carrying on discussion in an 'unlubricated' way, in short sharp jabs that are meant to go home – and yet not really meant to hurt. (1958, p.88)

Hoggart's seems a description of 'public' language as Bernstein formulated it: indeed it might well have helped to form the idea itself. In fact Bernstein sent Hoggart a copy of the 1958 paper, receiving in turn a very favourable reply (Bernstein, personal communication).

What must be emphasized to the reader not acquainted with English-language sociology of the 1950s and 1960s is that while Bernstein achieved a highly individual synthesis of sociological and linguistic currents, there was nothing unique about his portrayal of class differences in everyday life (as opposed to the inferences he drew from them). As I have suggested, his views on family and community were firmly rooted in major traditions of sociological research, and wider cultural discourse too.

There was nothing startling, for example, in his portrayal of working-class culture as being low in 'deferred gratification', as it was normally termed. The working-class actor was thought to be oriented primarily to the immediate and the concrete. For instance, in the working-class family:

> The specific character of long-term goals tends to be replaced by more general notions of the future, in which chance, a friend or relative plays a greater part than the rigorous working out of connections. Thus present, or near present activities have greater value than the relation of the present activity to the attainment of a distant goal. (1958, *CCC* 1, p.32)

The middle-class 'sensitivity to structure' is directly related to the way in which objects and activities are located within relationships which link present action with distant ends, through complex chains of effects and consequences.

Although it is not spelled out in detail in the very early papers, the implications of public and formal language use can be seen in two different domains. They have implications for a person's orientations to *objects* – located within a matrix of other objects and relations – and his or her orientations to *persons* – located in a matrix of social relations of power, authority, control, motive and feeling. In later work Bernstein makes more explicit use of the distinction between object-relations and person-relations: different modes of language use operate in different ways in these two domains.

In summarizing and commenting on Bernstein's earliest papers I have frequently, and deliberately, referred to 'language use' rather than language *per se*. This is consistent with Bernstein's own usage. He frequently refers to language use, although he is not internally consistent himself. He refers with equal frequency to the *form* of language. Sometimes Bernstein writes just 'language'.

This variation in terminology must have helped in creating some of the confusion concerning Bernstein's main purpose. He proposes a direct relationship between the *form* of linguistic usage, and its social *function*, but the stress upon the social contexts of language use alerts one to the fact that Bernstein was not – and never has been – engaged in the linguistic description of contrasting class dialects.

The forms and functions of language use are dialectically related in this view, and are related dialectically in turn to social structure. Indeed, the three aspects are mutually constitutive. As the author himself puts it:

> It may seem that there is something inherently circular in the method. One examines the language-use and infers social and psychological behaviour, but the latter originally determines the former – for the semantic function of a language is the social structure. What one is doing is simply looking at the social structure through a particular institution, the institution of language. (1959a, *CCC* 1, p. 54)

In the light of this it is hardly surprising that later commentators have sometimes been confused as to precisely where the emphasis lay. Does language use determine social structure and experience, or vice versa? Has Bernstein radically altered his position over the years? Has he reversed the polarity of his explanation? Some critics clearly feel this to be the case, finding a major difference between the earlier and later versions of the theory. This is certainly the view put forward by Jackson (1974) and Gordon (1981) among others, who claim that a complete reversal of this sort has taken place. Such views misread Bernstein, I believe. From the outset he wrote in terms of formal and functional relations between the various aspects of social organization, collective representations (through language), roles and identities, and individual perception. Even in the earliest and most 'coarse' versions of the theoretical programme, Bernstein avoids any simple reductionism or determinism. (This makes it difficult, of course, for those who wish to find a simple version in the work, or are capable themselves of only a crude interpretation!)

Of course, the problems of interpreting Bernstein arose initially because the early work was too readily assimilable to existing and later paradigms concerning 'educability'. As Robinson (1981) has pointed out, the notion of educability – that is, the 'propensity to succeed at school' – has had a career of its own, and has undergone a series of transformations. The formulations of public and formal language use, and their relationships with class and family structure were readily treated as congruent with existing theories and findings on socialization and educational attainment. Indeed, the way in which Bernstein arrived at these conceptualizations was no doubt guided by this general climate of work and opinion, as with contemporary views of class and community.

It is noticeable, for instance, that Bernstein's own early work includes a good deal of reliance upon psychometric techniques, incorporating as it does measures of verbal and non-verbal ability. This, coupled with Bernstein's discussion of the mismatch between working-class and schools' orders of meaning, is easily, if incorrectly, misread as an account of 'ability' and 'educability'.

Let us consider what Bernstein's early thoughts on social class and schooling actually were. While they include profound implications for pupils' experiences of educational institutions, they do not propose a straightforward account of failure through cultural or linguistic 'deficit'. He suggests that the school operates in accordance with a particular constellation of orientations which are congruent with those of the middle class and their use of formal language. In the school setting, Bernstein argues, items in the present are linked to ends in the distant future: there is thus a parallel between the temporal framework of the school and that of the middle-class child. There is likewise a congruence between the school and the middle-class family, in that both inculcate 'cognitive and emotional differentiation and discrimination': in both settings 'sensitivity to structure' and 'mediate relationships' are encouraged. Each is a universe of symbolic complexity and highly ordered matrices of relationships.

Hence the middle-class child who is adept at formal language use – and all that that implies – has available *two* orders of symbolic significance. Depending on the context, he or she operates with public forms when dealing with, say, peer groups, and formal language when sensitivity to differences in role and status is appropriate. This contrasts with the likelihood of infelicitous language use by the working-class child: 'the use of this [public] language in a superior–inferior situation (to a doctor, teacher, etc.) may often be interpreted as a hostile or aggressive (rude) response' (1958, *CCC* 1, p.34).

In addition to such social problems, the working-class pupil's attitudes to language and learning may lead to a mismatch with the aims of formal education. This is manifested in an apparent reluctance to extend his or her realm of experience:

> The working-class boy is often genuinely puzzled by the need to acquire vocabulary or use words in a way that is, for him, peculiar. It is important to realize that his difficulties in ordering a sentence and connecting sentences – problems of qualifying an object, quality, idea, sensitivity to time and its extensions and modifications, making sustained relationships – are alien to the way he perceives and reacts to his immediate environment. (1958, *CCC* 1, p.35)

The social contexts and conditions which Bernstein described here are those which it is claimed relate directly to language use. Language use in turn is a constitutive part of the array of perceptions and predispositions which impinge on schooling. Yet it is surely the case that Bernstein claims no simple and direct relationship between educational 'failure' and some posited linguistic 'handicap', 'deficit', 'incompetence' or whatever. The consequences of cultural and linguistic differences between social strata may be limiting in their effect, but this is a very different thing from a claim that working-class school pupils are intrinsically damaged or deficient.

Further, it is clear that while language use is an integral part of Bernstein's argument, it is not the whole story. The differences between the culture of the school and of the working-class home or family are, primarily, just that – *cultural* contrasts. Moreover, the differences so identified are similar to those enshrined in more 'mainstream' sociological accounts of class and educational aspiration or achievement. I shall go on to argue, however, that interpretations which focus exclusively on cultural and subcultural explanations of class difference misrepresent the core assumptions of Bernstein's *structuralist* sociology.

The problem is that much of Bernstein's thought was lifted out of its sociological context and placed – quite inappropriately – in relation to theories that were explicitly concerned with language 'deficit' and its 'remediation'. Bernstein's work was enthusiastically appropriated by writers espousing a deficit position. This position was then used by critics of 'deficit' to provide a framework for reading Bernstein himself as a deficit theorist. (For a sustained, erroneous reading of this sort, see Dittmar, 1976.) These and related issues will be taken up more systematically when I discuss the reception of Bernstein's ideas on language, the contentious area of 'deficit' and 'deprivation', and the entry of Bernstein into pedagogic discourse in more detail later.

A key empirical source for Bernstein's early thought was the study reported by Schatzman and Strauss (1955). They analysed accounts of a disaster (a tornado) by witnesses from different social class backgrounds. Schatzman and Strauss suggest, among other things, that their working-class informants were less likely than the middle-class members to employ 'explicit' references, and more likely to assume that their hearer shared their taken-for-granted background assumptions. For instance:

> Often terms like 'we' and 'they' are used without clear referents. The speaker seldom anticipates responses to his communication and seems to feel little need to explain particular features of his account. He seldom qualifies an utterance, presumably because he takes for granted that his perceptions represent reality and are shared by all who were present. Since he is apt to take so much for granted, his narrative lacks depth and richness and contains almost no qualifications and few genuine illustrations. (p.331)
>
> Among the devices readily observable are the use of crude chronological notations (e.g. 'then . . . and then'), the juxtaposing or direct contrasting of classes (e.g. 'rich' *v*. 'poor'), and the serial locating of events. But the elaborate devices that characterize middle-class interviews are strikingly absent. (p.335)

In a typically heavy-handed way Dittmar (1976, pp.42–3) insists on finding in such reports 'the most important hypotheses which appear in the investigations: they relate without exception to the verbal inadequacy of members of the lower class'. While it is the case that normative terminology is to be found in Schatzman and Strauss, it is abundantly plain that they are not concerned with verbal 'deficit' or 'inadequacy'. At root, their paper is an account of different ways in which respondents construct reality through the construction of personal narratives. It is not a description of the differential distribution of linguistic capacities, but the differential distribution of assumptions, presuppositions and conventional cultural resources.

One of the key issues relates to the speaker's sensitivity to the 'role of the other', and his or her deployment of the 'reciprocity of perspectives'. The speaker who presupposes his or her 'perceptions represent reality and are shared by all' will deploy narrative in a way which is relatively insensitive to possible differences in perception and perspective. It will not be found necessary or important to spell out the account in sufficient detail to take account of differences in background knowledge. Likewise, personal qualification and mitigation of the narrative will be diminished: the recounting will not be tailored with a view to personal differences between narrator and hearer. The symbolic world which is constructed through the medium of each narrative may be of a different order of complexity – of internal differentiation of time and place, in its causal relations and the like.

The Schatzman and Strauss study is an important source of early studies of language and social class (not only for Bernstein), but it is more than that alone. It provides for us a link with one of the major theoretical influences that Bernstein himself acknowledges – G. H. Mead. In the first place, Mead insisted on the way language is constitutive of our experience in and of the world: this is the work of the 'significant symbol':

> Symbolization constitutes objects not constituted before, objects which would not exist except for the context of social relationships wherein symbolization occurs. Language does not simply symbolize a situation or object which is already there in advance; it makes possible the existence or the appearance of the situation or object, for it is part of the mechanism whereby that situation or object is created. (Mead, 1934, p. 78)

Furthermore – and this is crucial for Bernstein's mature programme – for Mead language and the capacity for language use are constitutive of the social self and of mind. Mind, self and society – the key triad of Meadian thought – are not separate elements to be amalgamated like a societal construction kit. They are the three moments or aspects of the same general process and, in that process, language is the medium – in the dialogue between the self and the other and the inner dialogue of the I and the Me. According to Mead the constituents of the social process are the symbol and the conversation:

> The self . . . arises when the conversation of gestures is taken over into the conduct of the individual form. When this conversation of gestures can be taken over into the individual's conduct so that the attitude of the other forms can affect the organism, and the organism can reply with its corresponding gesture and thus arouse the attitude of the other in its own process, then a self arises. (Mead, 1934, p.167)

For a general review of Mead's social philosophy, the reader is referred to Miller (1973), and for an account of the origins and development of symbolic interactionism, which acknowledges Mead as progenitor, to Rock (1979). Throughout, it is clear that despite its importance to Mead, language as such is not subjected to detailed analysis. The particular mechanisms of language use did not preoccupy Mead, nor did he dwell on how particular social forms might be generated by specific forms of language. In Mead the processes referred to are of the most general: he refers to elementary social processes, but not to specific cultural variations.

For this latter sense of language Bernstein looked to Whorf and the so-called Sapir-Whorf hypothesis. In essence, this version of anthropological linguistics suggests that the lexis and morphology of a given language provide classificatory and combinatory principles and possibilities which constitute and are constituted by the cultural forms of a given language community (e.g. Whorf, 1956). Bernstein notes that this was an early influence on his thinking: he encountered the ideas in about 1956 (1974a, p.6).

Together, the social behaviourism of Mead, and the anthropological linguistics of Whorf provided a mutually reinforcing synthesis, the one mending what the other omitted. Winter (1973) makes this very point, in a paragraph which the author acknowledges to owe much to Bernstein himself:

> although Mead focuses on the sociological importance of language acquisition as a process, which Whorf merely assumes, he misses Whorf's insight into the cultural consequences of the process. It is interesting to wonder whether Mead missed the problematic character of this process, which he described in detail, precisely because he neglected the structural characteristics of both language and society (e.g. grammar and power respectively). (Winter, 1973, p.29)

The Whorfian view is, of course, thoroughly compatible with the essentially Kantian style of Durkheim's emphasis upon the specificity of cultural classifications (although the implied direction of causation is variable in Durkheim: cf. Thompson, 1982). When Bernstein's own views on language and cultural reproduction are considered, however, the Meadian component should not be lost from view. Bernstein is concerned with much more than the revelatory or inhibitory capacities of given linguistic resources: he addresses too how language use is itself constitutive of social structure, and of social selves, roles or identities.

In pursuing this programme Bernstein has developed a structuralist line of argument, rather than a throughgoing development of the Meadian perspective. It is, however, worth noting that there is a close family resemblance between the Whorfian notion of purely linguistic categories, and the notion of 'typifications' outlined in the existential phenomenology of Alfred Schutz (e.g. 1972). In their development (and domestication) of the phenomenological perspective Berger and Luckmann (1967) stress how linguistic categories embody and crystallize the sedimented experiences of shared cultural resources. Language is thus, *par excellence*, the medium of the social construction of reality.

When the 'new sociology of education' was proclaimed in the early 1970s (e.g. Young, 1971), its standard-bearers proposed a *mélange* of sociological styles, including the phenomenological. Bernstein's work on curriculum (to be discussed later) was widely regarded as part of the new canon, not least by virtue of his inclusion in the 'manifesto' (Young, 1971). Despite such contiguity and the similarities in the perspective just alluded to, Bernstein himself has done little to develop the phenomenological side of language use. It is congruent with this that Bernstein never allied himself wholeheartedly to the so-called 'new sociology'. In the last analysis his sympathies lie with the Whorfian rather than the Meadian strain in his intellectual inheritance. It is, as I have suggested, the Whorfian stress on classificatory and structural principles, rather than the Meadian reference to process with which he is most in sympathy. Sociologically a Durkheimian, Bernstein is temperamentally a structuralist.

Be that as it may, it is quite clear that even in the earliest papers on language and society, Bernstein is exploring different principles in the social construction of reality. Now, in the documentation of reality construction, a number of different approaches is possible. One is to describe the most general social features of intersubjectivity, procedures of everyday reasoning, the characteristics of common sense and scientific interpretation, and so on. Such an approach has relatively little to say about the culturally specific ways in which such reality construction is accomplished, and the differential distribution of such resources. Another approach – often associated with empirical work of an ethnographic nature – is to document the contents of social realities, symbolic worlds and the like – often in relation to institutional or occupational domains (cf. Strauss, 1978). Bernstein proposes a third. More culturally specific than the first approach, his is also more general and formal than the second. In drawing together the threads of Durkheim, Whorf and Mead, Bernstein was from the outset of his publishing career intent on locating different principles of reality-construction within the division of labour of a modern, differentiated society.

It is congruent with the structuralist tendencies in Bernstein's thought and the corresponding emphasis on the constitutive nature of language that, parallel to the sociology of Durkheim and Mead and to the linguistics of Sapir, Whorf and Malinowski, Bernstein should have turned for inspiration to the Russian psychologists: Luria and Vygotsky are major sources for the early essays. Finally, Cassirer's philosophy of the symbolic reinforced Bernstein's developing perspectives on collective representations, and the 'condensation' of shared experience into ritualized and symbolic forms.

Given the structuralist character of his thought, it is perhaps odd that in the development (under-developed though it is) of the psychological analogues of the sociology, Bernstein explicitly acknowledges no great debt to Piaget; this despite the fact that Piaget's project is itself structuralist (cf. Piaget, 1971; Gardner, 1976; Broughton, 1981a, 1981b). Piaget proposes different principles for the structuring of experience and understanding. Such features as Piaget's explorations of 'concrete' and 'formal' operations suggest the identification of different *principles* in the construction of world-views. They can be expressed in terms of a limited set of structural principles. Gardner summarizes his views in the following way; he sees intelligence

> as a product of the interaction between constantly evolving structures in the child's mind and ever-varying aspects of reality which the child becomes able to assimilate or accommodate. The world is not just 'out there', waiting to impress itself on a blank slate; it is a product of our actions upon it, of the relation between these actions, of the symbolic embodiments of those actions. (Gardner, 1976, p. 106)

In retrospect it is, perhaps, just as well that Bernstein did not draw on Piaget explicitly: commentators blind to the structuralist style of thought would have assimilated them both to equally crude views on developmental psychology. Formal analogies, for instance, between the public/restricted in Bernstein and the Piagetian concrete, and the equivalent homology of the formal/elaborated and the formal would no doubt have confused the issue for just too many. Interpretations of linguistic deficit would probably have been combined with equally crude notions of the development of thinking and intelligence in children and adolescents. In Anglo-Saxon circles, after all, there has been a tendency to see Piaget primarily in terms of developmental psychology, with much less attention to his more fundamental interests in structuralism and epistemology. This treatment of Piaget and its limitations are highlighted in the commentary on the Plowden Report by Bernstein and Davies (1969). Bernstein and Piaget have suffered similar fates: their complex ideas have been vulgarized, decontextualized and distorted in the creation and transmission of educational sociology and psychology respectively. This theme has emerged explicitly in Bernstein's more recent ideas on the construction of pedagogic discourse, which is not without such autobiographical connotations; Piaget is explicitly referred to in this latter context (see chapter 8).

In the early essays on language, then, we may not have as yet a fully matured sociology or anthropology of cultural reproduction. It is not yet a fully-fledged structuralist enterprise. The elements are there, as I have tried to outline. It was already a much more variegated line of thought than any simplistic interpretation of 'linguistic deficit' or 'educability' could ever do justice to. The mixture was, perhaps, too heady even for Bernstein himself fully to master at the outset. The assimilation of his later – most overtly structural – work to the European perspectives of the 'new' sociology was to reveal possibilities only latent in the early years. At the time, however, the tenor of British sociological and educational thought was not a sympathetic forum for Bernstein's emergent structuralism. The structuralist thrust was to take shape more explicitly with Bernstein's formulation of the theory of 'codes' and the distinction between 'restriction' and 'elaboration'. For many English-speaking commentators the full implications of this theoretical movement were too alien. Bernstein's contributions thus became entangled in successive debates in education and sociolinguistics, many of which were quite tangential to the nature of his own sociological imagination.

Note

1 This tradition of 'community' images continues to exert its power: the contemporary work of Jeremy Seabrook is a notable example. Oddly, it is this perspective which informs one of Bernstein's most persistent critics, Harold Rosen (e.g. 1973). On the other hand, Jackson (1968) incorporated Bernstein into his picture of the 'working class community'.

4 *The power of code and the coding of power*

While there is an essential continuity in Bernstein's sociology (and not just as it relates to his work on language), about 1962 there is a shift in the thought. The change is more than terminological, but it is marked by the new pair of terms. Public and formal language use are transformed into 'restricted' and 'elaborated' *codes*. The analogy is with a genetic code:

> I am suggesting that if we look into the work relationships of this particular group, its community relationships, its family role systems, it is reasonable to argue that the genes of social class may well be carried through a communication code that social class itself promotes. (1971a, *CCC* 1, p. 143)

This is clearly more than a handy simile or metaphor. The biological genetic code and the cultural communication code are formally equivalent in that they are mechanisms for intergenerational transmission whereby structural properties of similarity and difference are systematically reproduced. Such reproduction is managed by means of a relatively small set of elements, components or principles which in turn govern permitted combinations and permutations.

These components of 'code' will be explored in the next chapter. It will be emphasized there that the terminology of 'code', 'elaboration' and 'restriction' have precise reference. They have, however, been widely misinterpreted in terms of diffuse, evaluative connotations. In other words, it is all too easy to think of the terms as primarily metaphorical. The problem is that – as in all scientific fields – metaphorical usages take on a life of their own (cf. Edge, 1973). 'Public' and 'formal' were equally troublesome for many: a splendid example of confusion was perpetrated by de Cecco (1967) in an editorial introduction to a reprinting of 'Social structure, language and learning': 'The reader should recall that "public" in England refers to what we call "private" in the United States' (p. 86). With editors like that, who needs detractors to spread confusion?

The characteristics which are proposed as realizations of the two codes are derived from the features of language use that I have outlined already. The extreme form of restricted code would correspond to the *ritualistic* use of language. (It is noteworthy just how recurrent a theme ritual is.) A liturgical use of language, for instance, in which traditionally prescribed formulae were strictly adhered to, would reflect and realize restricted code. This particular aspect clearly refers to features of language use, since the surface form of the liturgy may be as 'simple' or 'complex' as you like. The point that Bernstein insists on here is that such ritualized language use is highly *predictable*. In the most extreme case, the language may be entirely predictable. Or at least, such predictability is culturally required: deviations from the prescribed forms will be negatively sanctioned and the social occasion regarded as spoiled. There is no room here, socially speaking, for significant innovation. The innovator in such a context is deviant – perhaps heretical.

It is, therefore, a context of *tradition*; the social conventions which regulate such activity serve to copy and transmit existing forms with utmost fidelity. Neither I nor Bernstein would wish to imply that in practice perfect copying takes place, however. There is no such thing as a perfectly frozen, unchanging 'tradition' which is perfectly transmitted from generation to generation in unmodified forms.

Predictability, then, is a hallmark of such language use. A church service, a collection of magical spells and formulae, a set of games and rhymes, proverbs and similar maxims, a legal code; these are all examples, to one degree or another, where a certain amount of predictability and faithful copying is valued. Consider for example the following examples of proverbial forms:

As plain as a. . . .
As sober as a. . . .
As drunk as a. . . .
As white as. . . .

I think you will agree that most native speakers of British English would readily find words or phrases to fill those slots, and they would be fairly predictable to other English language users. Most people would complete the first of these with *pikestaff*, and continue with *judge* and *lord*. Indeed, this sort of language use can become so much a matter of ritual and tradition that while *pikestaff* is the 'obvious' completion, few contemporary English speakers use that word in any other environment, and may have little idea of what a pikestaff might be or why indeed it should be so proverbially plain. The last example is a bit less predictable, in the dense that a wider range of proverbial fillers might be thought of quite readily. Depending on style or context one would accept at least *a sheet, snow, milk* or *chalk*.

There is no suggestion here that anybody is totally constrained by such habits or conventions. The innovator may artfully produce variations on such well-worn themes – often with startling and pleasing effects; compare, for instance, Dylan Thomas's 'Bible black' in *Under Milk Wood*. A wit can turn an epigram or *bon mot* by disrupting predicted utterance completions. But conventions do exercise constraint precisely by virtue of their conventionality. Predictability has considerable moral force in its own right, for good or ill.

In this sense, predictability does not tell us anything about the form or structure of the utterances in question. Proverbial formulae and the like do conform to elementary patterns and rhetorical tropes, but a prescribed ceremonial enactment may be couched in highly complex form while remaining totally 'predictable'. Now there are good arguments – and evidence – to suggest that even these enactments will tend to reflect elementary patterns, and these will be introduced subsequently. For the moment we should turn to a somewhat different – though closely related – issue concerning predictability, language and language planning.

A key development in Bernstein's academic career was his attachment to the Department of Phonetics at University College, London. There he came under the influence of Frieda Goldman-Eisler. Her own empirical work provided Bernstein with what he saw as a valuable method in the furtherance of his sociology of language:

> It was the most critical encounter of my academic life. Dr. Goldman-Eisler invited me to bring the tape-recordings of the various discussion groups to our next meeting, and gave me a number of her papers. I read them and immediately recognized that her theoretical and experimental work on the relationship between hesitation phenomena and types of verbal planning offered an exciting approach to the analysis of speech I had collected. (1974a, *CCC* 1, p.7)

As these remarks indicate, Goldman-Eisler's contribution was the analysis of linguistic features hypothetically related to verbal *planning*, and thus bearing directly on the notion of predictability. I shall not go into detail on the experimental methods and findings here, either of Goldman-Eisler or of Bernstein himself. I am more concerned with Bernstein's interpretation of the results, and – more importantly still – how that relates to his general sociological thesis.

In brief, then, the empirical techniques involve the enumeration and timing of pauses, hesitations and 'false starts' in spoken language, the measurement of mean utterance length between pauses, and the like. Such measures can be treated as indicators of 'fluency': speech which is fluent will be marked by relatively few hesitations and the mean length of unbroken utterance will be correspondingly longer. Now it is argued that fluency, in this sense, may be a reflection of underlying planning in speech production. In Goldman-Eisler's own work such fluency is held to reflect strength of habit in language use and low levels of planning. Complex planning on the part of the speaker is likely to result in raised levels of hesitation and depressed fluency. The more complicated and innovatory the linguistic planning involved, then, the less fluent the production is likely to be.

Bernstein examined the speech of working-class (day-release) and middle-class (independent school) boys using the Goldman-

Eisler approach. The findings indicated that the working-class sample were the more 'fluent', in that they spent less time pausing and had longer mean phrase length. (The relationship held when various measures of IQ were held constant.)

In drawing attention to Bernstein's emphasis on fluency, I want to emphasize that for many observers, commonsensically, verbal fluency is likely to be valued, and the association of working-class youths with fluent speech is likely to be counter-intuitive. For are they not typed more usually as 'inarticulate'? This counter-intuitive stress on fluency surely disposes of any suspicion that Bernstein ever claimed that working-class speakers were incapable of sustained speech, were 'lost for words' or whatever. There is an irony here, as the American sociolinguist Labov is sometimes thought of (and has thought of himself) as having 'refuted' Bernstein by demonstrating 'verbosity' or verbal fluency among lower-class Black Americans. This ironic contrast between Bernstein and Labov is developed in more detail in chapter 6.

The link between predictability and fluency should be clear in principle. The ritual or liturgical use of language with which I began this discussion will normally be fluent precisely in so far as it is predictable. Adherence to the 'traditional' forms will ensure these two features. I say that such language will 'normally' be fluent and predictable, not to hedge my bets, but simply in recognition that in practice the speaker may be under-rehearsed, may dry up with stage-fright and so on.

As might be extrapolated further from the 'liturgical' example, such verbal planning and production is likely to reproduce shared stocks of formulae and typifications. It is, Bernstein suggests, less well suited to the generation of personally individuated propositions. Whereas the 'ritualistic' use of language would correspond with (though by no means exhaust) the connotations of 'restricted' code, the elaborated code, by contrast, is regulative of the mediation of novelty and individual meaning. Here again, therefore, we are dealing – at the level of 'codes' – with the regulation of forms of social relationship:

> It is considered that an elaborated code facilitates the verbal elaboration of subjective intent whilst a restricted code limits the verbal explication of such intent. The codes themselves are

> thought to be functions of different forms of social relations or more generally qualities of different social structures. A restricted code is generated by a form of social relationship based upon a range of closely shared identifications self-consciously held by the members. An elaborated code is generated by a form of social relationship which does not necessarily presuppose such shared, self-consciously held identifications with the consequence that much less is taken for granted. (1962a, *CCC* 1, p.90)

Bernstein thus proposes at least a formal, structural relationship between: social relationships; modes of language use; linguistic forms themselves. It is no doubt this last element in the equivalences which is the most controversial.

It is extremely difficult to specify what counts as the manifestations of restricted and elaborated code in terms of linguistic forms *per se*. Quite apart from any theoretical niceties concerning the very possibility of such a programme, the complexity of language itself, and the multiple levels of linguistic analysis, mean that exhaustive analysis of language from a Bernsteinian perspective would be a daunting task indeed. He and his collaborators have, however, attempted to specify relations between crucial *contexts* of language use, social relations and semantics: these are not equivalent to grammars of sociolects.

Before outlining more specific aspects of the linguistic elements so defined, and Bernstein's hypotheses relating them to social forms, I want to try to outline in a simple and parsimonious fashion what I take to be the essence of 'elaboration' and 'restriction' in language environments. Before doing so, let me enter the *caveat* that 'codes' are not in themselves descriptions of language varieties: *codes are principles of structuration* which underpin linguistic and social forms, their variation and their reproduction. The relationship between 'code' and the surface manifestations of linguistic variation is a tricky one in Bernstein's writing, and gives rise to some terminological complexity and ambiguity.

Bernstein's contrasting codes can, I believe, be expressed in relation to one of the founding paradigms of modern structural linguistics. As has been suggested in an earlier publication (Atkinson, 1981a) the structural linguistics of Ferdinand de Saussure provide a ready conceptualization of code in language. It is perhaps surprising that Bernstein himself did not develop an explicitly Saussurean linguistics. Saussure himself provided much of the inspiration for structuralist semiotics, and had very close affinities with the Durkheimian school (Saussure, 1960; Culler, 1976).

One of the key components of Saussure's linguistics is the pair of terms *paradigmatic* and *syntagmatic*. These terms refer, respectively, to 'vertical' and 'horizontal' relations between linguistic units. They refer to two axes of distribution. John Lyons provides a succinct summary of how these axes operate:

> By virtue of its potentiality of occurrence in a certain context a linguistic unit enters into relations of two different kinds. It enters into paradigmatic relations with all the units which can also occur in the same context . . . and it enters into syntagmatic relations with the other units of the same level with which it occurs and which constitute its context. (1968, p.73)

At the level of words, Lyons cites the example of the context 'a pint of milk': here the word *pint* enjoys paradigmatic relations with such elements as *bottle*, *cup*, *gallon* and so on, and has syntagmatic relations with *a*, *of*, *milk*. In this formulation all linguistic elements partake of relations on these two dimensions.

While by no means exhausting the full implications of Saussure's linguistics, these two axes and the two types of relations thus expressed, provide an elementary framework for his expression of the structural, systematic character of language, composed of arbitrary signs. These dimensions of contrast and combination are equally central to Bernstein's programme. His work on language and on the organization of school knowledge simultaneously develop the implications of this structuralist perspective. For the moment we are concerned primarily with language, but it must be remembered throughout that, as in the structuralist movement generally, language provides an inspiration and a model which is then transferred to new cultural domains. It would be quite erroneous to extrapolate from this to assume that Bernstein is, like several of his detractors, first and foremost a theorist of language, only subsequently venturing beyond that specialized field into the domains of knowledge and cultural reproduction.

'Codes', then, are descriptive terms for regulative principles which are realized through *different possibilities of selection and combination.* As we shall see, these principles can be identified in analytic contexts other than the purely linguistic; indeed, their value rests precisely in their generalizability and their capacity to illuminate formal ('systemic') links. As demonstrated in the previous chapter, Bernstein was *never* engaged in the identification and description of two contrasting dialects. Language – and this cannot be said too often – is subsidiary, in that it is a means to understanding social relationships, structures and processes.

Hence, the crucial notions of restriction, elaboration, predictability and the like are to be apprehended as much from a sociological perspective as from that of linguistics. Bernstein never deals only in terms of formal linguistic categories, the distributional characteristics of linguistic features and the like. Language and language use are always understood in the context of a moral order: social roles and values; modes of social control and the exercise of power; the ordering of meaning and experience. 'Codes' regulate the transmission and reproduction of cosmologies and the very social structure itself. So while we consider language and language use in more detail, those more general concerns should be borne in mind.

The analysis of codes develops and draws upon the list of oppositions and relationships introduced in chapter 2. We return to a conceptual framework which itself elaborates the themes of the moral order, modes of social control, social roles, and message types. At its heart remains the Durkheimian formulation of the division of labour.

The essentially sociological character of the argument is stated repeatedly, although it has not always been appreciated by subsequent critics of the essays. For instance,

> the consequences of the form the social relation takes are often transmitted in terms of certain syntactic and lexical selections. Inasmuch as a social relation does this, then it may establish for speakers principles of choice, so that a certain syntax and a certain lexical range is chosen rather than another. (1965, *CCC* 1, p.124)

Or,

> According to this view, the form of the social relation or, more generally, the social structure generates distinct linguistic forms or codes and *these codes essentially transmit the culture and so constrain behaviour.* (1965, *CCC* 1, p. 122, emphasis in original)

It is equally the case that Bernstein avoids any hint of linguistic determinism. If anything, the social structure and the social division of labour are determining. Codes are mechanisms of reproduction, and to that extent regulate and constitute what is reproduced: at least, they set limits and create possibilities. There is a determinism in that sense, therefore, but Bernstein explicitly avoids the full implications of a Whorfian position. He also denies the Whorfian implication that there may be a common culture regulated by general features of a shared language (1965, *CCC* 1, p. 123).

The relations of social and language elements are summarized in the following diagram, derived from Bernstein (1965, *CCC* 1, p. 132):

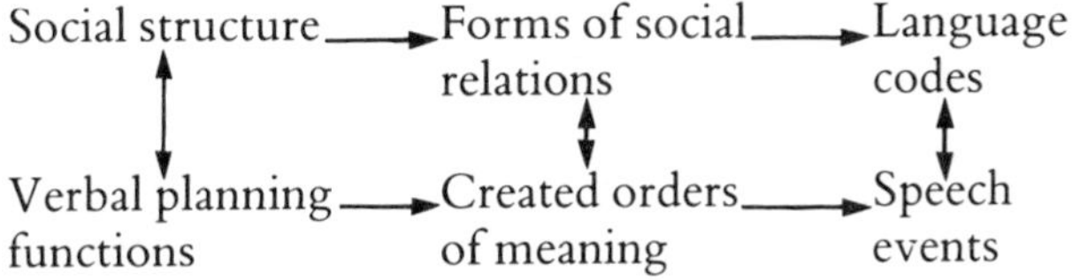

As will be seen, Bernstein proposes reciprocal or dialectical relationships within this model.

Let us begin our consideration with some definitions and consequences of the codes themselves. As we have seen, they concern planning and predictability:

> In the case of an elaborated code, the speaker will select from a relatively extensive range of alternatives and the probability of predicting the organizing elements is considerably reduced. In the case of a restricted code the number of these alternatives is often severely limited and the probability of predicting the elements is greatly increased. (1965, *CCC* 1, p. 125)

Predictability will clearly be closely related to the social context, and the nature of social relations within it. Predictability will not be founded upon purely formal criteria of language, but upon social circumstances, the shared knowledge, values and assumptions of the parties to the encounter.

The 'predictable' form of the 'restricted' code is determined by, and in turn regulates, social arrangements in which there is a high degree of shared orientation, which is taken for granted and/or reaffirmed. There is relatively little emphasis on or opportunity for the introduction of novelty or the elaboration of individual differences between interlocutors. In an extreme form, this would involve lexical prediction – where the very words are predictable to speaker and hearers. Such a degree of restriction is rare in other than pre-scripted ritual performances. In general, Bernstein hypothesizes predictability at a syntactic level.

Empirical evidence for this structural feature is adduced indirectly from evidence of hesitation phenomena (1962a, *CCC* 1, pp.76–94) and more directly from an analysis of the distribution of grammatical elements (1962b, *CCC* 1, pp.95–117). From the former, it is inferred that a degree of *fluency* indicates lower levels of planning (see above p.64). From the latter is inferred the selection of elements from relatively restricted sets and their combination in a relatively restricted range of ways:

> The restriction on the use of adjectives, uncommon adjectives, uncommon adverbs, the relative simplicity of the verbal form and the low proportion of subordinations supports the thesis that the working-class subjects relative to the middle-class do not explicate intent verbally and inasmuch as this is so the speech is relatively non-individuated. (1962b, *CCC* 1, p.109)

As is evident from this brief extract, in the empirical investigations referred to, Bernstein was comparing subjects of middle-class and working-class background (all male). But, as will be stressed again later, the distinctions between codes are not equated simplistically with social class differences: this is another of the many points which has often confused subsequent discussion.

The low level of syntactic elaboration of the restricted code realizations is related to other features of language use. The emphasis of restricted code use is upon an order of *implicit* meaning:

> The intent of the listener is likely to be taken for granted. The meanings are likely to be concrete, descriptive or narrative rather than analytical or abstract. In certain areas meanings will be highly condensed. The speech in these social relations is likely to be fast and fluent, articulatory clues are reduced; some meanings are likely to be dislocated, condensed and local; there will be a low level of vocabulary and syntactic selection; *the unique meaning of the individual is likely to be implicit*. (1965, *CCC* 1, p. 128, emphasis in original)

In contrast, the elaborated code regulates the expression of individuated, personal motives and meanings. By the same token, it is less dependent upon taken-for-granted, shared assumptions:

> The preparation and delivery of relatively explicit meaning is the major function of this code. . . . The code will facilitate the verbal transmission and elaboration of the individual's unique experience. The condition of the listener, unlike that in the case of a restricted code, will *not* be taken for granted, as the speaker is likely to modify his speech in the light of the special conditions and attributes of the listener. (1965, *CCC* 1, p. 128)

The contrasting principles and orders of meaning are paralleled by Bernstein's use of the contrast between *universalistic* and *particularistic*. These terms were appropriated from Talcott Parsons, but their Bernsteinian use is to be traced back beyond him to Durkheim. Universalistic refers to meaning which is explicated through language, while particularistic meaning is implicit – and, to that extent, context-dependent. This dichotomy does not map simply on the restricted/elaborated distinction. For there are *two* connotations to universalism and particularism generally. On the one hand, they refer – as I have just indicated – to the degree of context-dependence. On the other hand they refer to the general currency of language *models* which influence speech. Bernstein suggests that while restricted code is particularistic with respect to meaning, it is universalistic with respect to its models and their social availability. This latter is, perhaps, redolent of the connotations of the term 'public' in the earliest essays. By contrast, while elaborated code is universalistic with respect to its meaning, it is likely to be particularistic with respect to its models, or with respect to its 'special syntax'. In other words, the realization of elaborated code is thus particular to specific social positions.

The acquisition and use of language which is regulated by restricted and elaborated code is related directly to the moral order of the socializing agency – in particular, the family. The moral order is conceptualized in ways which are already familiar in the Durkheimian frame of reference, since they refer ultimately to the distinction between mechanical and organic solidarity, and their associated conceptual apparatus.

The intermediate concept refers to family types, which are distinguished in terms of positional and person-oriented families. These distinctions were applied to entire cultures by Margaret Mead (1937), who employs them to differentiate methods for the mobilization of 'public opinion' and collective action. In a manner congruent with the then current approach to cultural patterns, Mead distinguished between the Arapesh and the Iatmul as representative of personal and positional patterns respectively. Dell Hymes (1977) notes the convergence between Mead and Bernstein, and summarizes the former's analysis thus:

> [Arapesh type cultures] depend, for impetus to or inhibition of community action in public situations, upon the continuing response of individuals. The point of communication is to excite interest and bring together persons who will then respond with emotion to whatever has occurred. In the Iatmul type the societies depend upon formal alignments of individuals, who react not in terms of personal opinions but in terms of defined position in a formal sociopolitical structure. (Hymes, 1977, p. 39)

Bernstein (1971a, *CCC* 1, pp. 167–8) notes that his own use of the terms derives from an unpublished paper of his dated 1962, and a 1963 conference paper (where 'status' was originally used rather than 'positional'). Their use by Hanson (1965) is also acknowledged.

It was entirely congruent with the sociology of the day that

Bernstein should have expressed his ideas in terms of 'open and closed role systems' and the distinction between 'ascribed' and 'achieved' attributes. Families which are characterized as mobilizing 'positional' modes of authority and control are said to be organized in terms of ascribed characteristics – gender, age or generation. By contrast, within the person-oriented family there is much less emphasis upon such ascribed status. Here we are dealing with an interpersonal context where conduct is regulated through discussion or negotiation. Within the positional types conduct is regulated by appeals to authority which is vested in status or seniority. (Note that these are formal distinctions; it is not implied that 'seniority' would be allocated according to the same criteria in all cases.) One should also note Bernstein's own *caveat*, that the positional family is not necessarily 'authoritarian' or 'cold' (1971a, *CCC* 1, p.153). Hence we should not assume that the person-oriented counterpart is idyllically 'democratic'. Authority and control may be exercised in different ways – but that is not equivalent to a contrast between 'domination' and 'freedom'.

It is argued that the contrasting family types can be considered as different types of 'communication system' – 'open' and 'closed'. Here, as with other elements of the general theory, we are dealing with social and cognitive systems marked by variations in choice, planning and alternatives:

> Inasmuch as the role discretion (the range of alternatives of the role in different social situations) is wide, then individual choices can be made and offered. Verbal communication, of a particular kind, is generated. It is not just a question of more talk but talk of a particular kind. Judgments, their bases and consequences, would form a marked content of the communications. The role system would be continuously eliciting and reinforcing the verbal signalling and the making explicit of individual intentions, qualifications and judgments. (1971a, *CCC* 1, p.154)

Such verbal explicitness would be characteristic of the more 'open', 'person-oriented' social context.

In the contrasting positional type, there is a much smaller range of alternatives in the roles, and the communication system correspondingly reflects and regulates restricted personal selection from alternatives:

> Of course, within positional families, there is sensitivity towards persons but the point is that these sensitivities are less likely to be raised to a level of verbal elaboration so that they can become objects of special perceptual activity and control. (1965, *CCC* 1, p.132)

Here, therefore, we have a transformation of the contrast between implicit and explicit communication systems.

As we might expect, 'boundary' is a key element in this formulation. In both families there will be issues of boundary and boundary-maintenance. Within the person-oriented family, the boundaries will be matters of discussion, and by implication the boundaries themselves will be relatively permeable and flexible. In the positional family, on the other hand, boundaries 'might well become border disputes settled by the relative power inhering in the respective statuses' (1965, *CCC* 1, p.131). These boundaries – while not uncontested – will be treated by protagonists as more rigidly defined and demarcated. There will be less tolerance of ambiguity or fluidity here. This treatment of symbolic boundaries and the lines of cleavage or control are developed more vigorously later, in Bernstein's essays on school knowledge under the rubric of 'classification and framing'.

The basic and simplest version of the thesis at this point, therefore, rests upon a series of formal equivalences, which relate the levels of role systems, family types, modes of authority and control, forms of communication, boundary maintenance and symbolic universes. 'Codes', it will be recalled, are underlying principles which regulate and reproduce patterns of symbolic ordering which in turn dialectically relate these levels or domains.

They are not, however, linked in a simple uni-directional causal sequence. Gordon (1981, p.81) unhelpfully tries to summarize the thesis in such a way:

> Bernstein attempts to propose a series of causal relationships which seems to be as follows: social class → family structure → roles → modes of early socialization → roles . . . modes of

> perception . . . access to codes → codes → speech → educational attainment. (An arrow indicates a link clearly postulated as such by Bernstein, dots an obscure link.)

This is also quoted with approval by Stubbs (1983, p.60), who is as insistent as Gordon that there is not a satisfactory underlying theory.

While not wishing to disentangle all the elements at this stage, I wish to stress that formulations like Gordon's make the theory appear quite unnecessarily obscure by seeking to apply an inappropriate frame of reference. Gordon is mistaken in trying to reduce it to a single causal chain.

So far I have not discussed how social class enters into even this elementary scheme; this should be taken into account before the elaboration of the theory and its empirical exemplification. The important thing which must always be kept in mind, whatever aspect of Bernstein's theory is under consideration, is that there is no simple equivalence. It is not the case – nor was it ever – that Bernstein proposes restricted code as an exclusive characteristic of working-class contexts.

Moreover, although it is often portrayed in this way (even by Bernstein on occasion), it is not the case that the relationship with social class is simply a matter of differences in child-rearing practices. The differential distribution of 'codes' is *not* to be thought of as the outcome of more or less fortuitous distributions of class-related cultures, or of cultural lag on the part of the working class when it comes to the regulation of their children. It is related directly to the social distribution of knowledge and power in accordance with the social division of labour. And it is this aspect which also furnishes the full significance of the distinction between *universalistic* and *particularistic* orders of meaning. This is indicated in a key passage, which is worth quoting fairly extensively. Typically, this key passage is introduced by Bernstein almost as an aside ('let me glance at the social distribution of knowledge . . .'):

> We can see that the class system has affected the distribution of knowledge. Historically, and now, only a tiny percentage of the population has been socialized into knowledge at the level of meta-languages of control and innovation, whereas the mass

of the population has been socialized into knowledge at the level of context-tied operations.

> A tiny percentage of the population has been given access to the principles of intellectual change, whereas the rest have been denied such access. This suggests that we might be able to distinguish between two orders of meaning. . . . If orders of meaning are universalistic, then the meanings are less tied to a given context. The meta-languages of public forms of thought as these apply to objects and persons realize meanings of a universalistic type. Where meanings have this characteristic then individuals have access to the grounds of their experience and can change the grounds. Where orders of meaning are particularistic, where principles are linguistically implicit, then such meanings are less context independent and *more* context bound, that is, tied to a local relationship and to a local social structure. (1971c, *CCC* 1, pp. 175–6)

The two orders of meaning, therefore, are more than simply two different ways of using language for the same purposes and with equivalent outcomes. They imply different capacities for power, control, self-regulation and determination. Universalistic discourse, therefore, resides in and makes possible the privilege of symbolic control. The restriction of such control to a minority reflects and reproduces the distribution of control over material resources in this formulation. The class system, Bernstein argues, gives rise to a differential distribution of a sense that the world is 'permeable':

> We have three components, knowledge, possibility and invidious insulation. It would be a little naïve to believe that differences in knowledge, differences in the sense of the possible, combined with invidious isolation, rooted in differential *material* well-being, would not affect the forms of control and innovation in the socializing procedures of different social classes. (1971c, *CCC* 1, p. 175)

The child who is socialized into a permeable, controllable universe of meaning thus has access to the deep structural principle of elaborated code.

In other contexts, Bernstein makes fine discriminations *within* the middle class, as between members who own and control material goods and those who trade in the symbolic domain (the 'new' middle classes). Although it is not explicated in Bernstein's essays on language, there is more than a hint at various points that Bernstein is not really describing 'the middle class' as a unitary category. The specification of a class or class fraction who have privileged access to decontextualized modes of representation has important parallels with Mannheim's notion of an intelligentsia capable of transcending partial, social-context-dependent perspectives.

This latter observation is open to misunderstanding, since Mannheim's own perspective on intellectuals is often subject to unsympathetic reception. It is sometimes thought that Mannheim invoked the intelligentsia as a *deus ex machina* to escape from the problem of relativism, by granting them (and himself) total exemption from the cultural and historical limits of reason. But Mannheim's position, as sympathetically conveyed by Simmonds (1978), was that all social actors are potentially capable of a limited transcendence of their own position, by grasping the meanings of others. While all actors can perform this act of understanding, the intellectual is well placed actually to make the attempt. This does not mean, of course, that all such efforts can meet with perfect success.

Mannheim emphasized the extent to which his 'socially unattached intellectuals' are comparatively independent of the productive process, while being drawn from diverse social backgrounds. Mannheim's version of the intellectuals is undoubtedly much more restricted than Bernstein's characterization of the 'new' middle-class manipulators of symbolic goods. Yet there are very clear parallels between the 'intellectuals' and the new middle class, their capacity for de-contextualized understanding and their place in the social division of labour. As does Mannheim, Bernstein explores some of the implications of the division between cultural production and material production, and the educational consequences of such a difference: this will be dealt with at more length in succeeding chapters.

There is a further, and far from coincidental, continuity as well, in so far as Bernstein is himself the incumbent of the Karl Mannheim chair at the London University Institute of Education. Bernstein's career-long preoccupation with the social distribution of orders of meaning and control is in a direct line of descent from the spirit of Mannheim's work, if not the letter.

Whether or not Bernstein is as close to Mannheim as I have implied, their juxtaposition helps to raise one issue in the early Bernsteinian sociology of education which is, by any account, problematic. That is, the implied congruence between the moral and conceptual order of the elaborated code and the moral and cognitive order of the school. The equivalence is clearly implied by Bernstein, and has been taken up by other commentators, although it is by no means as strongly emphasized in the corpus of essays as might be thought. The issue is, then, to what extent schools operate in terms of de-contextualized meanings; to what extent they are 'intellectual' places.

Bernstein asserts that the school is concerned with the construction and transmission of universalistic orders of meaning, e.g.: 'The school is concerned with the making explicit and elaborating through language, principles and operations, as these apply to objects (science subjects) and persons (arts subjects)' (1970a, *CCC* 1, p. 196). This is stated, here and elsewhere, but is based on little or no detailed discussion of schools and classrooms themselves. Bernstein's bibliographies are not replete with references to studies of everyday life in educational settings. It is, nevertheless, a view which has recently been recapitulated by Holland (1981) in a further study of children's orientations to meaning; she too invokes the proposition that schools are settings for de-contextualized meanings.

Empirical studies which have inspected classroom life with an eye to Bernstein's model are far from endorsing his view of the school's moral and cognitive order. Cooper (1976), for instance, certainly takes Bernstein seriously, in that he codes classroom interaction in terms of the coding frame developed at the Sociological Research Unit (cf. Cook-Gumperz, 1973, pp. 48 ff.). He analyses classroom interaction in terms of two 'contexts' identified in Bernstein's sociology of language – regulative and instructional. On the basis of his analyses in two comprehensive school classrooms, he concludes that regulation is overwhelmingly a matter of 'imperative' language use, rather than through 'personal' appeal. Likewise, in the instructional context, the form of teaching implies passive student reception, while the content specifies particularistic rather than universalistic frames of reference. Cooper's argument, then, is that – paradoxically – the pedagogy of the observed classrooms corresponds more closely to communication regulated by restricted code. Cooper also notes that his own observations do square with Bernstein's formulation of 'visible' pedagogy, to be discussed in more detail in chapters 7 and 8.

Somewhat similar results are suggested by Young (1980) who attempts to relate studies of classroom discourse to Bernsteinian sociology. The analysis again emphasizes the extent to which classroom interaction is positional in form, and transmits what Young calls 'technicist' orders of meaning: that is, knowledge is reproduced in closed, non-negotiable, non-interpretative ways.

Indeed, the majority of studies of classroom interaction, based on observation and recording of everyday practice, suggest that processes of teaching and control approximate to 'restricted' code. It may well be that while the knowledge schools transmit is ideally understood through universalistic frames of reference, and conversely permits access to such meanings, in practice teachers' pedagogy militates against this.

This is a point underlined by Edwards (1981), who comments,

> Unlike Bernstein, I do not assume that the classroom is normally 'predicated upon elaborated codes and their system of social relationships'. Making deliberate reference to his own analysis of open and closed roles, I would typify meanings in the 'regulative context' as being realized largely through imperatives and through positional appeals in a restricted code, and describe pupils as having to 'step into' a predetermined set of 'instructional' meanings and 'leave it relatively undisturbed'. It is surely an unusual classroom in which pupils find frequent opportunities for 'disturbing or changing' a body of received knowledge, and so of 'achieving meaning' on their own terms. (p.292)

This is not the appropriate place to launch into a detailed review of the literature on classroom interaction: for recent surveys of relevant aspects see Edwards and Furlong (1978), Stubbs (1983) and Delamont (1983). The growing corpus of research in this area would certainly lend support to the reservations voiced by Cooper and Edwards.

This would suggest, I think, that schools resemble the mass media, in the way described by Marody (1981). Marody proposes the existence of 'quasi-elaborated code' (pp.27–8), a mode of discourse which 'joins the formal properties of the elaborated code and the cognitive properties of the restricted one' (p.27). Both mass education and the mass media, Marody argues, trade in knowledge and information divorced from everyday experience and from critical reflection (cf. Harris, 1978).

If we take these objections seriously – and I think we must – then any relationship between language codes and classroom discourse needs to be revised. Bernstein's later formulations of 'visible' and 'invisible' pedagogies – though by no means uncontroversial – are much more convincing in the light of empirical research, while remaining faithful to the general analytic framework. If the relationship between primary socialization, codes and educational experience were to be preserved, then a more sophisticated model is needed.

Young (1980) suggests one possible solution – arguing that the 'positional' discourse of classroom teaching means that teachers control high-level cognitive processes in an implicit fashion, and that it takes middle-class cultural competence to crack the meanings, and derive the universalistic propositions which are embedded. Hence Young proposes a 'school-deficit' hypothesis. Elaborated on in Young (1983) this suggests that the pattern of communication characteristic of schools is equally ill adapted to the cognitive needs of middle-class and working-class children. But the middle-class children cope more successfully with this deficit:

> Thus the following hypothesis appears to be a plausible one and worthy of research attention – that there is an association between the communication style of the majority of our classrooms and the class-related cognitive styles of pupils. The metacognitive skills of the middle-class children are more appropriate for learning by attention to the implicit and unreflexive cognitive work of typical teacher talk in the decontextualized environments of our classrooms. (p.12)

This is congruent with the general perspective argued by Bourdieu, who suggests that the cultural resources needed to control and manipulate the content of schooling remain implicit; hence only those already endowed with the relevant capacities can decode the culture of the school (e.g. Bourdieu, 1973, 1974).

The resolution of the apparent paradox appears therefore to lie in Bernstein's most recent discussions of 'pedagogic discourse' (discussed in chapter 8). Here Bernstein argues that knowledge (or texts) which schooling transmits and transmutes is necessarily elaborated. In classroom encounters, however, the exigencies of control may result in imperative and positional interactional modes. There is, therefore, scope for degrees of mismatch between knowledge and control. In Bernstein's most recent formulations one can think of relations between educational knowledge and classroom discourse in terms of different *contexts*.

Bernstein's later formulations of the problem are expressed in somewhat different – and more complex – ways, which also suggest that what is at stake is the pupil's ability to cope with and translate the different codings and transformations of knowledge rather than a simple correspondence model:

> Formal education acts selectively, abstracts from, and re-focuses procedures and performances acquired through the process of primary contextualizing. This process of selection, abstraction and re-focusing leads to *re-contextualizing*. At this level, the activities, meanings and social relationships, their inter-relationships, their sequencing, their evaluation and above all their relation to the procedures and performances acquired through primary contextualizing are a function of the *code* underlying the process of re-contextualizing. (1977b, pp.31–2, emphases in original)

This later account derives from Bernstein's analyses of pedagogy and pedagogic discourse which form part of the more mature structuralist programme, and to some extent supersede the earlier model. This discussion does, however, help to illustrate some of the difficulties encountered if Bernstein's analysis of class, codes and reproduction are treated too literally and simplistically.

5 *Codes, signs and structure*

Students and commentators routinely have some difficulty in coming to grips with the idea of a 'code' itself. As Bernstein himself has repeatedly made clear throughout his work, the term 'code' should never be taken to refer to the actual 'surface' manifestations of language, knowledge – or indeed of any other form of collective representation. People do not speak codes.

It is with the definition, exemplification and analytic significance of codes that one comes to the heart of Bernstein's structuralist programme. Since it is also one of the areas of greatest misunderstanding this is clearly crucial for a thorough appreciation of Bernstein's entire output. A warning is in order: it is difficult to offer anything other than a somewhat abstract characterization of 'code', and while illustration will be attempted here, in the last analysis it remains less than concrete.

This is not the outcome of deliberate mystification on my part, or on that of Bernstein. It reflects the analytic import of the idea itself. For code is not a 'thing' but a *principle*. In this sense, then, 'code' does not simply refer to a set of conventions in a given cultural domain (as in a notion of fashion or etiquette), but to fundamental sets of relationships within and between fields of cultural signification. In this latter sense, Bernstein's usage is close to the range of connotations of 'code' within semiological and cultural studies generally (cf. Corner, 1980). This is confirmed and developed in the most recent restatement and synthesis by Bernstein (1981), where code is defined as 'a regulative principle, tacitly acquired'; codes select and integrate 'relevant meanings', 'forms of their realization' and their 'evoking contexts'. The amplifications and developments contained in this most recent statement clarify and confirm that an essentially structuralist, semiotic approach unifies and underpins all of Bernstein's work. The essay and its various appendices summarize many aspects of the sociology. Moreover, it emphasizes the extent to which Bernstein's formulations of 'code' are representations of *power*.

What sort of a concept or principle is it, then? It refers to a regulatory principle which operates at a very fundamental or 'deep' level. Let us try to imagine that sort of principle with reference to the work of Claude Lévi-Strauss, and in particular to the anthropological treatment of the notion of 'social structure'. Lévi-Strauss takes issue with anthropologists who portray structure as a sort of jigsaw puzzle whereby the various institutional components 'fit' together to form a functional whole (system or organism). Lévi-Strauss himself proposes a different version of 'structure'. Retaining the metaphor of the jigsaw, Lévi-Strauss suggests an alternative level of analysis: that is, the mechanism which drove the jig that cut out the surface patterns in the first place. It is thus possible that the diverse patterns at the surface can be accounted for – in a parsimonious and elegant way – at this underlying or primitive level. For a Lévi-Strauss, therefore, the 'structure' to be investigated is this 'deep' principle which regulates the surface manifestations of cultural forms.

For Bernstein, 'code' has a very similar sort of analytic function, though one with more specificity than the views of 'structure' Lévi-Strauss himself or anthropologists of a similar persuasion would trade in. Overall, Bernstein's analytic use of 'code' has addressed many diverse social domains, institutions and practices: the school, the family, work, primary socialization, social control, curriculum, meaning, perception, the division of labour, language, ideology. The relationships between these varied social spheres, topics and levels of analysis are not expressed in simple structural–functional terms. Bernstein therefore does not attempt to show how they 'fit together' as in the first version of the jigsaw puzzle. Rather, he seeks constantly to uncover underlying principles governing the formal relationships between them, the structuring mechanisms which regulate their reproduction and transmission, and the transformation rules whereby their interrelationships may be expressed.

It is not the case that Bernstein has sought to *reduce* the diversity and complexity of cultural forms to a single all-embracing schema. Rather, the enterprise involves the search for a range of analytic concepts, which can be related through formal affinities, and which permit the principled and systematic exploration of the various forms: 'A major aim of the research has been to try and understand the basic social controls on the form and contents of symbolic orders transmitted initially in the family and in the process of education' (1973b; *CCC* 1, 2nd edn, p.237). Furthermore, when we talk of 'structuring' or 'regulative' principles, it must be emphasized that this should not be taken to imply a mechanistic view of the processes involved. The analyses should not be read as reductionist in that sense. As Bernstein himself points out, in one of his introductory reflections on the work:

> I should emphasize that because words like structure, codes, principles, are used, this is not to suggest a mechanical or simple process of transmission and reproduction. On the contrary, we should ask how it is that only at particular times is the relation between transmission and reproduction simple and complete. The distribution of power and the principles of social control *create structural relations* but these relationships contain contradictions, ambiguities, cleavages and dilemmas which inhere in the symbolic realizations of structural relations and in this way enter into mental processes to become the seeds of change. (1977a, *CCC* 3, p.20, emphasis in original)

The notion of a 'code' – and in particular the connotations of 'restriction' in such an environment – can be illustrated with a number of concrete exemplars. These illustrations are offered not as 'proof' of the validity of Bernstein's formulations but rather to display the general *form* of the principle of 'codes'. Furthermore, they are an attempt to illustrate the generality and range of the idea. It is certainly not confined to those areas of application essayed by Bernstein himself.

Let us begin with an example far removed from ideas of spoken and written language, and from the world of education. Take the idea of *clothing*. It is possible to think of dress as a sort of cultural domain governed by fundamental semiological or semiotic principles: indeed authors such as Barthes (1967) and Leach (1976) have done just that. In the act of putting on a collection of garments any wearer is engaging in a *system* of clothing conventions, and as in all such systems of signification, the elements (garments) partake of relations of *selection* and *combination*. That is, any individual piece of clothing will be selected from a class of possible garments, and will be combined with elements from other equivalent classes.

Our own system of clothing, for instance, provides a number of garment 'slots' to be filled by the appropriate selection of one or more from a garment category. These garments are arranged primarily on the basis of two dimensions – from top to bottom (head to toe) and from inside to outside (underwear to outer garments). At the top, the slot 'hat' may be filled from a diverse collection (top hat, bowler, cap, pork-pie, trilby, headscarf, pill-box, snood, bonnet, turban, cloche, panama, boater, etc., etc.) or may be left unfilled. At the other end, the feet may be shod from an equally diverse range (brogues, sandals, trainers, carpet slippers, court shoes, clogs, boots, etc., etc.). Likewise, for the various intermediate slots which are variously realized by skirts, trousers, shirts, jackets, pullovers and so on, there is normally a range of choice. Many other categories will be optional, but for most purposes *some* garment must be selected for at least one such garment slot.

Now, my intention here is to illustrate what the notion of 'code' – and especially a 'restricted code' – might give rise to in such a semiotic context. In Bernstein's terms, remember, the code will regulate the selection and combination of cultural elements, and will articulate that array with social occasions and contexts of use. Now, there are obviously many constraints operating on any individual's use of clothing. There are 'system' constraints, as in any such environments, so that it is rarely 'grammatical' to wear 'two hats' at once, or 'odd' shoes. There are also constraints of 'fashion' which at least some users will seek to conform with, and which limit the availability of garments for any potential dresser. There are also aesthetic constraints, such as the matching of colours, combinations of pattern and so on. The choice of garments is rarely entirely open and free, then, any more than in any other system of signs. There are always degrees of restriction and constraint. Without them there could be no sense either of 'grammatical' or 'felicitous' productions; we should be in the realm of meaningless chaos.

On the other hand, one can think of contexts where there are very severe conventional restrictions in operation. What in clothing systems we refer to as *uniforms* are subject to extreme restriction. By definition, uniforms (such as military dress) admit of no flexibility or personal preference. Instructed to dress appropriately for ceremonial duty at Buckingham Palace, a member of the Brigade of Guards has no options to exercise. He cannot choose whether or not to wear the bearskin cap, or the scarlet tunic: these elements are required. Likewise, the system of uniforms eliminates choice as to the permitted combination of elements. Our guardsman's red tunic cannot, as a matter of whim or changing fashion, be combined with khaki fatigues and a forage cap. Each 'uniform' specifies a unique or highly restricted selection and combination of elements.

In these terms, then, the uniform system of, say, the military realizes a restricted code in this precise sense: the selection and combination of elements (garments) is fixed. Moreover, such clothing requirements are directly related to social contexts. The restrictions of dress correspond to a fixed, closed set of social roles and occasions which our hypothetical guardsman is required to participate in. The military example is nicely paralleled by the behaviour of the flight attendants on major airlines: the stages of the journey and the division of labour are precisely and nicely marked by prescribed changes of uniform, and the addition or removal of specified garments.

I realize that military uniforms and occupational liveries are rather 'obvious' examples. It comes as no surprise that such clothing systems operate in the way they do. Indeed, that is why they are offered by way of exemplification here. Their very familiarity and concreteness make them readily accessible. Furthermore, it draws attention to some further features. Uniforms absolve their wearers from problems of planning and choice, since there are no options to be exercised. By definition, they promote relations of identity ('uniformity') among the wearers: differentiation between *individuals* is at a minimum. On the other hand, uniforms also clearly demarcate grades and categories (e.g. ranks). While individual differences are slight, contrasts in position or status are sharply marked. Likewise, a relatively small set of different social contexts or functions is delimited.

In practice, most uses of clothing fall between the extreme restriction of uniform and completely open-ended choice. By and large, the opposition between 'restricted' and 'open' use corresponds to the polarity between 'formal' and 'informal'. Formal occasions call for highly restricted selections and combinations from within the garment system. Leach reminds us:

> Until very recently it was common practice in certain sections of contemporary English society to mark invitation cards for an evening dinner party with one or other of three formality indicators. 'White Tie' meant 'very Formal'. Males were expected to wear a stiff-fronted white shirt, white tie and black tail coat. . . . 'Black Tie' meant 'Semi-Formal'. Males were expected to wear a dinner jacket (tuxedo), with soft shirt and a bow tie of some sort. This could never be white, but need not be black! 'Informal Dress' meant what it says. (1976, p. 56)

Leach cites this as an example of how socially significant messages can be encoded very elegantly and parsimoniously in terms of binary oppositions (white/not-white and bow tie/not bow tie). Such metonymic codings are possible because of the degree of uniformity or predictability involved in the system. As we move from the most formal towards the less formal, so the predictability diminishes. White tie admits of no choice, black tie permits some choice, and informal provides even more latitude. Events which are formal enough to have such invitations do not imply total freedom, of course.

We could go on in increasing detail about garment codes, but that is not the main purpose here. What we have is just one example of a semiotic code by which message-systems and social contexts are constituted. Note here some further, more general features. In the examples already cited, the formal restricted occasions and their markers are largely matters of 'tradition'. They change slowly, if at all, and admit of little personal – or indeed collective – innovation. Spontaneity and invention are largely subordinated to collective uniformity. What is valued is a form of social conformity: *savoir-faire* and felicity reside in the successful matching of identity to occasion, rather than the creation of innovatory personal style. Moreover, the clothing example parallels how features may have differing significance under differing codings. In uniform, for instance, fine gradations of shine, creasing, or the angle of a cap may have very specific 'meaning'. This may be compared with the extent to which extra-verbal features attain enhanced salience the greater the strength, or predictability, of language code. (I am grateful to Basil Bernstein for this observation.)

My next example is equally removed from debates concerning education and social class. It concerns the genre known as 'oral epic'. This is a widely spread form of narrative art, which has been documented in many cultures. In the European literary tradition it is most familiar through the Homeric poems *The Odyssey* and *The Iliad.* Abstruse though this may appear at first sight, these epic narrative verses exemplify the general theme quite appositely: I first proposed it in 1981, since when Ong (1982) has drawn a similar analogy.

While we have the Homeric epics in written form, they derive from a tradition of oral production, predating the construction of written texts. The pioneering work in the recognition of their oral character was done by Milman Parry (e.g., 1971), who drew on comparative evidence of contemporary oral composition, in the Balkans especially. Prior to Parry's writings, classical scholars had noted distinctive features of the Homeric corpus, but it was Parry who displayed their full significance. The most noticeable thing about Homer's verse is the repeated use of a relatively limited repertoire of 'stock' phrases and descriptions. The poet had available standardized, formulaic forms of words. These were used and distributed with a high degree of economy, and their use related very precisely to the requirements and constraints of the verse metre (hexameters). For example, while Homer had to hand several ways of describing 'wine', they were all different in terms of their metrical equivalence: each was available to fill a different segment of the line. Moreover the economy of the system allowed little redundancy. For a given metrically defined position there may be only one filler, or very few alternatives available to the composer. Kirk (1965) provides a succinct account of the formulaic character of oral epic, illustrating its parsimony and efficiency, while modern – rather different – examples of such improvization in the Greek language are reproduced in Fermor (1958) and Loizos (1981).

To a considerable extent, therefore, *The Odyssey* and *The Iliad* consist of a predictable deployment of set formulae. The function of such a mode of composition is quite clear. The oral poet or bard does not commit entire epics to heart and simply repeat them by rote. Rather, the bard's skill lies in extemporizing. Yet such compositions cannot be produced absolutely afresh on each new occasion. The bard cannot try out new forms and construct the epic from scratch. Hence the use of formulae is perfectly adapted to the fluent composition of the verse. The 'artistic' originality normally valued in written verbal arts is here subordinate to the functional requirements of oral composition. Mary Renault (1978) has written an excellent fictionalized (or mythologized) account of the tension between the 'restricted code' of the oral bard and the compositional style of the literate poet.

While it does not correspond to our normal canons of creative aesthetics, the skill of the bard is highly developed. His or her competence is embedded in a highly evolved tradition, and skill resides in the artful manipulation of the traditional resources. The improvised composition of oral verse must be generated with a smooth assurance, and there is little place for 'artistic' redrafting, musing, and waiting for inspiration.

The tradition and skills associated with oral epic thus depend upon a high degree of restriction in the system. Operating within the overall constraints of the metrical line, the composer selects from a relatively restricted range of alternatives: the stock of formulae is limited. Likewise, these metrical elements or building-blocks can contract only a restricted number of permitted combinations, given their highly economical deployment in different positions in the line.

Here again, therefore, we find a semiotic system characterized by a degree of restriction in terms of *selection* and *combination*. While Homeric epic and military uniforms are very different cultural manifestations, they appear to share this common feature, which is related directly to shared functions. Both are functionally suited to the elimination of personal, individual planning and choice. In these contexts the identity of the wearer or the bard is largely subordinate to the demands of the semiological system itself. As we shall see, features of this sort are central to Bernstein's own formulations.

In emphasizing notions of 'restriction' here, no inference need be drawn concerning 'inadequacy' or 'incompetence'. On the contrary the semiology of such systems is evolved, functional and economical. They convey their messages with remarkable efficiency. A 'Homer' is clearly a different sort of author from a contemporary literate novelist or poet. Yet few, I believe, would care to suggest that Homer was the perpetrator of inadequate or deficient compositions.

Bernstein's general scheme may be illustrated further with more brief examples. Consider, for instance, the verbal 'art' of a particular and familiar sort of stand-up comic. While it is by no means hard-and-fast, many such comics rely on a fairly limited repertoire of stock characters, stock situations and narratives, and stock verbal formulae. At its most elementary and basic: 'Take my mother-in-law, what a woman . . .'; 'There was an Englishman, an Irishman and a Scotsman . . .'; 'A funny thing happened . . .'. (I do not wish to suggest that many contemporary comedians can actually survive on quite such hackneyed and impoverished material!) These elemental building blocks are highly functional to the situation of the comedian and the audience. They facilitate the instantaneous recognition of predictable contents and formats. The audience can be expected to 'know' how and why Irishmen or mothers-in-law are supposed to be funny according to the conventions of the genre. Originality (in this sense) is not as important as a rapid-fire recognition. The sort of stand-up comic I am referring to rarely evokes novel characters and situations. Rather, comic and audience share and re-create well-known assumptions and stereotypes. The 'jokes' can often be very brief indeed, since they readily index underlying stocks of knowledge and belief. Of course, I do not deny any element of 'creativity' on the part of the comic and the scriptwriter. Stale jokes are occasions of failure, not success. But novelty is often forged out of the manipulation of a limited (restricted) range of existing archetypes – a kind of 'molecular roulette' played with the formulae of the comic genre.

Note again how this characterization of a form of restriction emphasizes its relationship to a social context, to which it is highly adapted. Nobody would suggest that the format employed by a one-line comedian is ideally suited to the production of a PhD thesis; but the compositional formats of most doctoral dissertations would probably go down rather poorly on most club nights. Here, as throughout, we are not dealing with mere niceties of style. Bernstein certainly claims far more than stylistic, conventional differences for the codes he describes.

My examples from Homer and the world of the stand-up comic can be paralleled again by reference to other verbal arts. Many cultures value verbal skills – often of a competitive nature – which call for the rapid production and exchange of verbal tokens between contestants. Dundes, Leach and Özkök (1972) for instance, have documented verbal 'duelling' among young Turkish males, who compete in the exchange of rhyming insults on a turn-by-turn basis. Many such verbal forms have been described among black Americans, and they are identified in terms of various folk-types, including rapping, shucking, jiving, signifying, and playing the dozens. (See, e.g. Kochman, 1972; Gilmore, 1981; Hannerz, 1969.)

Labov (1972b) has collected and analysed many examples of the exchange of 'ritual insults' among urban black males. He comments on their ritual features:

> The ways in which sounds [insults] are delivered, and the evaluation of them by the group, follow a well-established ritual pattern that reflects many assumptions and much social knowledge not shared by members of other sub-cultures. (p. 127)

These ritual insults and other characteristics of black English vernacular in use are often used to counter the (supposed) claims of Bernsteinian sociology. In much of the 'standard' secondary literature in this area, Bernstein and Labov are juxtaposed; Labov is widely held to have exposed the 'errors' of deficit models in general, and of Bernstein in particular. The 'debate' is chimerical, for while each author makes passing reference to the other, in critical vein, they have not in fact engaged in sustained confrontation.

Such naturalistic accounts of Afro-American language skills certainly dispose of any notion that linguistic competence *per se* is missing or undervalued, but I intend to ignore the Labov–Bernstein juxtaposition for now: it will be returned to in the following chapter. Rather – with deliberate perversity – I use Labov's findings to illustrate Bernstein's own concept. Here I wish to note the formal similarity between these ritual insults and the semiotic forms already exemplified. As Labov's own designation indicates, the insults have ritualized features, and this implies much more than being delivered without serious intent. They follow set patterns and stock themes. Labov's analysis involves the explication of the *rules* involved in the collaborative production of ritualized sequences. The successful practitioner needs to master the repertoire of culturally available paradigms, themes, formulae and patterns of insult. These are not just memorized by the adept performer, but provide a resource to be deployed.

As Labov himself shows, there are elementary forms which provide the basis for such insults. They include:

Your mother is (like). . . .
Your mother got. . . .
Your mother so . . . she. . . .
Your mother eat. . . .
Your mother raised you on. . . .
I went to your house. . . .

Labov describes these and similar sequences as 'basic formulas', a characterization which recalls the formulaic nature of the Homeric epic. These formulae are built on in the course of insult exchanges, but they furnish the basic 'grammar' for such sequences. The combination of themes ('your mother', 'your house' and various obscene attributes) provides for a fair degree of *restriction* in this semiotic system. The successful insult-maker will not search the entire cultural universe for felicitous insults ('your bank manager . . .'; 'your probation officer . . .'; 'your second cousin . . .') but for the most part will select from a limited class of items. Likewise, the basic formulae reflect only a limited range of patterns and 'slots' to be filled. Thus, while there is certainly room for innovation, embellishment and personal style, the overall system displays restriction, in the sense we are dealing with here. The user selects from a restricted range of paradigmatic possibilities, and these are combined in a restricted number of ways. Again, we can see that this feature of the system aids fluency: like the bard or club comic, the protagonist in an exchange of insults has no time to stop and think up an entire domain of brand-new offerings, while the audience and adversary have no time to cue in and respond in an appropriate fashion. These oral traditions, therefore, all depend in various ways on the promotion of fluency.

The elements of ritual and tradition in such oral culture played their part in Bernstein's early thinking. This is clear in his review essay (1960b) on *The Lore and Language of Schoolchildren* (Iona and Peter Opie, 1959). It is worth noting that although it was a book review, Bernstein accords that short piece sufficient significance to warrant inclusion in the first volume of *Class, Codes and Control* (pp.71–5). In the Opies' repository of children's rhymes, games and the like, Bernstein finds an example of 'public' language use (the terminology reflects the date of the publication). He cites the work of Goldman-Eisler on the fluent reproduction of habitual 'words, phrases and sequences as tags or social encounters':

> The language of children used in the peer group bears all the hall-marks of old, practised, well organized speech. The speech is not specially created by the child, except by the innovators; rather the child's task is to learn when and how to apply the sequence appropriately and adroitly. (1960b, *CCC* 1, p.72)

As he notes himself, this may require a highly developed communicative competence, in terms of adequate 'sensitivity to the norms of his sub-culture', but it is not a medium well suited to the expression of individually subjective motive or intention. Even the innovative child, according to the Opies, expresses creativity through the felicitous selection from an existing set of terms.

Given Bernstein's enthusiastic reception of the Opies' book, it is bizarre that any critic of his should ever have suggested that he was unaware or dismissive of the rich variety and expressive capacity of such oral culture(s). It adds special piquancy to the quite misplaced way in which Labov's documentation of 'ritual insults' is often used to 'demonstrate' the error of Bernstein's ways.

Now it might be objected that while these various things share common features, this is unremarkable, as *all* such systems of collective representation exhibit formal restriction. And in one sense that is quite right. Any spoken, written, graphic, material or musical composition will be constituted through the conventions of style, genre, fashion and the like. No author creates completely afresh: speech and writing are always conducted within or against the boundaries of cultural convention. On the other hand, it must be remembered that 'restriction' in our sense, is always in principle a matter of degree rather than absolute difference. The types referred to above seem to be particularly restricted in terms of the two principles of selection and combination. They are certainly not 'restricting', in so far as they are very well suited to the promotion of fluent production and comprehension. Hence they do not hamper or prevent communication and the user is not at a loss or communicatively handicapped. On the contrary, the adept user can generate highly artful and effective performances.

The point is that such cultural resources are highly specific. They are very good indeed for particular purposes, but not very flexible or adaptable to new contexts. Labov's ritual insults are magnificently fashioned for the vigorous expression of sexual insult, obscenity, competitive masculinity and so forth. They are – as far as I can judge – very poorly suited to the exploration of nuances of personal feelings and the generation of novel insights. This remark leaves open whether the users' verbal skills and communicative competence more generally might be transferred to other social contexts and other verbal skills.

Zijderfeld (1979) draws on G. H. Mead to make a similar point concerning the social function of verbal formulae:

> In order to be able to communicate efficiently in social life, we must conduct the greatest part of our social interactions as routine. Daily social life would simply be impossible if we had to ponder every single sentence and move, investing cognitive and emotive energy in every situation that occurred. Clichés are the indispensable and rather ingenious means for the realization of this social objective. They enable us to communicate without the need to reflectively internalize the attitudes of our interaction partners and to mentally and emotionally anti-

cipate the further course of the interaction. . . . By means of clichés we are able to interact and communicate smoothly, routinely and in a facile manner. It must be stated emphatically, therefore, that clichés are indispensable to social life. (pp. 57–8)

In Zijderfeld's monograph the old rhetorical notion of *prolepsis* is given a new lease of life. In its original usage it referred to a speaker's capacity to anticipate and pre-empt objections to the argument. Zijderfeld extends it to mean the realization in language of the Meadian concept 'taking the role of the other'. This insight is directly parallel to the following observation from Bernstein, commenting on the relationship between verbal planning and the reciprocity of perspectives in face-to-face encounters. Parties to the encounter, he suggests, will attempt to achieve some equilibrium in mutual perception; through speech each actor will attempt to internalize the other's intent. The nature and range of such internalization is related directly to code, by reference to 'verbal planning'. Hence

If the code is *restricted*, by definition so is verbal planning; consequently the range and type of others who can be so internalized is limited. By implication the social tie to those who can be so becomes a very powerful bond which is both positively and negatively strengthened by the code. (1961a, p. 260)

This feature of 'coding' incidentally serves to reinforce the conceptual link to G. H. Mead, whose presence is implicit in so many of Bernstein's texts.

Further exemplification along these lines is provided by Widdowson (1976) in a discussion of 'traditional' forms of learning and social control in lower-class families; the analysis is based primarily on fieldwork in Yorkshire. He instances the form of *dites* (such as formulaic explanations of natural phenomena) and proverbs. Widdowson emphasizes that they are highly functional:

Insofar as such usages encapsulate certain aspects of the familial and cultural *mores*, they clearly have an important part to play in the socialization of the child. Their brevity, pithiness,

> structural patterning (including balance, antithesis, alliteration and assonance), word play and metaphorial form, reinforced by frequent repetition in similar contexts, present the child with opportunities to extend his receptive competence, and also, through imitation, to improve his expressive competence and performance. (p. 51)

Widdowson bases his discussion on a cautious reading of Bernstein, in a way congruent with the view of 'code' presented here, with no implication of 'deficit'.

Consequently, when we talk of 'restricted' code in Bernstein's work, it must be in the sense outlined and exemplified above. It has sometimes been suggested that Bernstein himself was ill-advised to use the term 'restricted'. For too many of his readers it has carried strong connotations of 'inadequancy' or 'deficiency'. The terminology has fuelled the misunderstanding of Bernstein's own intentions and has run counter to his own protestations to the contrary. On the other hand, if my own characterization is apposite, then it becomes clear that 'restriction' can be given a precise formulation where the terminology itself is highly appropriate, and which can be related to well-established semiological principles. In addition, such a view of restriction, as I hope has been demonstrated, in no way implies an absence or inadequacy of communicative competence on the part of the user. There are surely few readers who would want to suggest that *The Iliad* or *The Odyssey* were the outcome of linguistic or cognitive 'handicap'.

These exemplifications do not exhaust the connotations of Bernstein's notion of 'restriction' in relation to 'codes'. My own examples are open to misinterpretation: they should not be taken to mean, for instance, that 'restricted code equals oral communication' with the corollary that 'elaborated code equals written language', or that restricted code is necessarily to do with 'primitive', pre-literate cultures and sub-cultures.

It is already the case that conceptual muddles exist on this score. Some have suceeded in equating 'elaborated' with 'written' and 'restricted' with 'oral' productions. Harrison (1971) invokes Bernstein to help deal with the relationship between the language of literature and the language of the street, while Hill and Varenne (1981) manage to equate restricted code with speech and elaborated code with written text. Strachan (1979), somewhat unhelpfully, suggests that 'literature' approximates to elaborated code (on the grounds of low predictability), and may therefore be the basis for a heightened awareness of language through literary studies. (This manages, it would appear, to miss the co-presence of condensed, metaphoric and metonymic orders within 'literary' texts.) Of more value in the literary domain is Fowler's (1977) analysis of restricted and elaborated codes in D. H. Lawrence (*Sons and Lovers*). Indeed, Fowler suggests that Lawrence subscribed to the same 'model' or 'schema' and constructed his characters in accordance with it (p.115).

In the last analysis, however, such considerations are tangential to the main sociological argument; we should not become too preoccupied with the exemplification of codes. The semiology of codes, the principles of selection and combination, and the orders of meaning they give access to, are of more profound significance than matters of style, genre or cultural conventions. If code is a fundamental regulative principle, then we must look to equally fundamental sociological issues.

We have seen hitherto that some of Bernstein's early papers of codes relate them to a *gemeinschaftlich* view of working-class 'community'. This can lead to misunderstandings, however, which mask the true significance of the analyses. For understandable reasons codes have been interpreted theoretically and deployed empirically in terms of class and community cultures. For instance, Lumby (1976) attempts to use Bernstein to analyse talk between homosexuals, and between homo- and heterosexuals, in terms of a restricted code in the 'closed' gay social world. Easthope (1976) writes of restricted codes within the Catholic and Protestant 'communities' in Northern Ireland: such restricted code, he argues, 'limits the perceived possibilities of action and reinforces the pressures to conformity produced by localism' (p.435). Allan (1977) affirms this trend, citing Bernstein in the general context of working-class community studies. A general interpretation of this sort is endorsed by Gumperz (1982), who cites both Sapir and Bernstein in support of the view that 'exclusive interaction with individuals of similar background leads to reliance on unverbalized and context bound presuppositions in communication, and that the formulaic nature of closed network group talk reflects this fact' (p.71). The upshot is that many interpretations stress cultural rather than structural features, emphasizing 'closed' cultures, bounded by linguistic 'barriers' (cf. Hartig, 1977).

Now there is more than an element of truth in such interpretations, quite properly reinforced by Bernstein's own insistence on the significance of 'boundary' in his own sociology, but a purely cultural interpretation is inadequate, and leads to a thoroughly mistaken view of Bernstein's own intentions. The mistaken inference is that Bernstein does no more than juxtapose contrasting class sub-cultures. This is a view articulated by Goldthorpe and Bevan (1977) in a general review of British studies of social stratification. They identify, and are critical of, approaches which address 'class as culture', and include Bernstein in that category; Goldthorpe and Bevan themselves advocate, in contrast to such cultural viewpoints, ideas of class expressed through *power* relations.

Goldthorpe and Bevan here highlight an important issue in the interpretation of code. It has been argued by a number of authors that Bernstein contains an inadequate representation of social class, by virtue of the absence of power in his sociology. Bisseret (1979) provides a particularly strong and articulate version of this critique:

> Bernstein separates and dichotomizes so as to compare, as if it were a question of comparing, like an ethnologist, heterogeneous culture systems and not two sub-systems which define each other. In fact, when he talks of social structure, the expression 'social structure' does not refer to the whole society, but to each particular class. (p. 103)

Bisseret goes on to gloss Bernstein's view of class as a representation of a 'closed society'.

My own view is precisely the reverse of this. Far from being absent, power informs all of Bernstein's sociology, as does a notion of social structure which is radically different from a pluralist juxtaposition of class, ethnic or regional cultures. It is not always recognized, however, because power is treated in a specific manner, alien to much 'mainstream' sociology. To some extent the treatment of power and structure are implicit in the earlier essays, and emerge more clearly as the structuralist thread is discerned more clearly. It is confirmed in the most recent affirmation of the theory of codes (Bernstein, 1981). The most general position is enunciated most emphatically in the opening statement:

> 'Class relations' will be taken to refer to inequalities in the distribution of power and in principles of control between social groups, which are realized in the creation, distribution, reproduction, and legitimation of physical and symbolic values that have their source in the social division of labour. (p. 327)

In other words, power and control are inscribed in the cultural forms which Bernstein addresses. This most recent reformulation of Bernstein's theoretical position leaves no doubt as to the centrality of power and control to the entire sociological programme. Power relates to *message* while control relates to its realization (or 'voice' in the most recent conceptual reorderings). The relations of power and control thus underpin the earliest work on role systems (and the positional/personal contrast) as well as the later work on school knowledge, to be discussed in chapters 7 and 8. The forms of communication and consciousness so generated 'position' persons ('subjects') by virtue of such differential distribution. Hence, in most general terms, codes are 'culturally determined positioning devices', and 'More specifically, class regulated codes position subjects with respect to dominating and dominated forms of communication *and* to the relationship between them' (p. 327).

Bernstein conceives of 'power' as a matter of boundaries and 'positions': of the distinction between the 'thinkable' and the 'unthinkable'. At its most general 'power' is to silence as 'control' is to communication (Bernstein, personal communication). This principle underlies the work on language *and* on educational knowledge. Indeed, at root both sets of analyses play out the same underlying relationships. The 1981 'modalities' paper makes this clear, as the most general and inclusive (if highly condensed and abstract) statement of Bernstein's sociology.

The distribution of codes, therefore, does not simply follow a functional diversity within the division of labour. It is not innocent. It is a reflection of the hegemony of the dominant class:

> If agents become specialized categories of the social division of labour, and their location is fixed and so nontransposable, then coding orientations become specialties of position within the social division of labour. The condition for these conditions is the *principle of the social division of labour itself.* The group that dominates the principle of the social division of labour determines the extent to which positions in the social division of labour give access to specialized coding orientations. (1981, p.333)

This, then, is quite the reverse of the position attributed to Bernstein by Bisseret and others. The work is suffused with notions of power. But 'power' is by no means a simple relation. Rather, his position – especially in the most recent essays – seems much closer to that of Foucault, who insists that power is multi-faceted, diffuse and ubiquitous. Power, for Foucault, is to be found in the complex of sites, institutions and relationships throughout society. Power, for both Foucault and Bernstein, is not separate from other relationships, of production and knowledge, but immanent in them (cf. Sheridan, 1980, pp.183–4 for a succinct summary of Foucault on power).

Hence, the 'positioning' of categories and subjects in the division of labour and the codes that are generated (and generative) in that process, are regulative of *structuration*, to use the term given wide currency by Giddens (e.g., 1980). As Elchardus (1981) has pointed out, there is a close affinity between Bernstein's position and the view of structuration via 'the reproduction of common life experience over the generations' (Giddens, 1980, p.107). It is in this way that the structural and the cultural are fused. Grimshaw (1976), in one of the best short appreciations of Bernstein's work, is one of the relatively few authors explicitly to have recognized the thrust of the sociology in this vein. He comments that Bernstein's goal is the construction of a model which specifies relations between the realities of class, power and ideology, and their relation to principles of interpretation.

We can at this point comment briefly on the relevance of the so-called 'deficit' versus 'difference' debate to Bernstein's project. On the one hand, Bernstein is certainly claiming far more than the mere documentation and comparison of contrasting cultures, language varieties, world-views, socialization practices and so on. On the other hand, he displays little or no interest in attributing differential life-chances to persons' moral qualities – linguistic, cognitive or cultural. His is neither a bland relativism, nor an attempt to blame the victims for their own disadvantage.

What Bernstein is attempting to do, rather, is to account for the differential positioning of persons (subjects) within the division of labour. Such positioning is a function of power, and the coding of power is implicated in language. It is not only a matter of class: power pervades relations of ethnicity and gender as well (Bernstein, 1981, p.336). Here, too, we must recognize that Bernstein's interest is in the coding of dominating/dominated relationships, and not in questions of style, self-presentation and so on – the terms in which his contribution is too often interpreted.

As established at the start of this chapter, the basic theory of 'elaboration' and 'restriction' has a very specific range of referents. They were not chosen with a careless reliance upon their evaluative connotations. As used by Bernstein, the codes have clear and specific (if abstract) definition in relation to a structuralist semiotic. Codes articulate principles of selection and combination, and, as the most recent paper makes plain, this is crucial. A fundamental property of the division of labour is the imposition of boundaries of insulation between social categories – what Bernstein refers to as 'classification'. The creation, manipulation and legitimation of such categories are manifestations of power. Bernstein thus proposes a formal, structural or systemic correspondence between principles of power, coding and classification.

6 *Bernstein and the linguists*

In a book of this scope and length it would be quite impossible – and inappropriate – to try to review all the literature which uses, comments on and criticizes Bernstein's language theories. My view, indeed, is that much of that literature is rendered all but irrelevant, since it is based on erroneous interpretations of Bernstein. As indicated already, Bernstein's work should never have been thought of as a version of sociolinguistics attempting to describe two contrasting dialects or their equivalent. Critics who upbraid Bernstein for an inadequate representation of 'styles' are equally wide of the mark. In this chapter, therefore, I refer to some of the critics among the linguists in order to expose the irrelevance of their remarks to Bernstein's structuralist semiotics, and to introduce, by way of contrast, linguistic thought which is relevant to that programme. No attempt is made even to approximate to a comprehensive review of the literature on class differences in language acquisition and use, or on the relationships between language, ability and attainment. I have singled out for attention a small number of authors whose work has entered directly or indirectly into debate with Bernstein, and who themselves make a significant contribution to linguistics. I have not devoted attention to other figures who enter into merely polemical and contentious disputes.

There have been a number of readily available secondary sources which cover the sociolinguistic debates (e.g. Edwards,

1976; Robinson, 1978; Gordon, 1981; Stubbs, 1983), although they exhibit the problem I have just alluded to. Hence I shall outline and exemplify some of the main problems only. Further, it is by no means the case – some commentators to the contrary – that linguists have been united in opposition to Bernstein: some account must be taken, therefore, of how some linguists have interpreted the work from a sympathetic perspective. I shall, however, go on to argue that in the last analysis the approach of conventional linguistics and sociolinguistics is not readily compatible with the sort of structuralist anthropology-cum-sociology implicit in Bernstein's whole work, despite many surface similarities and a shared vocabulary. From this point of view there is a major divide within the literature relating to Bernstein, which reflects a greater division within the sociology of communication and structure. Bernstein's work straddles that gulf somewhat uneasily.

Some of the confusion in this area has been compounded by the fact that some of the 'debates' and controversies are mistaken constructs of observers. Stubbs (1983, p.79) has pointed out that the supposed opposition between Bernstein and Labov is just such a mythological construct. In the production of lecture courses, textbooks and the like, there is an understandable tendency to 'tidy up' fields of discourse, and arrange protagonists into competing 'camps'. This is the stuff of myth and legend: Labov is supposed to wrestle with Bernstein as Beowulf grappled with Grendel's mother. This drama is attained at the expense of accuracy, however. I shall comment on this pedagogical fate of texts in a later chapter.

Stubbs cites the following comment by Tough (1977, p.31) as evidence of this particular myth: 'there have been many criticisms of Bernstein's work, most notably by William Labov' (Stubbs, 1983, p.79). This misrepresentation can be multiplied from many sources. Even where there is no implication of direct confrontation, many discussions juxtapose Bernstein and Labov as if they were representatives of two opposing 'sides'. Where that is done, of course, they are treated as the respective champions of 'deficit' and 'difference' positions. This renders the confusion particularly muddled: whatever their origins and consequences, Bernstein's theories have never embraced a 'deficit' position – at least not in the way that is normally understood.

It has been observed that Labov's few early strictures on Bernstein were not based on first-hand knowledge of the work, but derived at second hand from American authors who incorrectly drew on Bernstein to support a thoroughly 'deficit' view, especially as it related to the socialization and educability of young black Americans from the urban ghettos and the south-eastern states. As Robinson (1981, p. 59) summarizes the history of the confusion:

> Labov groups Bernstein with deficit theorists like Bereiter and Engelmann, a misunderstanding which appears to be a consequence of forming a view of Bernstein based on Jensen's (1968) account of one of Bernstein's earliest papers, 'Language and Social Class', published in 1960. At that stage Bernstein was still exploring 'linguistic differences, *other than dialect*' which occur between middle- and lower-working-class groups; the concept 'code' had not been introduced, nor had the development of the thesis into a theory of cultural transmission been accomplished. Yet Labov is particularly concerned with the relation between concept formation on the one hand, and *dialect differences* on the other, a project which is different to [*sic*] Bernstein's, more akin to linguistics and less to the sociological assessment of the consequences of different speech forms. (emphases in original)

There is no doubt that Labov was quite justified in taking issue with the crude deficit theorists of the 1960s in the United States. There were current some quite extraordinarily crass and ill-informed views of language, culture and cognition. Bereiter and Engelmann, for instance, conveyed a singularly bleak view of the linguistic capacities of lower-class black children (1966). According to them, language for such youngsters was not a tool for the acquisition and processing of information, and was poorly developed for the conduct of logical analysis. Regrettably Labov has continued to misrepresent Bernstein as a deficit theorist, bracketed with Bereiter and Engelmann, even in his most recent publications (Labov, 1982).

Labov took issue with such views on a number of grounds: verbosity, logic, and the quality of the linguistic environment or culture. Although Labov's work is widely regarded as providing important refutations of the deficit position, several of the 'key' papers are based upon fragmentary and highly selective evidence. Their power rests upon their plausibility and the inherent good sense of the argument rather than an overwhelming weight of empirical evidence. This is in contrast with some of Labov's other work, for instance that on the stratification of English in New York City (1966). Labov's papers do have the undoubted strength of being based on the collection of actually occurring speech under natural conditions, coupled with a thorough grounding in linguistics.

Labov demonstrated to his own satisfaction that an apparent lack of 'verbosity' on the part of supposedly 'deficient' children was an artifact of the testing situations under which the standard sort of data were collected. Youngsters certainly do produce monosyllabic answers, interspersed with lengthy silences, but Labov argues that this is a characteristic of a social situation defined as a 'test', administered in a relatively formal fashion, by a white adult. When the conditions are varied to approximate more closely to an egalitarian, informal encounter, then the young respondents will readily produce much more verbose talk. Such a demonstration was certainly based on sound sociolinguistic perspectives, and helped to explode the more simple-minded versions of linguistic deficit. It had remarkably little to do with Bernstein, however, in so far as the public language/restricted code was originally formulated in terms of *fluency*. There is no implication that restricted code regulates talk which is quantitatively diminished or sparse. Indeed, it will be remembered that Bernstein's use of the Goldman-Eisler approach is quite at odds with the equation of silence and hesitations with his version of 'restriction'.

Labov also sought to refute any notion that the speech of lower-class black Americans displayed a lack of logic. In a celebrated contribution he claims that logically coherent propositions can be expressed in Black English Vernacular, as in any other style or dialect. A key passage in the argument is the following, in which a young BEV speaker expresses beliefs concerning life after death. The extract is from a conversation between Larry and an interviewer, John Lewis (Labov, 1972a, p.173):

J.L.: What happens to you after you die? Do you know?

L.: Yeah, I know. After they put you in the ground your body turns into – ah – bones an' shit.

J.L.: What happens to your spirit?

L.: Your spirit – soon as you die, your spirit leaves you.

J.L.: And where does the spirit go?

L.: Well it all depends . . .

J.L.: On what?

L.: You know, like some people say if you're good an' shit, your spirit, your spirit goin' t'heaven . . . 'n' if you're bad your spirit goin' to hell. Well bullshit! Your spirit goin' to hell anyway, good or bad.

J.L.: Why?

L.: Why? I'll tell you why. 'Cause, you see, doesn' nobody really know that it's a God, y'know 'cause I mean I have seen black gods, pink gods, white gods, all colour gods, and don't nobody know its really a God. An' when they be sayin' if you good you goin' t'heaven tha's bullshit, cause you ain't goin' to no heaven, 'cause it ain't no heaven for you to go to.

In his demonstration of the logical adequacy of this series of responses by Larry, Labov translates them into a series of propositions. Labov himself is somewhat misleading about the nature of this translation exercise, giving the impression that the differences between the two formats is a matter of style, claiming that he is involved in 'setting out the Standard English equivalents in linear order'. The 'argument' is represented as eight numbered propositions, as follows:

1 Everyone has a different idea of what God is like.
2 Therefore nobody really knows that God exists.
3 If there is a heaven, it was made by God.
4 If God doesn't exist, he couldn't have made heaven.
5 Therefore heaven does not exist.
6 You can't go somewhere that doesn't exist.
7 Therefore you can't go to heaven.
8 Therefore you are going to hell.

Now it is surely obvious that Labov's act of translation is far more than a transposition from the style of BEV to Standard (American) English. He re-orders and re-creates the 'thesis' that Larry is interpreted as proposing. The interesting thing to ask is how and why Labov performs this translation or recuperation of the text constructed out of Larry's replies to Lewis's prompting. My contention is that the recension of the text is a highly dubious activity anyway, which Labov does little or nothing to warrant. The actual translation 'lifts' and reconstructs an argument which is embedded and implicit in Larry's speech. The act of translation into an ordered sequence of propositions moves the language from an implicit, highly contextual performance, to the relatively context-free format of a propositional logic. This seems analogous to the act of recontextualization performed by Willis (1977) on the utterances of his 'lads'. Labov makes of his informant a sophisticated logician, while Willis reconstructs his as a spokesperson of working-class 'resistance'.

In Bernsteinian terms, the notion of 'illogicality' is a straw argument. He never proposed that working-class (or any) form of language use was 'illogical' *per se*. That absurdity would be confined to other authors. On the other hand, Labov's so-called 'translation' seems an excellent exemplification of the move from 'restricted' to 'elaborated' code. The difference between the implicit, embedded logic of Larry and the propositions of Labov is irrefutably much more than is implied by Labov's own insistence on 'style'.

Bernstein never denied that restricted code regulated meaningful or comprehensible communicative acts. Indeed, such acts may be highly efficient. What is at issue is *how* those acts are performed and their relation to the social situation of which they are part. The demonstration of 'sense', even of 'logic' does nothing to undermine Bernstein's own position. Indeed, the irony is that Labov's own treatment of the issue illustrates Bernstein's own thesis rather nicely. It does not 'prove' it either, of course.

In a highly elegant, if somewhat eccentric, interpretation of this same passage, Silverman and Torode (1980, pp.171 ff.) also argue that Larry's speech is clearly identifiable as 'restricted' in form. Their analysis rests on an interpretation of Bernstein which is related to – but by no means identical with – mine. They emphasize the extent to which Bernstein's notion of the universalistic elaborated code embodies a commitment to a transcendental subject. Codes regulate persons' understanding of the relation between appearance and reality, and of the nature of the knowing subject.

The analysis depends on a close reading of the text in terms of 'pictures' (constituent elements) and 'voices' (which are not coterminous with speakers) representing different viewpoints or moral positions within the text. They outline to begin with an 'interpretation' of the text which, it is argued, is entirely congruent with that of Bernstein. The interviewer (J.L.) can be heard to express a particular viewpoint reflecting elaborated code, while Larry realizes restricted code:

> The conception of the world as comprising human subjects (*you* seeking to *know* the underlying essence or *spirit*) is an elaborated one, and indeed in the conversation here recorded, the speech which articulates this conception . . . is itself 'elaborated'. By contrast, the conception of the world as comprising *bodies* and *shit* is a restricted one, and the speech which articulates it here . . . is itself 'restricted'. The terms 'elaborated' and 'restricted' are here being used in the sense of *elaborating* the difference between 'appearance' and 'reality' on the one hand, and of *restricting* 'reality' to an identity with 'appearance' on the other. (Silverman and Torode, 1980, p.181, emphases in original)

This interpretation goes well beyond the conventional reading of Bernstein, although it certainly preserves and develops the underlying spirit of the work. Silverman and Torode's analysis of 'voices' goes even further, suggesting that the questions and answers of Labov's text reflect a number of voices whereby Larry can participate in elaborated code speech, but he does so in order to reaffirm his own identification with a restricted code:

> The restricted code speaker finds his singular voice to be under attack from the elaborated codes which impinge upon it without showing awareness of its existence. More specifically, the 'restricted' speaker finds his viewpoint that reality is as it appears to him constantly assailed by the 'elaborated' assertion of the existence of realities beyond appearance. (ibid., 1980, p.186)

The analysis of pictures and voices in the text depends upon a close line-by-line reading, and unfortunately it cannot be reproduced here. In any event I am not totally convinced by the particular analytic devices that Silverman and Torode propose: in many ways the force of different modes of expression seems overemphasized. None the less their reading of the Labov extract does suggest that a truly Bernsteinian reading goes far beyond the somewhat simplistic view of Labov himself, coupled with an equally simple view of 'style'. Silverman and Torode also go on to apply the same 'voices' analysis to a Labov example of 'elaborated' speech – from a college-educated black respondent, Charles Morris, who is being interviewed by Clarence Robbins:

> C.R.: Do you know of anything someone can do to have someone who has passed on visit him in a dream?
>
> C.M.: Well I even heard my parents say that there is such a thing as something in dreams some things like that and sometimes dreams do come true I've never dreamed that somebody was dying and they actually died or that I was going to have ten dollars the next day and somehow I got ten dollars in my pocket I don't particularly believe in that I don't believe it's true I do feel though that there is such a thing as – ah – witchcraft I do feel that in certain cultures there is such a thing as witchcraft or some sort of *science* of witchcraft I don't think that it's just a matter of believing hard enough that there is such a thing as witchcraft I do believe that there is such a thing that a person can put himself in a state of *mind* or that something could be given to them to intoxicate them in a certain – to a certain frame of mind that could actually be considered witchcraft. (Labov, 1972a, p. 197)

Labov himself is again somewhat insensitive to this text. He identifies it as 'elaborated' only in terms of style – and, hardly surprisingly, satisfies himself that differences between the speech of Larry and that of Charles Morris are purely stylistic. He 'translates' the latter text also into a series of propositions. The fact that he can transpose the first part of the utterance into but three propositions he takes as evidence that the educated speaker's speech is merely verbose and redundant. The derived propositions are:

1 Some people say that dreams sometimes come true.
2 I have never had a dream come true.
3 Therefore I don't believe 1.

Likewise, the second part is reduced to 'But I believe in witchcraft. I don't think witchcraft is just a belief'.

Silverman and Torode suggest that in fact Labov was unwittingly more acute than his own insensitive analysis allowed, since the second interview extract really does display 'elaboration' in precisely the same way as the first displayed restriction:

> The interviewer's formulation is notably concrete compared to that of the interviewee. 'Do you know of anything that someone can do . . .?' invites a response in terms of anecdotes about someone known to you, the interviewee. The interviewee reformulates this subjective orientation. His feeling and belief suggest that with regard to the topic at hand knowledge may not be the appropriate mode. He also reformulates that topic: something replaces someone so that what is at issue is his intellectual activity rather than his stock of personal acquaintances.
>
> His subsequent transformation of the topic of dreams to that of witchcraft also shifts the conversation from a potential interrogation of his personal experiences (everyone has dreams) to a topic external both to himself and the interviewer (most people are not witches). Finally, when he constructs his own two voices, within which he states 'it's [a matter] of mind' his discourse raises issues which go beyond the particularities of both the speech and the topic formulated by the interviewer. (ibid., pp. 192–3)

Thus, Silverman and Torode suggest, the speaker is able to construct his speech in such a way as to transcend the interview format whereby he (as respondent) simply answers the interviewer's questions from within the same frame of reference. This 'elaborated' speech thus universalizes the particularistic discourse which the interviewer initially proposes. Again, the detailed analysis of 'voices' cannot be recapitulated here, but Silverman and Torode employ it to trace a very different attitude to 'appearance' and 'reality' from that identified in the restricted code extract. The idea of a voice in this sense has subsequently reappeared in Bernstein's own work (1981), as a borrowing back from Silverman and Torode.

It will be apparent that I have some reservations about Silverman and Torode: their own view of language is idiosyncratic. None the less, we do not have to subscribe fully to it in order to appreciate the inadequacy of over-simplified interpretations of style, and to display the poverty of the conventional treatment of the Labov–Bernstein contrast. Very recently Cooper (1984) has also subjected the two Labov arguments to critical scrutiny. He shows quite convincingly that Labov himself engages in illogical argument, and in the reconstruction of the two interview extracts begs some of the questions he claims to answer.

As Bernstein has also pointed out in direct dialogue with American colleagues, part of the difficulty arises from the particular, reductionist, approaches to socialization underlying the conventional American perspective. His own theoretical stance demands a much more complex integration of sociological and anthropological views of socializing agencies (Bernstein, 1966b). Bernstein has commented, somewhat ruefully, on the reception of his work in the United States, and the tendency to make him a scapegoat for American researchers' sins of commission. He remarks, puckishly: 'Perhaps Americans have some difficulty in acknowledging the potential or actual influence on Americans by Americans. Indeed, it took me a little time to free myself of the standard USA work on socialization' (1973b, *CCC* 1, p.250).

The irony is, in my view, not only that Labov's criticisms are wide of the mark, but that the key examples he uses actually lend credence to Bernstein. I have in fact already cited one of the other key Labov examples – the collection of ritual insults – in just this way. These are, quite properly, used by Labov and subsequent commentators, to show that, for some purposes, the language environment of BEV is 'rich'. Bernstein's views never suggested that the reverse was the case. His early review of the Opies' book shows his own alertness to the selfsame issues, as do the following remarks from the early formulation of 'public' language:

> A *public* language contains its own aesthetic, a simplicity and directness of expression, emotionally virile, pithy and power-

> ful and a metaphoric range of considerable force and appropriateness. Some examples taken from the schools of this country have a beauty which many writers might well envy. (1959a, *CCC* 1, p. 54)

The full irony, as I tried to show, is that Labov's 'ritual insults' are in fact excellent demonstrations of Bernstein's restricted code. It is a complete travesty to contrast Bernstein's view of the differential distribution of power and performance with supposedly egalitarian notions of universal competence. The profound intellectual and disciplinary differences between Bernstein and Labov do not, however, imply a lack of mutual respect.

The association of Bernstein with some version of 'deficit' theory lies behind many of his opponents' counter-arguments. Dittmar (1976) has provided one of the most sustained assaults in a detailed book-length diatribe against the deficit perspective. The book purports to concern itself with sociolinguistics more generally; in fact it deals almost obsessively with this one concern. As with other authors, Dittmar credits Bernstein with considerable influence in the development of American views on deficit and compensation. Dittmar goes into a fair degree of detail in his sustained attempt to discredit Bernstein's work and that of his SRU collaborators. His huffing and puffing are to little purpose in the long run, however, as the thesis he attacks is not Bernstein's thesis anyway. This is revealed in the very opening statement of Dittmar's first chapter. Bernstein's view is summarized thus:

> Instead of analysing the manifest differences between the two linguistic varieties according to their various functional capabilities, the linguistic characteristics which divide the speech behaviour of the lower classes from that of the middle class are interpreted as a deficit phenomenon on the basis of an *a priori* normative scale of values. That is to say, they are interpreted as precisely those linguistic attributes which lower-class speakers lack, in order to achieve the same social success as the speakers of the middle class. This central assumption that the speech of the lower class is more limited in its competence than the speech of the middle class will be termed the *Deficit Hypothesis* throughout. (Dittmar, 1976, p. 4)

It is all very well to call that – or something like it – a deficit hypothesis, but it is a caricature of Bernstein's own position, albeit a caricature believed and appropriated by many others. Dittmar's fevered assault on Bernstein as the arch-fiend of deficit is quite erroneous. Dittmar provides a very detailed and closely argued review of Bernstein's sociology of language, but it is rendered irrelevant for the most part, in so far as it rests on false premises.

Dittmar's failure is particularly unfortunate since his work is that *rara avis*, a sustained treatment of the topic from a Marxist perspective. Like Bernstein, therefore, Dittmar has a particularly acute sense of the relationship between theories of language and theories of class and the division of labour. Unfortunately this is expressed in terms of a crudely polemical assault on all versions of sociolinguistics ('deficit' and 'difference' theories together). The advocates of a 'culturally relativist' perspective are assailed as but more sophisticated apologists for class divisions in capitalist societies. He argues throughout his book that sociolinguistic investigations are not prompted by the desire to emancipate the working class, but by a desire to integrate it into the existing social order. Sociolinguists are dubbed 'pacification specialists' (p.244 ff.). Dittmar's attack is as much a reflection of the vulgarity of his own Marxism as it is a justified critique of 'bourgeois' theorizing.

Paradoxically, indeed, Dittmar seems to converge with Bernstein in recognizing that the use and evaluation of differing modes of reality-construction are related directly to the division of labour. As Atkinson, Kilby and Roca (1982) gloss this, Dittmar

> regards the issue of codes as one related to the needs of production in post-industrial societies, where the priority given to information-processing requires the handling by the worker of systems with features closer to those of the elaborated code. (pp.352–3)

Such an insight is surely very close to Bernstein's own perspective on social change and the division of labour (albeit that he takes his inspiration from Durkheim as well as from Marx).

Michael Halliday is one of the relatively few linguists who has not only been sympathetic to the Bernsteinian view, but has also been so from a well-informed perspective. It is noteworthy that Halliday, the linguist, insists upon the value of his *sociological* imagination: 'What interests me about Bernstein is that he is a theoretical sociologist who builds language into his theory not as an optional extra but as an essential component' (Halliday, 1978, p.36). Halliday goes on to list his own preoccupations – as a linguist – with the role of language in the transmission of culture, the communication of the social system through everyday language use. Bernstein, he maintains, provides a theoretical framework which is pre-eminently suited to the investigation of such problems.

Halliday is under no great illusions: the questions we can ask are perhaps more exciting than the answers we can furnish with any degree of precision and empirical warrant:

> We are still far from being able to give a comprehensive or systematic account of the linguistic realizations of Bernstein's codes or of the ways in which language operates in the transmission of culture. But the perspective is that of language and social man [*sic*], and the functional investigation of language and language development provides the basis for understanding. (Halliday, 1978, p.27)

There is indeed a very close affinity between Halliday and Bernstein. Bernstein reappears in citations throughout Halliday's work. By the same token, Halliday's own approach to linguistics was extremely influential in shaping the empirical work of the SRU.

We shall examine the influence of Halliday a little later. For the moment, the important thing to note is the extent to which he realizes the appropriate 'level' for Bernstein's theories. He acknowledges that Bernstein's is not a characterization of the surface structure of language behaviour, but should be thought of as a 'social semiotic', located at a level 'above' the linguistic system *per se* (1978, p.68). He correctly sees that 'codes' are not language varieties, but are principles which articulate language use with social contexts or situations.

In contrast to the actual or implied criticisms of Labov or Trudgill (1975), Halliday is quite clear that the notion of 'dialect' is quite irrelevant to Bernstein's programme. For Halliday, the key notion in the sociolinguistic repertoire is 'register'. Register differs from dialect in so far as it captures the sociosemantic system, rather than the morphological features described as dialect. Both register and dialect, of course, are used to describe variation – and both relate to social distribution of variation. Whereas dialect refers to the spatial and hierarchical distribution of phonology, lexicon and grammar, register refers to the social distribution of 'ways of meaning'.

Halliday suggests that one of the key differences between dialects and registers can be summed up in this way: dialects are, in principle, 'ways of saying the same thing', while registers are 'ways of saying different things'. The variables which determine the distribution of dialects include: class, caste, provenance, generation, age and gender. Those which relate to register are of a different order – referred to as *field, tenor* and *mode.* (For a summary representation of the dialect/register distinction, including further features, see Halliday, 1978, p.35.)

A brief explanation of Halliday's use of field, tenor and mode will help to clarify the articulation of his theory with that of Bernstein. (The terms are not unique to Halliday.) Halliday himself cites (1978, p.33) Pearce (1972, pp.185–6) by way of summary:

> Field refers to the institutional setting in which a piece of language occurs, and embraces not only the subject-matter but the whole activity of the speaker or participant in a setting. . . .
>
> Tenor . . . refers to the relationship between participants . . . not merely variation in formality . . . but . . . such questions as the permanence or otherwise of the relationship and the degree of emotional charge in it. . . .
>
> Mode refers to the channel of communication adopted: not only the choice between spoken and written medium, but much more detailed choices.

In so far as these features describe the general determinants of register, then, it is clear that we are dealing with the articulation of language with contexts of meaning, domains of social action, qualities of interpersonal relations. This is a very different notion from the distributional idea implied by 'dialect'.

The Halliday view of language thus incorporates a sensitivity to the relationship between language and social order: acknowledged sources of inspiration include Firth, Malinowski and Cicourel. His view of language as a 'social semiotic' stresses the *functional* aspects, and 'code' relates directly to them:

> Seen from a linguistic point of view, the different 'codes' . . . are different strategies of language use. All human beings put language to certain types of use, and all of them learn a linguistic system which has evolved in that context; but what aspects of the system are typically deployed and emphasized in one type of use or another is to a significant extent determined by the culture – by the systems of social relations in which the child grows up, including the roles he himself learns to recognize and to adopt. (Halliday, 1978, p.27)

The functions Halliday indicates are: experiential, logical, interpersonal and textual. For him, the codes regulate which functional resources will be emphasized in which contexts of use.

It is in this spirit that several of the empirical projects in the SRU were conducted by Bernstein and his associates. It is impossible to make adequate sense of the work on language codes without due acknowledgement of the significance of Halliday's inspiration. It is noticeable that several of the texts which launch sustained 'linguistic' assaults on Bernstein in fact make little or no reference to the close relationship between his work and Halliday's linguistics. It would be easy for readers of such sources to gain the impression that no linguist of any repute has any sympathy or affinity with Bernstein.

Halliday's own foreword to *Class, Codes and Control,* volume 2, is ample testimony to his own insight into Bernstein's programme and of their mutual influence at a personal level. He opens the book by encapsulating the work and the problem of its interpretation:

> The work of Professor Basil Bernstein has sometimes been referred to as 'a theory of educational failure'. This seems to me misleading; the truth is both more, and less, than this implies. More, because Bernstein's theory is a theory about society, how a society persists and how it changes; it is a theory of the

> nature and processes of cultural transmission, and of the essential part that is played by language therein. (*CCC* 2, p.ix)

Moreover, he is capable of seeing well beyond the confines of his own discipline, in recognizing that the theory is a very general one of a primarily *sociological* nature.

It is recognized by Bernstein himself that the earliest formulations were linguistically under-developed, although that does not detract from a view that the general *sociological* perspectives were clearly established from the outset. The influence of Halliday's linguistics provided Bernstein and his collaborators in the SRU with a coherent and relevant model of language and linguistics.

The relationship between Bernstein and Halliday is more than a little reminiscent of the mutual regard and influence between the linguist J. R. Firth and the anthropologist Bronislaw Malinowski. They supported one another in a view of language as a means of social action, and in an emphasis on the analysis of the 'context of situation' in addressing 'meaning' as a function of social behaviour. As Henson (1974) documents, their shared interests and programmatic statements (e.g. Firth, 1934; Malinowski, 1923) did not in fact lead to a sustained focus on language by British social anthropologists – an absence also noted by Ardener (1971). That was left largely to American scholars in the English-speaking world, and to anthropologists in the French tradition. It is notable that Bernstein himself has been paid relatively little attention by British social anthropology (Mary Douglas excepted), although he has been acknowledged by American anthropologists such as Dell Hymes. Henson (1974, p.68) makes a brief passing reference to Bernstein, linking him with Firth and Douglas. Henson's definition of anthropology is characteristically narrow, however; no attempt is made to explore the extent to which the Bernstein–Halliday version of social semiotics is the real British heir to the Firth–Malinowski programme. There is certainly direct continuity here, as Halliday is in direct line of descent from Firth, as representative of the London school of linguistics. Halliday himself explicitly acknowledges the contribution of Firth, as well as that of Malinowski (e.g. Halliday, 1978, p.28).

The interplay between Bernstein and Halliday is nowhere

more apparent than in the empirical work at the SRU by Adlam, Cook-Gumperz, Hawkins, Robinson, Rackstraw, Turner and others. In their work 'code' is fleshed out and operationalized in a suite of closely related empirical studies. The bulk of the empirical work was based on samples of children in two London boroughs. The data collected included samples of elicited speech from the children at ages five and seven, interviews with the mothers, mothers' scores on a 'communication index' measures of socioeconomic status. Several of the empirical studies reported in the various papers and monographs (in the 'Primary Socialization, Language and Education' series) go over the same data base in complementary ways. As Edwards remarks (1976, p.98). 'The apparent accumulation of evidence is, to some extent, a repetition of evidence.' But as he goes on to acknowledge, 'Nevertheless, the main findings provide some justification for Bernstein's early "explorations".'

The distinctively Hallidayan approach is pervasive. Code is conceptualized in essentially functional terms, and more attention is paid to relationships between context and function than was the case in Bernstein's earliest papers. (Note in this connection the presence of Halliday's own essay on functional analysis as an appendix to *CCC* 2, 1973, pp.343–66.) The SRU research is organized in terms of four major contexts of language use: regulative, instructional, interpersonal and imaginative (see e.g. Adlam, 1977). Bernstein himself suggests that this fourfold classification was implicit at the very outset of the SRU research programme, but Robinson (1978, p.66) expresses some scepticism in this retrospective account:

> The original differences between the speech tasks posed to the children were described in terms of types of speech, e.g. narrative, descriptive, explanatory, and not four contexts of socialization. It looks more like a fortunate coincidence than a deliberate plan that two of the picture-story sequences suggested narratives which could be linked subsequently to a section on discipline in the maternal interview schedule (regulative context).

Bernstein is perhaps justified none the less in claiming the *implicit* model at the outset of the research. The congruence between the research design and the analytic framework can hardly be as fortuitous as Robinson's somewhat dismissive remark suggests. Certainly he does not claim that the Halliday approach to language was fully and explicitly incorporated into his thinking from the word go. In his introduction to the collected volume of SRU papers Bernstein acknowledges, 'It is a matter of great personal regret that my own work until recently was insufficiently developed, was insufficiently explicit, to take full advantage of Halliday's researches' (*CCC* 2, p.8).

Various of the SRU empirical studies develop and exemplify the key notion of 'implicit' versus 'explicit' orders of meaning. Of particular importance here is the analysis of *reference* based largely on Hasan (1968), a close collaborator with Halliday. The distinction is made, in analysing principles of narrative cohesion in texts, between anaphoric and exophoric reference. Anaphoric reference is made ('backwards') to elements already introduced in the text; exophoric reference is made 'outwards' to the context of situation, or the environment of the speaker. Hawkins (1969; 1977) analyses texts of speech of five-year-old children from this point of view, and finds social class differences in use of types of reference. In both narrative and descriptive texts, Hawkins reports 'substantial evidence that the working-class children in our sample are using not more pronouns, but more pronouns of the exophoric kind, which rely heavily for their interpretation on the surrounding context' (1969, *CCC* 2, p.90). In other words, there is a class difference in the relationship between language-use and the speaker's background assumptions concerning the hearer and the context. The working-class child appears to base reference on the assumption that speaker and hearer share a common frame of reference and stock of background knowledge relevant to the immediate talk. The middle-class child seems to assume a lower degree of shared knowledge in the immediate context or situation.

This mode of analysis is furthered elsewhere in the SRU corpus (e.g. Turner, 1973; Adlam and Turner, 1977). Commenting again on descriptive language use, Adlam and Turner conclude that the working-class child is more likely to rely upon exophoric, context-dependent reference. Data were collected – as in Hawkins's experiment – by recording children's descriptions of scenes depicted on stimulus cards. Here are examples that Adlam cites, derived from descriptions of a wedding scene:

> i) Middle-class child
> There's a man got a sword, he's a guard I expect. There's two dogs, one's running about and the other's going to the toilet. Three people at the gate. There's a church and three houses in the background and two cats up on the roof of the house. Lots of flowers in the garden. And steps leading down to the ground from the house. There's a tree. There's flowers in a vase on the posts above the gates.
> ii) Working-class child
> They're all having a party. She doesn't feel well. All the animals haven't got anything to eat. They've had theirs and they think that's not enough for me, let's go and have all that.
> That lady up there she thinks that's not fair they've got all that and she hasn't anything. She's not sitting down because of that fat lady and he's not going to sit next to that fat lady. That lady doesn't mind sitting next to that fat lady nor does that one so they all sat and they all sit down to eat their tea.
> All the animals are going away from that fat lady 'cos they don't like her one bit. (p.79)

There are clear differences between these two extracts in the extent to which the text rests upon a shared knowledge of the context and the circumstances (here, the original stimulus picture). This is not a straightforwardly evaluative matter, nor is it presented as such by Hawkins and the other SRU authors. The second child arguably appears to be offering the researcher a more vivid, imaginative and creative response. The middle-class respondent provides a rather dull, literal description. The former's description is in contrast to the latter's narrative performance, associated with context-dependent language use (cf. Lineker, 1977).

The issue of context-dependence has been oddly misunderstood by some commentators. Those linguists who insist on finding some version of a 'deficit' model – where none exists – see experiments like those reported by Hawkins, Turner and Adlam as evaluative. They assume – with little justification – that the context-dependent mode is regarded as inferior. Understandably this straw argument is readily demolished. Dittmar (1976, p. 57) includes in a detailed critique of Hawkins the following:

> we do not know whether Hawkins's test situation was such that an unspecified use of exophoric pronouns can justifiably be interpreted as poor communicative behaviour. The children were shown picture cards and asked to say what they had seen. Since we can assume that the child and the interviewer had the same opportunity to look at the picture, there is no reason why the child could not have described details in the cards which the interviewer was not able to recognize and identify.

Stubbs (1983, p. 51) makes a similar point:

> One can stand Hawkins's argument on its head and say that the WC version takes appropriate account of the listener's knowledge; while the MC version is full of redundant information. This is completely the opposite of Hawkins's conclusion: perhaps it is the MC children who are incapable of adapting their language to the context, since they treat the researcher as someone who must have the most obvious things explained to him!

These and equivalent objections would have considerable force had Hawkins and the others been concerned with the imputation of poor communicative behaviour. The point is *not* that the middle-class respondents have a superior approach, nor that the working-class use of language is defective. Rather, the point is precisely that the working-class child *does* assume (perfectly reasonably) a different relationship between speech and situation. The working-class and middle-class children operate with *different* ways of reporting – and hence constructing – social reality. And this is precisely the force of 'code' in the general theory.

I am ready to acknowledge that Hawkins's interpretation implies that the middle-class elaborated code, which is less context-dependent, has greater flexibility. To that extent there is indeed an evaluative component, which is consistently implied in the Bernsteinian distinction between 'explicit' and 'implicit' orders of meaning. Notably, Hawkins promotes the view that the explicitness of the elaborated code provides the user with possibilities not otherwise available – most notably, of course, 'the middle-class child can be understood outside the immediate context'. This can hardly be equated with a crude model of linguistic deficit.

Some authors, such as G. M. Young (1982, 1983) have in recent years attempted to provide a specification of 'code' which derives even more explicitly from a functional model. This analysis goes some way to confirming the close affinity between Bernstein and Halliday, although Young also claims to have developed the model beyond Halliday's. A detailed exposition is not possible here, but its existence further weakens the argument that Bernstein's approach to language is totally out of keeping with linguistically informed approaches, although I shall shortly suggest that there are indeed some very profound problems in bridging the disciplinary divide.

It is, however, less than fair of commentators like Gordon to imply that Bernstein's approach to language cannot be specified in terms more sophisticated or up-to-date than the original features of the very early papers. It is, however, true that the more complex and sophisticated versions of 'code', 'context' and 'control', such as found in Cook-Gumperz (1973) for example, render simple formulations increasingly problematic. Yet there is no doubt that the majority of unsympathetic commentators have been content to oppose simplistic, often apocryphal 'Bernsteins' rather than engage with the full ramifications of the research. A detailed review and synthesis which adopts a perspective in sympathetic understanding of Bernstein's sociology of language is yet to be undertaken.

In this chapter no attempt has been made to review and evaluate all of the now very substantial literature which uses, develops or criticizes Bernstein's sociology of language. A highly selective account has been provided, intended to illustrate some of the issues and problems of interpretation. What is clear throughout the corpus of literature – that referred to here and that omitted – is that there are recurrent difficulties in mutual perceptions and sympathies between linguists and sociologists or anthropologists. This is clearly not total; as I have shown, Halliday is one of the major figures who has attempted to bridge the divide.

Labov (1978) has noted and commented on that 'gulf', but like others of a similar persuasion tends to attribute the problem to the sociologists' lack of training in the empirical study of language (a sort of 'linguistics deficit' explanation). Labov includes Bernstein in these strictures, of course – with a brief but equivocal reference to Halliday's influence. There is no doubt something in this general argument. Bernstein would agree that his early understandings of language were 'bootstrapped' and lacking in system, but it really would be wrong to assume that Bernstein's starting-point was a naïve belief in 'primitive' language based on an equally primitive linguistics. As we have seen, the starting-point is actually a sophisticated view of the relationship between language and the construction of reality.

Herein lies a problem which goes well beyond the linguistic training of particular scholars in sociology or anthropology. Indeed, it runs deeper than the normal sort of cross-disciplinary bickering and incomprehension which is always liable to occur. At root, I believe that the sort of treatment of 'language' proposed in Bernstein's general anthropology is not readily compatible with the sort of analysis espoused by contemporary empirical linguists. Because we find ourselves dealing with disciplines and theories which address 'language' we should not assume that they deal with 'the same' phenomenon. On the contrary, disciplines construct the objects of their own discourse (a perspective which Bernstein's own version of the social construction of reality is congruent with). There is thus no guarantee that the versions of 'language' so constructed will be congruent or readily commensurable. I do not want to make too much of this and go so far as to suggest that each discipline or theory group is hermeneutically sealed; but there are very important differences in emphasis and approach. The apparent consensus of common terminology, or borrowed models and metaphors often serves merely to mask the underlying differences. This is the case with 'language'.

Structuralism and post-structuralism have treated 'language' as a central preoccupation and 'linguistics' has furnished major analytic perspectives. The foundations of structural linguistics laid by Saussure and Jakobson, with their emphases on the systematic relations of arbitrary signs in relations of difference and opposition are also the foundations of structuralism and semiotics. While language occupies this central position, however, it is not normally expressed in terms of a detailed specification of syntax or discourse. The intellectual rococo of a Derrida, say, owes little to the detailed analysis of actual language use, such as preoccupies Anglo-American linguists and socio-linguists.

By way of exemplification of one sort of extreme, consider the following, from Bisseret's commentary on Bernstein:

> Doubtless, if Bernstein had been aware of linguistic changes in time he would have realized that class languages slowly took shape as an expression and instrument of social hierarchy in the making. During the whole of the nineteenth century the bourgeoisie forged its class identity and gradually defined itself as 'subject', inasmuch as its practices as a whole, including its language practices, allotted to the dominated social categories an identity as objects. (1979, p. 108)

It is far from clear – to me, at any rate – how such global historical perspectives could readily be translated into an empirical specification in terms of modern descriptive linguistics, though I do not deny the potential importance of Bisseret's remarks.

The divide is also exemplified by Henri Pêcheux, who mounts a thoroughgoing critique of conventional linguistics which questions the very basis of that 'science', in terms reminiscent of Bisseret's:

> I believe that a reference to history *vis-à-vis* linguistic questions is only justifiable in the perspective of a materialist analysis of class relationships on what can be called the 'linguistic practices' inscribed in the operation of the ideological apparatuses of a given social and economic formation; given this it becomes possible to explain what is going on today in 'the study of language' and to help to transform it, not by repeating its contradictions but by grasping them as derivatory effects of the class struggle in a 'Western country' under the domination of bourgeois ideology. (1982, p. 8)

In this context Pêcheux argues against what he calls the 'formalist' tendency (including Chomsky) and the 'historical' tendency (including Labov and Bernstein) (p. 6) in terms which few if any of their English-speaking adherents would be able to engage with at all. (I do not expect the reader necessarily to grasp what Pêcheux is getting at here; that is illustrative of my point.)

Even where linguists and sociologists/anthropologists draw on 'the same' concepts – such as when Lévi-Strauss uses the phoneme as a model, or when literary critics use Jakobson's distinction between 'metaphoric' and 'metonymic' orders of meaning (cf. Lodge, 1977), the linguistic elements are used in essentially 'metaphorical' ways. They are not generally used to construct sociological accounts on foundations of linguistic analyses.

Although it cannot be developed in any detail here, the disciplinary difference is perfectly captured in contrasting discussions of 'language' and psychiatry. On the one hand we have Lacan (1977a, 1977b) and his followers, whose starting-point is the observation that 'the unconscious is structured like a language', and whose opaque pronouncements are based on a structuralist reinterpretation of Freud. Lacan's discussion of classic psychoanalytic themes through the theory of the sign is by no means grounded in the technical apparatus of contemporary linguistics and a detailed empirical investigation of language use in psychoanalytic settings. Indeed, such analyses would be quite irrelevant to his task. On the other hand, it comes as no surprise whatsoever that Labov's interest in the psychiatric encounter (Labov and Fanshel, 1977) takes the form of a very detailed analysis of recordings of psychiatrist–client interaction. The two approaches to 'language' are as different as chalk and cheese, despite a superficial similarity in subject-matter.

In this context it is worth noting that Bernstein's early papers make passing reference to psychiatric encounters – albeit in a highly speculative fashion – and one is devoted solely to the topic (1964b); it is not widely cited, and has not been anthologized in the *Class, Codes and Control* volumes. It builds directly on the features of language use claimed for the codes:

> From this point of view the psycho-therapy relationship involves, for an individual limited to a restricted code, a relationship where the signals are antithetic to his own way of making relationships. For the status relationships are ambiguous, give no indication for here-and-now behaviour. It is a person-oriented relationship which increases the tension upon

> the individual to structure and re-structure his experience in a verbally unique way. For the patient it involves a loss of social identity which his very code promotes, and exposes the patient to the reflections on his personal identity in a social relationship which from the patient's point of view is unsupporting. A lack of insight into the sources of motivation combined with the dependency of the patient will tend to force the therapist into taking, from his point of view, too active or dominant a role in the relationship. (1964b, pp.63–4)

In a relatively small literature, Bernstein's remarks have been taken up by a few authors in the field of psychiatry and psychotherapy (e.g. Meltzer, 1978). His is not a major contribution to that literature, nor is it a major part of his own work. His position is, however, illustrative of general features in his sociology and of a somewhat ambivalent orientation towards language. I mention his speculations on the psychotherapeutic encounter for illustrative and comparative purposes, therefore, and not in order to evaluate their accuracy.

Characteristically, in these embryonic remarks, Bernstein's position is an intermediate one. He attempts to relate general features of the therapeutic relationship to equally general cultural forms, mediated by class differences in language use. 'Language' here is more specifically grounded, sociologically speaking, than in Lacanian usage: Bernstein points towards key elements in an ethnography of speaking in psychotherapeutic settings. On the other hand, Bernstein's approach is not grounded in the sort of detailed analysis of talk such as Labov trades in, and is addressed to more general problems of structure and culture.

It has been characteristic of Bernstein throughout his career to adopt similar betwixt-and-between positions. He has always sought expression of highly abstract and general sociological themes, while attempting to relate them to features of language and interaction. In terms of academic cultures, therefore, he is a sort of 'marginal man', poised between the French and the Anglo-Saxon, between anthropology, sociology and linguistics. (Anthropologically speaking we know that such 'trickster' figures can become highly charged, symbolically, as Bernstein has.) The tension is detectable within the corpus of essays and books produced by Bernstein and his SRU colleagues. There are differences of emphasis, from work which stresses the 'linguistic', with little reference to the general anthropological themes, to those reflecting the opposite tendency.

Given these contradictory and ambiguous themes in the work it is perhaps understandable that Bernstein's position on language codes and social structure should have been received in the puzzled and puzzling ways it has been.

7 The boundaries of knowledge: the thinkable and the unthinkable

Hitherto we have seen how Bernstein has drawn on an interpretation of Durkheim's sociology. He has developed the basic notions of Durkheim's treatment of the division of labour, as well as those aspects of the *Elementary Forms of Religious Life* that have already been touched on.

While Bernstein's self-characterization as a Durkheimian by inclination tells us a good deal about his underlying approach, we must be alert to two things. First, as I have commented already, Bernstein's is not a slavishly literal re-working of Durkheim's sociology. (See Cherkaoui, 1977, 1978 for a discussion of parallels and differences between the two.) Secondly, we must be clear from which version of Durkheim Bernstein draws inspiration, for there is no single orthodoxy.

Over the years there have been several 'versions' of Durkheim and his school. These differences in interpretation have been associated with different national schools of sociology and anthropology. If we are to go on to make full use of the Durkheimian theme, then we must make some preliminary appraisal of these rather different traditions. Briefly, I shall mention what I take to be the less interesting and illuminating of the major traditions, and then turn to what I believe to be (a) more exciting, and (b) closer to Bernstein's own understandings. It is this latter – essentially structuralist – view of Durkheim's legacy which provides the key to understanding Bernstein's entire sociology.

Bernstein comments, somewhat self-deprecatingly, that when he was first moved by reading Durkheim, as a student, he turned a blind eye to his supposed shortcomings. He is and was reacting against that view of Durkheim which portrays him in the history of sociological thought as the arch-positivist, and as the fountainhead of a conservative structural-functionalism.

Durkheim's supposed contribution to structural-functionalism had been established by those two major interpreters and builders of twentieth-century social theory (sociology and anthropology respectively) – Talcott Parsons and Radcliffe-Brown. Thompson's introductory text provides a clear statement:

> It is one of the quirks of intellectual history that the eventual successful re-entry of Durkheimian sociology into America was partly in the form of an adaptation re-exported from Britain. It was taken there by the anthropologist A. R. Radcliffe-Brown, who went to the University of Chicago for several years in the early 1930s. Radcliffe-Brown's adaptation was suited to the study of societies with little if any written history. It lost sight of Durkheim's original problematic – that of resolving the divisions and problems of a modern industrial society and of reconciling individualism and social solidarity. Radcliffe-Brown's structural-functionalism was inspired by Durkheim's studies of religion and kinship. . . . When applied to American society and the topics such as social stratification, as in the work of W. Lloyd Warner and Talcott Parsons, the integrating function of kinship was still given prominence. Indeed, for Parsons, who did more than anyone else to promote this structural-functionalist version of Durkheim's sociology, stratification itself was an integrating function in the social system. (1982, p. 20)

There is, however, a version of Durkheim and his heritage quite different from that of Parsons and Radcliffe-Brown. Whereas the structural-functionalist view is (or was) a distinctively Anglo-American reading, the alternative – structuralist – is pre-eminently a French perspective. Indeed, the structuralist movement in general, and various 'post-structuralist' developments, have played a dominant role in the social sciences in modern France. Its influence has been felt in a wide range of 'human sciences': sociology, anthropology, psychology, linguistics, literary theory, studies of mass communications. The collection of papers in translation edited by Lemert (1981) is an excellent introduction to contemporary French sociology in this vein. For general introductions to structuralism in a broad range of disciplines, see Hawkes (1977), Macksey and Donato (1972), Culler (1975), Kurzweil (1980) and Sturrock (1979).

While its influence is discernible in his earliest work, Bernstein makes there little explicit reference to the structuralist movement. Nevertheless, the subsequent directions taken by his thinking indicate that a broadly structuralist programme was always at least implicit. In the latest and most mature work, there is an increasingly explicit debt to structuralist authors.

Bernstein himself has drawn attention to this. In a paper which captures many of his preoccupations, he comments on the profusion – indeed, confusion – of paradigms and 'approaches' in sociology and reaffirms his own allegiance to Durkheim. At the same time he mourns the partial understanding of Durkheim prevalent in the English-speaking world:

> the attack of [Jack] Douglas (amongst others) on Durkheim is based almost wholly upon *Suicide* and the *Rules of Sociological Method*. Douglas ignores almost completely *The Division of Labour in Society, Primitive Classification* and *The Elementary Forms of the Religious Life*; books which have had a vital influence upon French anthropology and contemporary sociology. If Douglas had asked how it was that *Suicide* had had such a powerful effect on American sociology, then we might have obtained a rather more general understanding of the development of sociology in two cultures. (Bernstein, 1974b, pp. 145–6)

As we shall see, it is only relatively late in the development of the sociology that Bernstein has embarked on a thoroughgoing exploration of the French tradition as it is reflected in structuralist and post-structuralist thought.

Bernstein's structuralist programme is most clearly and readily apparent in his papers on the organization and transmission of school knowledge. As has been pointed out already, this structuralist anthropology of schooling developed *pari passu* with the language-based investigations of the Sociological Research Unit. It draws on precisely the same sociological tradition and deploys what is essentially the same repertoire of concepts. Indeed, the bare bones of the project are perhaps easier to discern in the context of curriculum studies, if for no other reason than the fact that they have not been obscured by the sort of dispute occasioned by linguists' criticisms, or by the misunderstandings evoked by the moral and political connotations of 'deficit' debates.

The 'knowledge' papers continue and develop the themes and variations apparent from the very outset of Bernstein's work, and which were outlined in chapter 2. The project is built upon thoroughly Durkheimian foundations, and returns repeatedly to the nature and consequences of change from mechanical to organic solidarity in education systems. Corresponding changes in the moral or sentimental order are explored; implications for the reproduction of orders of meaning and the reproduction of social identities are suggested. Bernstein's own papers in this area are not based directly on reports of empirical research in educational institutions. Characteristically he has been concerned primarily with the initial generation of suggestive, sensitizing theoretical schemes at a high level of generality. But, as we shall see, despite criticism from some quarters, other researchers have found Bernstein's formulations of considerable value in ordering empirical enquiry in a wide range of educational (and other) settings.

Bernstein's work on the sociology of educational knowledge will be used to exemplify the most thoroughly structuralist element of his output. At the same time, I shall argue that the full development of his insights has not been achieved, either by Bernstein himself, his followers, or his critics. Here, as in the work on language codes, the structuralist framework remains under-developed. Most of the links are there, but many of them are implicit. The more explicitly acknowledged debts and influences (such as Mary Douglas or Pierre Bourdieu) are undoubtedly fruitful, but they do not constitute a fully formed theoretical justification. Other authors within the structuralist tradition have not been incorporated. This observation does not derive simply from fusty pedantry on my part, or from some accusation that Bernstein has not done his 'homework'. Rather, my point here – as elsewhere – is that the author and his interpreters have not always done full justice to the ideas, as their potential has not always been recognized. Some attempt to remedy that will be made here.

The essential continuity in Bernstein's thought is indicated by the use of the notion of *code*, which is as fundamental to his work on curriculum as it is to that on language. This continuity in terminology is not to be taken as in any sense adventitious, or as a reflection of mental laziness whereby existing conceptual tools are recycled and made to do a hand's turn for lack of anything better. Bernstein is something of a *bricoleur* – like all of us – but he is a good deal more systematic and principled than that. In the two contexts *code* performs precisely the same analytic function, and has the same theoretical status and pedigree. Bernstein's theory of language and his theory of knowledge are formally equivalent. Ultimately, they are but two (of the many) possible manifestations of a single theoretical vision.

I have already tried to convey how 'code' may be identified in a range of different cultural domains, and how 'restriction' or 'elaboration' may be so understood. With but minor modifications, that earlier demonstration can be transposed to the domain of school knowledge. In all contexts of application, Bernstein's codes regulate the selection and combination of cultural elements into permitted arrangements. This regulation or structuration relates such cultural forms to the social division of labour. Moreover, it will be recalled, the codes give access to and are constitutive of different modes of understanding and meaning.

Bernstein's views on curriculum are therefore formulated in terms of principles of selection and combination. Thought of in formal, abstract terms, any 'curriculum' (in a broad sense of that term) is a reflection of two complementary principles: educational contents must be constructed as separate units or domains, and educational contents must be combined. Curricula may therefore be described and compared in terms of how these principles are realized.

The principle that knowledge contents are subject to some degree of selection and separation is clearly a prerequisite to anything recognizable as a curriculum. Without some such classification, the curriculum would be coterminous with the entire universe of possible knowledge and experience. In so far as any curriculum must propose a version, or set of representations of that universe (or selections from it), then the first principle of organization is a *sine qua non*. In fact, this single principle of structuration covers two closely related operations. First, there is the question of the external boundary: how is the curriculum to be distinguishable from any and every other domain? What is to be counted in and what counted out? What marks its contents as 'curricular' or 'educational' as opposed to any other knowledge domains? Secondly, there is the question of its internal differentiation. How is this domain of educational knowledge partitioned? What is the nature of its units? What is the nature of its internal boundaries?

Together, these two define curricular units and their distribution within the curricular domain. They define the culturally available class or classes of curricular units. If we restrict ourselves to the simplest exemplification, we can think in terms of school or college 'subjects'. The two principles of selection and differentiation operate simultaneously in order to generate domains (e.g. English, Science, Mathematics, Languages, etc.) which are recognizably differentiated from each other and which select our particular domains from the entire range of conceivable possibilities.

This is what Bernstein refers to as the *classification* of school knowledge. Classification is therefore a matter of boundary, the definition, maintenance and validation of domains of knowledge: 'classification thus refers to the degree of boundary maintenance between contents' (1971b, *CCC* 1, p.205; *CCC* 3, p.88). Classification relates to the organization of knowledge into *curricula*, or the various domains of educational activity.

The work of classification and boundary-maintenance is part and parcel of what Raymond Williams calls the 'selective tradition' (1965, pp.67–76). Commenting specifically on the literary field, Williams discusses how certain works are selected for special treatment and evaluation. The boundaries so constructed create the stability of 'tradition' (which is itself a matter of construction) and of change:

> In a society as a whole, and in all its particular activities, the cultural tradition can be seen as a continual selection and re-selection of ancestors. Particular lines will be drawn, often for as long as a century, and then suddenly with some new stage of growth these will be cancelled or weakened, and new lines drawn. (ibid., p.69)

Williams's comments on literature here are strongly reminiscent of Kuhn's construction of scientific 'paradigms', which represent the 'selective tradition' of the scientific community (Kuhn, 1970; see also chapter 9 below).

Within the literary field the starkest exemplar of classification and selectivity is the approach associated with F. R. Leavis and 'the great tradition' (Leavis, 1962). The Leavisite method and its translation into curricular prescriptions rests upon a very strong boundary indeed. As is well known, the Leavisite approach proposes a very clear separation between authors, and indeed between works by the same authors (even, in the case of *Daniel Deronda*, within the same text) between those treated as canonical and those relegated beyond greatness. The spirit is conveyed in the first sentence of Leavis's book: 'The great English novelists are Jane Austen, George Eliot, Henry James, and Joseph Conrad' (p.9). This style of literary thought has exercised considerable influence in the study of English literature – in secondary schools and universities – through the construction of syllabuses and reading lists. The result is a strongly classified 'tradition', marked by a high degree of consensus among an intellectual community as to what is included and what is not (see Parsons, 1979, 1981, for empirical evidence of such stability and consensus as manifested in public examinations; and St John-Brooks, 1983, for exemplification of such classification in the construction of the 'practical curriculum' in school).

Leavis himself couches the task in terms of discrimination and distinction:

> It is necessary to insist . . . that there are important distinctions to be made, and that far from all of the names in the literary histories really belong to the realm of significant creative achievement. And as a recall to a due sense of differences it is as well to start by distinguishing the few really great. (1962, p.10)

These distinctions are not, of course, posited as conventional, still less as matters of personal taste, but as embodiments of self-evident truths. The rhetoric of 'scrutiny' appeals to the untrammelled 'gaze' of the dispassionate but discriminating reader (cf. Foucault, 1973). (For critical discussions of Leavis see Lawford, 1976; Mulhern, 1979; Belsey, 1982.)

The classificatory process in educational settings therefore partakes of more general cultural activities of boundary construction. Such boundaries mark what is thinkable, or what is regarded as good 'taste'. Dimaggio (1982a, 1982b) has explicitly drawn on Bernstein to describe how 'cultural entrepreneurs' in nineteenth-century America shaped and institutionalized 'high culture'. Dimaggio writes of how Boston Brahmins legitimized their position as a status group through the culturally exclusive divide between 'high' and 'popular' forms. For an equivalent account of contemporary management of the arts which draws on Bernstein in a similar fashion, see also Dimaggio and Useem (1978).

The implications of classifications for a hierarchical ordering of knowledge – the two coalesce nicely in the connotations of 'discrimination' – is one of the many specific ways in which Bernstein's sociology of knowledge grows near to that of Bourdieu (e.g. Bourdieu and Passeron, 1979) who argues, in a general discussion of the legitimization of high culture in France, that it serves to demarcate caste (cf. Douglas, 1981). It corresponds to the organization of exclusiveness by 'cultural curators' as Goffman (1951) called them.

Classification is paralleled by the notion of *framing*. Framing is also related to the nature of strength of boundary, but in a somewhat different sense. Whereas classification characterizes curriculum, framing refers to the context of knowledge transmission – that is, the pedagogic encounter. 'Frame refers to the strength of the boundary between what may be transmitted and what may not be transmitted, in the pedagogical relationship' (1971b, *CCC* 1, pp.205–6; *CCC* 3, p.88). This is, therefore, a matter of the options available to teachers and taught in the encounter. Where framing is strong, then the range of options and freedom of movement is limited. Where it is weak, then there are more degrees of freedom available to the participants: 'Thus frame refers to the degree of control teacher and pupil possess over the selection, organization, pacing and timing of the knowledge transmitted and received in the pedagogical relationship' (ibid.).

Bernstein notes another aspect of frame, which bears directly on the notion of boundary. That is, the degree of insulation between what is defined as 'proper' educational knowledge, and the everyday mundane knowledge possessed by teachers and taught: 'Thus we can consider variations in the strength of frames as these refer to the strength of the boundary between educational knowledge and everyday community knowledge of teacher and taught' (1971b, *CCC* 1, p.206; *CCC* 3, p.89). In practice, this latter aspect of boundary seems equally a matter of classification and frame, since it is often related directly to the relative purity and strength of membrane of curricular contents. Empirical research tends to reflect this overlap and ambiguity.

It is entirely in keeping with Bernstein's most general theory that curriculum and pedagogy should be thought of in essentially semiotic terms. They are referred to as *message systems*, to which is added the third, evaluation: 'Curriculum defines what counts as valid knowledge, pedagogy defines what counts as a valid transmission of knowledge, and evaluation defines what counts as a valid realization of this knowledge on the part of the taught' (1971b, *CCC* 1, p.203; *CCC* 3, p.85). The concern is with the formal ordering of these three message systems, and their systemic relationships. Classification, framing and evaluation direct attention to structural principles rather than to contents *per se*.

Just as it operates with language-based message systems, code is held to be a regulative principle which underlies these various message systems, especially curriculum and pedagogy. While the empirical realizations of these codes and messages are diverse, Bernstein suggests an underlying model based on two varieties of code: *collection and integrated codes*.

To begin with, two curricular types are identified. A *collection* type is said to consist of strongly classified and bounded domains. The student who needs to satisfy the requirements for such a curriculum – such as selecting courses and enrolling for examinations – has to select a number of such clearly separated contents (subjects, courses, credits). A student will thus construct his or her educational knowledge by making up a set of such units (with or without choice). An integrated type of curriculum, on the other hand, will consist of contents which 'stand in an open relation to each other' (1971b, *CCC* 1, p.205; *CCC* 3, p.88). Here, therefore, insulating boundaries are relatively weak.

It must be emphasized – as on previous occasions – that these are ideal types: the underlying coding is what is at stake rather than the specification of many and varied curricula. While some actual curricula may approximate to the collection and integrated types more closely than others, they are not held to exist in a pure form. Indeed it is difficult to see how a 'curriculum' could exist, located and practised in a real organization, which corresponded to the extremes.

From the two types, Bernstein proposes two codes, which are fundamental to the boundaries of classification and frame. These are then developed into a further typology, but for the moment I shall deal with the most straightforward cases. As we have seen, collection codes regulate strong classification. For the most part in England and Wales they also underpin highly specialized and 'pure' forms of selection and combination. (Scotland is distinctively different in furthering broader, less specialized subject combinations.) Here the pupil or student is required to select a relatively small number of self-contained elements. Moreover, in this system (the specialized 'English' mode) the number of permitted combinations may be tightly restricted. In other words, at 'A' level or university degree level, for example, the range of permitted combinations has traditionally been restricted. Thus, the available 'packages' at 'A' level would be of the form 'Latin, Greek, Ancient History', 'Maths, Physics, Chemistry', 'English, French, History' and so on. Similarly, the single or joint honours degree allows for little option outside the required package of courses and subjects.

The sort of model I have just alluded to is clearly recognizable as the 'traditional' and 'academic' curriculum of the grammar school and public school. The strong boundaries reflect and construct the domains of knowledge as 'pure' and 'sacred'. It is a highly *selective* mode. Teachers, pupils and their knowledge are specialized, segregated and selected.

This was the perspective emphasized in Bernstein's somewhat transitional paper 'On the curriculum' (effectively the first draft of the classification and framing essay) which is reproduced in

CCC 3 (pp.79–84). This brief sketch for the later work is useful in that it provides some clue as to the origins of the more developed analysis. It is apparent that Bernstein includes at the outset the symbolic significance of such segregation and selection:

> The specialized form of collection, indeed any form of collection, involves a hierarchy whereby the ultimate mystery of the subject is revealed very late in the educational life. And education takes the form of a long initiation into this mystery. Knowledge partakes of the sacred, it is not ordinary or mundane. And this enhances the significance of the subject and those who profess it. A very powerful form of control. Now the receipt of this knowledge is not so much a right as something to be won, or earned. This is called discipline. The educational relationship tends to be hierarchical and ritualized, the educand seen as ignorant with little status and therefore few rights. (*CCC* 3, p.82)

The jerky style of that passage reflects its status as a draft paper.

There is a clear allusion here to the Durkheimian notion of 'the sacred' as a domain separated from the surrounding context of 'profane' everyday experience. The pupil is thus in a position analogous to that of the religious novice or postulant. Education 'in depth' in one of the sacred areas thus becomes a protracted *rite de passage*. The novices must be screened carefully before they embark upon such an ordeal; their worth established and their vocation kept up to scratch:

> Pupils and students are also carefully screened to see who belongs and who does not belong. And once such screening has taken place, it is very difficult, sometimes impossible, to change one's educational identity. With specialized education the sheep have to be very quickly separated from the goats and the goats are invested with attributes of pollution. (*CCC* 3, p.82)

Such a form would, of course, facilitate the 'sponsored mobility' of an elect band (cf. Turner, 1961).

The metaphors of ritual, sacredness, purity and pollution remind us not only of the Durkheimian heritage, but also of

Bernstein's debt to Mary Douglas. Bernstein himself has recounted his first meeting with Douglas, after he had presented the 'ritual in education' paper at a conference on ritual convened by Julian Huxley:

> She came up to me after the paper, delivered the following and disappeared: 'It's the Convent of the Sacred Heart all over again! See you in September.' It was then late June. What could one do, except read her work? (1977a, *CCC* 3, p.6)

The key work of Mary Douglas which establishes her approach to structuralist anthropology, *Purity and Danger* (1966) is concerned with the classification of natural categories and classes, their arbitrary arrangements, and the consequences of ambiguities or anomalies in such systems of representation. It is this work which provides the key link with that of Bernstein.

Douglas seeks to answer the long-standing anthropological puzzle as to how and why certain natural species and objects are treated as 'taboo', with the dual connotations of being particularly 'sacred' on the one hand, and 'dangerous' and 'polluting' on the other. The phenomenon is identifiable from many cultures and the various cultural configurations have a number of common features. The collections of categories so identified are often recondite assemblages of very different sorts of natural categories. There is nothing inherent in their nature, nor is their 'special' status directly attributable to common functions and uses.

Without going into unncessary detail here, suffice it to say that Douglas proposes a very general solution, based upon the very logic of such classificatory systems. There is, for instance, nothing inherent in all the different sorts of things that can be identified as 'dirt' and 'pollution'. Their common feature is the fact that – according to the logic of the given culture – they count as matter which is 'out of place'. The culture consists of classes and categories which define persons, objects and events in terms of 'proper' kinds. These categorizations are essentially arbitrary, cultural impositions rather than pictures of a natural order. There is no perfect correspondence between the natural world and the cultural system. There will be areas of ambiguity, anomaly and interstitial elements. These threaten the logic of classification, which deals with them and solves the cultural puzzles they pose by insulating the anomalies and placing them in a special category of dirt and sacredness. In other words, the boundaries and categories of the system are preserved by a sort of symbolic *cordon sanitaire*.

Douglas exemplifies her argument by – *inter alia* – a most elegant discussion of Judaic dietary laws enshrined in the Abominations of Leviticus. These laws proclaim certain animal categories as 'unclean' (the pig is probably the best known, but there are many more, and they comprise a very varied list). Douglas suggests that what they all have in common is that they each contravene relevant dimensions of the classification system. To take just one example, crustacea are impure in that they do not conform to the proper category for a water-living creature. A proper fish, for example, has scales, and swims with fins, while something like a lobster is anomalous – having a shell and claws, crawling rather than swimming.

Here, then, in Douglas we find a ready exemplification of the structuralist anthropology of knowledge, complete with an account of the symbolic significance of boundary-maintenance. It reflects the general principles of a structuralist theory of knowledge:

> If the names of abstractions are organized into a classification system, they form a perceptual *code*, a set of conventions for looking at the world. They link and signify. A theory of meaning is a theory of coding. These codes are necessary and perhaps the fundamental precondition of knowledge and systematic learning. . . . They permit persons to define fundamental relations, places, times (to mark days, cycles, ceremonies), to sort out obligations and entitlements, to speculate about the meaning of events, and to engage in ordered interaction. (Manning, 1982, pp.60–1)

Modern anthropology is replete with exemplification of this general principle, as well as this specific issue of cultural ambiguities and anomalies.

Bernstein draws inspiration from this structuralist. Durkheimian tradition. The anthropological interest in such systems is indeed represented in Durkheim's own work. It is most clearly apparent in one of his shorter works (important, for all that) co-authored with Marcel Mauss (1963). The gist of the argument concerned the character and origin of the elementary categories which shape our perceptions of the world: how we compartmentalize our experience of time, space, natural classes and the like. The Durkheimian perspective has come to be known as 'sociological Kantianism'. Whereas the philosopher Kant saw the categories of experience as *given* or *a priori*, Durkheim saw them as socially or culturally determined. In a parallel way, too, just as Durkheim rendered Kant's categories into sociological phenomena, Bernstein 'sociologized' the philosophy of Peters and Hirst (e.g. Hirst 1974; Dearden, Hirst and Peters, 1972). At its weakest the Durkheim–Mauss argument suggests that there is a parallelism between distinctions and classifications in society itself, and the axes of that society's cosmology. They also suggest a stronger version: that natural categories are reflections or realizations of prior social categorizations. It is not necessary to subscribe to the latter claim to appreciate the general perspective. Tiryakian (1978, p.212) comments on its significance:

> Although Durkheim himself may not have realized the full import of this essay, I think it may be argued that his treatment of the social basis of classification is a major innovation or anticipation of phenomenological sociology: for if the modes of organizing and classifying objective reality are collective representations, then it follows that these a priori structures . . . are constitutive of the social world we seek to understand. To understand the structure of a collectivity's classification of the world is, in effect, to understand its rules or principles of social organization. This may well be considered as one of Durkheim's greatest insights and discoveries.

The important issue here, then, is the view that categories of thought are 'collective representations'. That is:

> (1) they are socially generated; (2) they represent social concerns; (3) there is a structural correspondence with social organization; (4) once formed they become relatively autonomous and combine, separate, and are transformed, according to their own laws. (Thompson, 1982, p.62)

Such collective representations have become the subject matter of subsequent structuralist sociology and anthropology, as we have seen. Claude Lévi-Strauss, for example, offers this summary of the scope of such studies:

> Myths, popular legends, religious conceptions of all sorts, moral beliefs, etc. reflect a reality different from the individual's reality; but the way in which they attract and repel each other, unite or separate, may nevertheless be independent of their content and may depend uniquely on their general quality as representations. . . . We need to investigate by comparison of mythical themes, popular legends, traditions, and languages, the manner in which social representations adhere to and repel one another, how they fuse or separate from one another, etc. (cited in Thompson, 1982, p.62)

The parallels between Bernstein and Mary Douglas are further emphasized through a brief consideration of her later formulations of 'group' and 'grid'. This convergence is not surprising since – as we have seen – there was a longstanding relationship of mutual influence between the two after their first meeting. Douglas herself has a sensitivity to matters of collective representation which is born of anthropology and Catholicism – a combination with which Bernstein is in far greater sympathy than sociology and Protestantism. The ideas of group and grid were first formulated in Douglas (1970) and later refined in a subsequent essay (1978). More recently still, Douglas has edited a collection of essays (1982) by a number of authors who variously apply the conceptual framework to the 'sociology of perception', including studies in the sociology of science and belief.

The ideas that Douglas proposes are somewhat elusive. Indeed, in relating them to Bernstein we are in danger of approaching *ignotum per ignotius*. Yet the parallels are instructive and are worth persevering with. At root, the two dimensions of group and grid refer respectively to whom one interacts with and how one interacts with them. Group, then, is an axis which identifies the strength of 'social incorporation': that is, it describes the strength of boundary circumscribing membership and the strength of allegiance a group demands from its members. Grid, on the other hand, refers to the strength of regulation exerted on members' conduct. Douglas herself (1982, p.3) summarizes the two as 'group commitment, grid control'. Douglas's scheme suggests that these two dimensions can vary independently.

Although they are not intended to be in any way 'the same' the Douglas and Bernstein frameworks are formally very close. Group and classification both refer to boundary phenomena: group to boundaries between social collectivities, classification to boundaries between fields of knowledge and their implications for social relations. Ultimately, the two dimensions are equally references to aspects of cosmology. Ostrander (1982, p.24) summarizes the similarity and the difference:

> The typologies have in common a focus on boundaries between social entities; the classification boundaries are between cognitive entities, fields of knowledge. Thus, while Douglas is using two social dimensions in order to derive social environments with predictable cosmological correlates, Bernstein is placing a social dimension against a cosmological dimension in order to derive socialization environments.

Likewise, grid/frame both refer to regulatory codes for the control of interaction. Ostrander also comments on the group/grid scheme in terms which are also broadly applicable to Bernstein's framework:

> 1 It is a relative rather than an absolute tool, constructed of continuous rather than dichotomous variables. . . .
> 2 As it classifies social environments, it is technically incapable of distinguishing (as it stands) whole social systems or pan-system institutions. . . .
> 3 The grid/group classification is not a causal model. . . .
> 4 It is not the only classification possible, or extant, which links social structure to symbolic structure. (p.15)

There can be no doubt, therefore, that there is a very close affinity between the theories of Bernstein and Douglas. Indeed, in the sociology of science, one network of scholars recognizes a Douglas–Bernstein approach to the articulation of knowledge, cosmology and social organization. Recent studies which exemplify and explicate this link include: Shapin (1975) on phrenological knowledge and social structure; Shapin and Barnes (1977) on science and control in Mechanics' Institutes; Wilde (1982) on matter and spirit in eighteenth-century natural philosophy; see also Bloor (1982) on mathematical knowledge.[1]

In noting these features of the structuralist tradition, we can readily understand how Bernstein's papers were assimilated to the so-called 'new sociology of education'. As the extract from Tiryakian indicates there is a direct parallel between the post-Durkheimian analysis of collective representations and the phenomenologists' attention to the 'social construction of reality' (e.g. Berger and Luckmann, 1967). They have common roots in Kantian and post-Kantian theories of knowledge. It was thus possible for Bernstein's structuralist essay to be placed happily beside papers which stressed much more thoroughly the perspectives of Meadian symbolic interactionism and Schutzian phenomenology. The papers edited by M. F. D. Young (1971) which constituted the original manifesto of this self-consciously rebellious movement reflected a variety of perspectives, which addressed a common (if rather fuzzy) set of themes.

In various ways those papers drew upon the traditions of the sociology of knowledge in directing attention to the social production and organization of the contents of schooling. There can be no doubt that the papers enjoyed considerable *succès d'estime*, but their freshness, enthusiasm, novelty and strangeness helped to gloss over the many internal differences. The papers by Bernstein and Bourdieu shared a common tradition, largely French in inspiration and informed by a similar anthropological frame of mind, but they differed from the orientations to be found in, say, Young, Esland and Keddie which derived much less from a structuralist than from an action frame of reference. Bernbaum (1977) provides an excellent critical review of the 'new' movement which helps considerably in disentangling some of the contradictions and inconsistencies. While damning the emergent paradigm as self-defeatingly relativist, Bernbaum is much more sympathetic to Bernstein's contribution – rightly seeing it as a sociology of power, not of pluralism.

While both the structuralist and action traditions share a common emphasis upon the 'social construction of reality' the structuralists – as we have seen – emphasize knowledge as consisting of 'collective representations' which are themselves structured and coded. The interpretivists, on the other hand, make much more of the work of individual actors in the construction and maintenance of meaning through social action/interaction. The structuralist will thus tend to see significance in the systems of classification and ordering; the interactionist will see meaning as the emergent outcome of transactions between actors or groups of actors. For a recent summary of these contrasting positions in relation to curricular knowledge, see Goodson (1981).

It is, I think, for these reasons that in Bernstein's treatment of classification and framing, classification is more clearly defined and is more readily identified by others. For classification, operating as it does in the curriculum message system clearly refers to the realm of the structural. In terms of classic semiotics and linguistics, the notion of classification operates in terms of *langue* (i.e. language as a system of relationships). Framing, on the other hand, may at first sight appear to sit slightly less happily here, since it refers to pedagogical encounters, and so operates at the level of *parole* (i.e. use of the system's potential, or its realization, in actual communicative acts). The latter is less directly attributable to structural features of the cultural field.

'Frame' is, none the less, a structural notion, and Bernstein's use of the term to relate structural and interactional analyses is more than terminologically similar to Goffman's 'frame analysis' (Goffman, 1974). Goffman is concerned with ways in which actors demarcate and discriminate between different versions or orders of reality. As Manning (1980) points out, Goffman's frame analysis confirms him as an author in the structuralist tradition of Durkheim and of Simmel's formalism (see also Gonos, 1977). Similar notions of the structuring and bounding of experience in face-to-face interaction are to be found in Bateson (1972) and among several anthropologists of language (e.g. Tannen, 1979; Frake, 1977; Gumperz, 1977).

We have seen how Bernstein proposes the notion of a 'collection code' as a summary statement of the form of message system whereby contents are relatively well insulated from one another. It is clear that the Mary Douglas-like structuralist approach most fully fits this curricular type. Such a form of educational knowledge most clearly reflects the principles of categorization and boundary-maintenance, the preservation of 'pure' categories and so on. Bernstein does not fully develop and follow through the implications of such an approach. The anthropological precedents would suggest that such tightly bounded symbolic systems would pose considerable barriers to mixed categories, boundary-transgression and so forth.

Such a view is implicit in all Bernstein says. He makes passing reference to the exclusion of pupils as 'polluting' if they are not selected for the protracted *rites de passage*, but he provides little exemplification of what might happen if the symbolic boundaries are perceived to be under threat or undermined. We should certainly expect such a system to be very strongly resistant to the introduction of novel categories – especially those which overlap with existing classes or which do not fit into existing ones. Such 'impure' or 'profane' contents would be seen as ritually defiling – as threatening 'proper' standards, representing 'debased' knowledge, introducing dangerous innovations. It is not difficult to think of examples for oneself from diverse school and higher educational contexts. Commentary which uses the rhetoric of 'non-subjects' trades on such symbolic systems: a current example is the widely reported debate on 'peace studies'. Sociology itself is often subject to such attacks as are degree courses in such exoteric subjects as home economics, catering or tourism. It is worth reflecting on the symbolic significance of the fact that the opponents – who defend esoteric knowledge – are often called 'purists'.

This is admirably exemplified by Johnston (1978), in a case-study of boundary-enforcement. Based on an analysis of parental complaint about classroom content and conduct, Johnston's discussion draws on Mary Douglas and Bernstein in demonstrating the social construction of 'dangerous' knowledge. The classification of knowledge was reaffirmed in order to prevent the transgression of boundaries, while simultaneously encoding the social typing of actors. The symbolic coding of persons was based on the following formal equivalences:

> young:old :: female:male :: innocent:experienced :: vulnerable:invulnerable :: unprotected:protected

The collection code is contrasted with the so-called integrated code. As we should expect, the strong boundaries of the former are weakened. The code does not regulate a closed system of options and combinations. Bernstein makes it quite clear that this is intended to refer to something more fundamental than just 'interdisciplinary' borrowing or trans-disciplinary co-operation: 'Integration, as it is used here, refers minimally to the *subordination* of previously insulated subjects *or* courses to some *relational* idea, which blurs the boundaries between the subjects' (1971b, *CCC* 1, p.209; *CCC* 3, p.93, emphases in original). The idea of integration only makes sense in terms of its opposition to the former term. Moreover, it would appear that since Bernstein talks of 'previously insulated subjects' integration is to be thought of as a reflection of *change*.

The heuristic value of the framework, therefore, lies in the analysis of difference and change in a *relative* fashion. Strength of classification and frame are not calibrated on an absolute scale. This may be illustrated through a clutch of recent papers on medicine and nursing. (For a general discussion of the relevance of Bernstein and Bourdieu in this context, see Atkinson, 1983.)

Jacobsen (1981) in a study of Danish higher education develops the Bernstein framework in contrasting Medicine and Danish. The two disciplines are transmitted in very different ways. Medicine is found to approximate to a system of strong classification and framing: the structure of knowledge is hierarchical, as are its social relationships; it is arranged in tightly specified temporal and spatial units. Danish, on the other hand, is 'loosely structured' in comparison. Jacobsen makes no attempt there to make distinctions within the medical school – although it is a highly variegated organization (cf. Atkinson, 1977). Colditz and Sheehan (1982), on the other hand, draw on Bernstein to make distinctions within the curriculum of the first year at an Australian medical school: Chemistry, Physics and Zoology are strongly classified and framed, while Social and Preventive Medicine and Medical Sociology more weakly so. Likewise, Armstrong (1980) writing from a British viewpoint argues that the preclinical years are characterized by collection code and the clinical phase by principles of integration. There is too a process of change over time in professional education, as the organizing principle – in terms of rhetoric if not always in practice – shifts from collection to integration: this is documented in the context of nursing by Webb (1981) and Davies (1980).

Bernstein's general anthropology of educational transmissions, therefore, is concerned with a process of transformation. At root it is the same social change which underlies all: the shift from mechanical to organic solidarity. And here we begin to detect the continuity which lies beneath the work as a whole. It can be illustrated through Bernstein's discussion of the introduction and development of integrated code curricular types – and which incidentally reveals the implications of the collection code.

Consider first the social organization of knowledge itself. While under collection codings contents stand in closed relations of segmentation or juxtaposition, under conditions of integration they are subordinated to over-arching general principles: 'there must be some relational idea, a supra-content concept, which focuses upon general principles at a high level of abstraction' (1971b, *CCC* 1, p.217; *CCC* 3, p.101). There will therefore be a reduced emphasis upon the 'surface structure' of fine-grained particulars. Stress will be placed on the 'deep structure' of subjects. Curriculum and pedagogy would thus be less concerned with the assimilation and recapitulation of 'facts'; rather, these would be treated as secondary to an understanding of the general 'ways of knowing' characteristic of the intellectual domain. For instance, in the field of 'science' an integrating principle would be something like 'the scientific method' rather than classic demonstrations of chemistry, physics, biology.

Hence, as Bernstein himself expresses it: 'With integrated codes, the pedagogy is likely to proceed from the deep structure to the surface structure' (1971b, *CCC* 1, p.218; *CCC* 3, p.102). This contrasts with the specialized collection code whereby the deep structure is a 'mystery' to be revealed as the outcome of a protracted apprenticeship.

The organization of knowledge is mirrored in the educational philosophy embedded in each code. The collection code implies didactic teaching whereby the *facts* are inculcated. The integrated code is implicated in a theory of teaching and learning predicated on the self-regulation of individuals or groups of students. This theory of learning is fundamental to that weakly classified and weakly framed mode Bernstein refers to under the rubric of 'invisible pedagogy'.

We are now in a position to trace out more explicitly the continuities in Bernstein's formulation of 'code' as well as to refer back to the general structuralist anthropology with which the exposition of the sociology began in chapter 2.

While they should not be thought of as identical, there is a formal relationship between language codes and knowledge codes. In a manner already familiar to us, the general argument is:

restricted : elaborated :: collection : integrated

Both collection code and restricted code rest on the principle of restriction of choice and limited methods of permitted combination. Integrated and elaborated regulate selection and combination with more degrees of freedom.

Just as I suggested in relation to the model of language use, the organization of knowledge may be expressed in terms of Saussure's framework of paradigmatic and syntagmatic relations. Both classification and framing can be conceptualized in a similar manner. (In my earlier discussion of this point (Atkinson, 1981a) I ran the two together; I now believe this simplification to be unwarranted.)

For classification, the paradigmatic axis defines what may be defined as content units, and hence the universe from which appropriate selection is to be made, while the syntagmatic axis defines how such contents can be put together to make acceptable 'packages' of course, options, degree schemes and so on. For framing, the paradigmatic axis defines what may be counted into pedagogic encounters (what is admissible) and separates out what is inadmissible. The syntagmatic axis regulates how such contents are combined to produce orderly instruction (lessons, courses, etc.).

The parallels and continuities go much further, of course. The two analyses deal with socializing agencies (families, schools) in terms of their modalities of social control, their internal differentiation, the organization and allocation of roles, identities, motives and meanings.

I do not wish to recapitulate all the detailed comparisons that could be made here. Let me begin by a summary outline of some of the parallels and equivalences implied in Bernstein's work. It will be recalled that in primary socialization, the restricted code is identified as a regulator of family types which are 'positional'.

Roles are distributed according to a small number of attributes treated as 'given' and unquestionable – notably gender and generation. Individual identities are constrained within the restricted degrees of freedom of such allocational possibilities. The formal equivalent is the segmented school in which teachers' and pupils' identities are constrained by equally positional attributes of age, gender, ability and subject loyalty. (Links between Bernstein's later work on knowledge codes and the earlier papers referred to in chapter 2 should start to become apparent here.)

Control is conceptualized in parallel ways. In the positional family, control is vested in the positions themselves. It is explicit, in the sense that control is manifest in the formal status of parent and child, and may be realized through appeals to shared, public norms which are held to regulate such statuses (cf. the original connotations of the 'public' variety of language use). Likewise, the collection code is characteristic of schools wherein control relies upon the positional statuses of teachers and taught. By contrast, the personalizing family and the individualizing school, regulated by elaborated and integrated code respectively, encourage the verbal exploration of individual motives and identities. Here, then, control is less overt; it is a matter of negotiation and influence rather than power and status. Note that the suggestion that control is less manifest or explicit bears no implication that control is absent: quite the reverse, the 'implicit' or 'invisible' mode may be a particularly strong one – as we shall see.

There is, too, a parallel in the organization of knowledge and experience in the two analytic contexts. The elaborated code, as we have seen, regulates the explication of meanings. Bernstein, it will be recalled, proposes that 'universalistic' propositions are facilitated under conditions of elaboration. Likewise, the integrated code is predicated on the explication and clarification of general propositions which locate educational contents in frames of reference which spell out their rationale.

There is, therefore, complete continuity between the two sets of ideas. Moreover, the notion of curriculum code also links directly with Bernstein's more general papers on the organization and rituals of schools. While the ideas pass through various transformations there is an element of almost obsessive preoccupation with the same set of themes. The themes are, admittedly, sufficiently general in their scope and implications as to occupy more than one academic career.

At root, as ever, is a concern to map and understand the process of change in social organization and the moral order. It is argued that modern English schooling is marked by the transition from the mechanical solidarity of the segmented school towards the organic solidarity of the differentiated school, with its more weakly bounded curriculum and pedagogy. This movement, Bernstein maintains, is reflected directly in the internal organization and division of labour within the school.

The collection code will reflect and reproduce an essentially mechanical, segmental and hierarchical mode of organization in the school. The school staff will be composed of relatively self-contained (i.e. strongly bounded) segments. The mode of social solidarity will be that of juxtaposed or competing units of functional equivalence. There will be little in the way of co-operation and collaboration across such departmental boundaries (what Bernstein refers to as 'horizontal' links), while 'vertical' ties within departments will be strong. The integrated code will regulate organically defined relationships. The integrated curriculum, and developments like team teaching presuppose much stronger horizontal relationships, with more permeable inter-departmental membranes. Intra-departmental, vertical relations of formal authority will have a correspondingly diminished importance.

Just as there is a change in the way pupil identities are constructed, so too are teacher identities based on contrasting principles. Confined within strongly bounded and vertically integrated disciplines and departments, teachers in the 'traditional' system are defined primarily in terms of ascribed characteristics (subject taught, level to which it is taught, seniority). The pedagogic encounter is primarily a private matter and classroom organization isolates each individual teacher. The teacher's own work thus mirrors the curriculum and its timetable: it too is tightly classified and rigidly framed. With the weakening of symbolic and organizational boundaries under the new, organic, regime, the teacher's professional identity is not so determined, but is a matter for achievement in the context of interpersonal negotiation between colleagues.

The collection code – by virtue of its strong internal boundaries – permits the coexistence of diverse professional ideologies among a school staff. The development of the integrated code requires shared adherence to the principle of curriculum and pedagogy which inform the code and its realization. This is indicated by Bernstein to be one of the conditions necessary for the successful implementation of integrated practice: 'There must be consensus about the integrating idea and it must be very explicit. . . . It may be that integrated codes will work only when there is a *high* level of ideological consensus among the staff' (1971b, *CCC* 1, p.222; *CCC* 3, p.107). Consensus is needed over pedagogy and evaluation: in comparison with collection code, the organic solidarity of integrated code will 'reduce differences between teachers in the form of the transmission and assessment of knowledge' (*CCC* 1, p.222; *CCC* 3, p.107).

Further, the staff must understand the principles for the realization of the integrating device:

> The development of such a co-ordinating framework will be the process of socialization of teachers into the code. During this process, the teachers will internalize, as in all processes of socialization, the interpretative procedures of the code so that these become implicit guides which regulate and co-ordinate the behaviour of the individual teachers in the relaxed frames and weakened classification. (1971b, *CCC* 1, p.223; *CCC* 3, pp.107–8)

The organizational implementation may require committees, working parties, curriculum groups and so on. Bernstein suggests that pupils may also become involved in this process.

We should expect that the transition from collection to integrated code could be a particularly troublesome one – and that particularly interesting troubles may arise. The collection code, after all, trades on the importance of *purity*. Contents are treated as sacred mysteries. Such bounded systems – as we have seen in relation to Mary Douglas – locate anomalies and boundary transgressions as manifestations of 'danger' and 'pollution'. The normative connotations of classificatory systems describe what is 'proper' and deviation from that is *ipso facto* improper. We should thus be led to suppose that the weakening of classification and frame would lead to a response which treated the essentially secular integrated approach as wrong, polluting and deeply threatening.

I do not think it is difficult to call such responses to mind, nor is it difficult to find evidence of such general reactions to perceived threats of that sort. Such contention is part and parcel of the recurrent debate concerning 'standards' and the dispute between 'traditional' and 'progressive' approaches to curriculum and pedagogy. The growing corpus of sociologically informed histories of school subjects include illustration of such boundary disputes. One case in point is outlined in Goodson's account of the dispute between 'pure' geography and 'environmental sciences' (Goodson, 1983). The geographers' stance was particularly ironic, as Goodson shows, in that their own 'discipline' emerged historically as an 'integrated' coalition.

Although Bernstein indicated some of the potential organizational problems associated with integrated code, and some of the preconditions to its realization in practice, he himself did little to document actual problems of transition of the sort I have just outlined. Although there are passing references to notions of 'purity' and 'danger' Bernstein does not explore the conditions under which change is seen as a symbolic threat, such that moral pollution is experienced.

Likewise he offers tantalizingly brief remarks at the end of the 'classification and frame' discussion which are highly suggestive but not developed. These observations – almost throw-away lines – suggest a fascinating paradox. (The unsympathetic critic will see it as one of those typical moves whereby Bernstein elaborates his argument to the point of impenetrability and renders empirical testing all but impossible.) If I understand these remarks, they go something like this. The inception of the integrated code is predicated on a complex division of labour and the celebration of individual differences. It is thus a matter of individualism and organic solidarity, as opposed to the earlier mechanical form predicated on collectively ritualized beliefs and values. Yet the organizational requirements of the newer order demand teacher and pupil understanding of and adherence to the overt principles of knowledge organization. The social arrangements of the school and the sentimental order thus tend towards a new public value system and collective representations. The integrated code thus sows the seeds of newly constituted mechanical solidarity. Likewise, the collection code can actually allow for the development of differentiation within its segmental framework.

The collection code thus has as its output a highly differentiated division of labour (such as the strongly bounded specialists and specialisms of subject-based expertise). The integrated code, on the other hand, produces output (in terms of knowledge and student identities) whereby differences are less emphasized, tending towards the re-creation of mechanical solidarity. This is clearly very puzzling. Bernstein's own comments here do little to clarify the issue:

> the covert structure of mechanical solidarity of collection codes creates through its specialized outputs *organic* solidarity. On the other hand the overt structure of organic solidarity of integrated codes creates through its less specialized outputs *mechanical* solidarity. And it will do this to the extent to which its ideology is explicit, elaborated and closed *and* effectively and *implicitly* transmitted through its low insulations. (1971b, *CCC* 1, p.225; *CCC* 3, p.110, emphases in original)

His remarks conclude: 'Inasmuch as integrated codes do accomplish such socialization, then we have the covert deep closure of mechanical solidarity. This is the fundamental paradox which has to be faced and explored' (1976b, *CCC* 1, p.225; *CCC* 3, p.110).

This certainly is a paradox, it would seem, but Bernstein does little to follow it up or attempt to resolve it himself. In one version of the paper, the final remark has a footnote attached which does little to disentangle things for the uninitiated. It does offer a clue, however, in a brief reference to the paradox whereby the modern art school attempts to 'repeat the unrepeatable'. Here the problem is the collective adherence to shared beliefs and values which include the celebration of individual difference combined with weakly framed and unpredictable contents. Here the 'paradox' is revealed less as a muddle in the analytic framework but as a trouble inherent in the implementation and reproduction of a particular cultural form. It is closely analogous to the problem of the reproduction of charismatic authority and its translation into routinized or bureaucratic forms.

Note

1 Such imaginative development and extensions of Bernstein's contribution to the sociology of knowledge are in sharp contrast to the grudging reception afforded by King. In a series of papers (e.g. 1976, 1979, 1981a, 1981b, 1982) and most recently in an introductory text (1983) King has devoted himself to an assault on Bernstein's sociology of the school. I have not made reference to all the points of difference in this book: to have done so would have held up the argument unduly. At root, King's espousal of a version of Weberian action theory renders him suspicious of Bernstein's structuralist perspective (cf. King, 1980).

8 *Production, reproduction and the fate of the text*

The discussion of classification and frame returns one to the themes and structures of the earlier 'anthropological' papers outlined in chapter 2. The style of thought has shifted somewhat. The earlier papers were fairly straightforwardly Durkheimian in character, with more than a smattering of the conceptual apparatus of Mertonian sociology. The later papers reflect the maturation of Bernstein's perspectives, and the Durkheim who exerts his influence is now more obviously the originator of the French tradition. The sociology of collective representations has been resolved into the complexity of a structuralist semiotics and its codes.

It will be remembered that the early papers were by no means confined to an examination of the moral order of schools. In various ways Bernstein explored the structural relations expressed in the triad of school/family/work. This triplet has indeed lain at the heart of all the themes and variations so far encountered. At times one or two of the terms have received more attention, but in reading Bernstein one must always bear in mind that what is significant is the set of systemic relations between those domains.

The significance of that triad is ultimately reducible to a yet more elementary structural theme. That is, the systemic relations between *fields of production* and *fields of reproduction*.

This is true of the later cluster of papers on school knowledge.

That on classification and frame appears, perhaps, to be addressed primarily to changes in the organization of schools and their contents. Reference 'out' to other domains is relatively limited there, but two other papers (1973b, 1977b) – which have received relatively less attention – start to fill in some of the relevant relationships. Both begin with principles of curriculum and pedagogy, but the links with family and production are more explicitly drawn.

A key distinction is made at the level of pedagogy: between *visible* and *invisible* pedagogies. The distinction is derived from the methods by which either explicit or implicit message systems and modes of control are regulated in the pedagogic encounter. The key here is the modern development, Bernstein claims, whereby education for pre-school and infant-school children has shifted markedly towards a form characterized by weakened classification and framing. This is associated with the rhetoric of 'progressivism', and displays the following characteristics:

1 Where the control of the teacher over the child is implicit rather than explicit.
2 Where, ideally, the teacher arranges the *context* which the child is expected to rearrange and explore.
3 Where within this arranged context, the child apparently has wide powers over what he selects, over how he structures, and over the time-scale of his activities.
4 Where the child apparently regulates his own movements and social relationships.
5 Where there is a reduced emphasis upon the transmission and acquisition of specific skills.
6 Where the criteria for evaluating the pedagogy are multiple and diffuse and so not easily measured.

This package of features is referred to as 'invisible pedagogy'. The two types are distinguished specifically in terms of three criteria. The visible pedagogy reflects: explicit hierarchy, explicit sequencing rules, explicit and specific criteria of assessment. The invisible pedagogy reflects: implicit hierarchy, implicit sequencing rules, and implicit criteria.

Two points should be made at the outset. First, pedagogy is 'visible' or 'invisible' from the point of view of the 'receiver', not the sender. Secondly, the notion that such matters are implicit in the invisible form does *not* mean that they are absent; nor does it mean that they are by definition beyond the inspection of the sociologist.

It realizes a particular theory, or set of theories, about teaching and learning. That is, it can be understood in terms of what is 'visible' for the socializing agent. Such 'theory' is not to be thought of as identical to a specific set of psychological propositions as embedded in the academic discipline, although it is clear that the theories of particular psychologists (such as Piaget) are incorporated. The 'theory' of the invisible pedagogy is much more 'practical': a work of *bricolage* which translates any such theories into a more or less coherent assemblage of recipes and doctrines.

Bernstein suggests that the pedagogical theory is constructed out of elements of diverse theories: Piaget, Freud, Chomsky, plus 'ethological theories of critical learning' and Gestalt psychology. While by no means identical in all respects, Bernstein suggests that these theoretical positions can be used to warrant the pedagogy in so far as they satisfy the following requirements:

1 The theories in general will be seeking universals and thus are likely to be developmental and concerned with sequence. A particular context of learning is only of interest inasmuch as it throws light on a sequence. Such theories are likely to have a strong biological bias.
2 Learning is a tacit, invisible act, its progression is not facilitated by explicit public control.
3 The theories will tend to abstract the child's personal biography and local context from his cultural biography and institutional context.
4 In a sense, the theories see socializers as potentially, if not actually, dangerous, as they embody an adult-focused, therefore reified, concept of the socialized. Exemplary models are relatively unimportant and so the various theories in different ways point towards *implicit* rather than explicit hierarchical social relationships. Indeed, the imposing exemplar is transformed into a *facilitator*.
5 Thus the theories can be seen as interruptors of cultural reproduction and therefore have been considered by some as

> progressive or even revolutionary. Notions of child's time replace notions of adult's time, notions of child's space replace notions of adult's space; facilitation replaces imposition and accommodation replaces domination. (1973a, *CCC* 3, pp. 122–3)

Bernstein makes two rather important points about this collection of theories and theorists. First, it is a very mixed bag. It is, as I have implied, the outcome of *bricolage*: that is, the cobbling together of whatever bits and pieces are to hand, rather than custom-built design. (Lévi-Strauss, 1966, uses the term *bricolage* to describe aspects of the 'concrete' mode of thought of *pensée sauvage*, such as the logic of myth.) Second, the 'theory' so constructed brings together the infant-school teacher and the university-based academic. In part, therefore, Bernstein is concerned not only – perhaps not even primarily – with the documentation of actual innovations in schoolroom practice, but with those processes whereby such educational 'theories' are produced, and the circumstances whereby they become current. We shall see how this leads towards an increasing concern with the construction and reproduction of 'discourse' in educational contexts in an intellectual move which in recent years has brought Bernstein even closer to the French schools of structuralist and post-structuralist thought, and to Michel Foucault in particular.

For the time being, however, let us concentrate on the invisible pedagogy itself. We have seen roughly what it is, and some of its pedigree (or at any rate, its mythological charter). Does it have any significance beyond the exemplification of aspects of classification and framing?

It does. Among other things, invisible pedagogy provides a link between the organization of school knowledge and family types. These are in turn related to issues of social class (though not in terms of a simple middle-class/working-class dichotomy).

Bernstein argues that the invisible pedagogy realizes some of the cultural assumptions embedded in the ideology of the 'new middle class'. This new middle class, he argues, celebrates weakened classification and framing, whereas 'the old middle class were domesticated through the strong classification and frames of the family and public schools' (1973a, *CCC* 3, p. 124). These contrasting fractions of the middle class are identified in the following terms: 'The new middle class is both a product and a sponsor of the related expansion of education and fields of symbolic control' (ibid., p.127). Whereas the old middle class is concerned primarily with the manipulation and control of the means of production, the new middle class has a more indirect relationship to such material means, while being directly committed to means and relations of symbolic or cultural reproduction.

There are difficulties in recognizing 'invisible pedagogy' on the ground in contemporary schooling. Arguably, the 'progressivism' of infant and primary schooling is more a matter of 'myth' than 'reality'. As Simon (1981) argues, while there *have* been changes in the organization and relationships of schooling, they hardly amount to a major 'revolution' in educational practice. Sharp and Green (1975) document an ironic contrast between progressive rhetoric and classroom practice, in a study which derives in good measure from Bernstein's interests (cf. Davies, 1976, pp.162–4). This does not mean, however, that the ideas are devoid of heuristic value in describing pedagogy (see e.g. Atkinson, 1981b, p.120). Simon (p.24) concludes his essay by asking how and why the disputes over 'progressivism' became so important and so highly charged, if the effect on practice was relatively undramatic. The answer, if we follow Bernstein, is that its real significance lies at the level of mythological or ideological dispute.

The difference – indeed the conflict – between the two pedagogies 'is an ideological conflict within the middle class'. Whereas the old middle class could reproduce itself through strongly classified and framed systems, the new middle class reproduces itself through cultural systems characterized by much weaker boundaries.

One of the key cultural elements of the new middle class, Bernstein argues, is the role of women as agents of cultural reproduction. Within the old middle class the woman is abstracted from the reproduction of the means of production (such as the inheritance and control of property). With the emphasis shifted to symbolic 'goods', 'the woman is transformed into a crucial preparing agent of cultural reproduction' (1973a, *CCC* 3, p.132).

The significance of women in the cultural reproduction of the middle classes is a relatively neglected theme in Bernstein's sociology. The significance of Bernstein's insight has been recognized by David (1978), in that 'it acknowledges the crucial connections, in social reproduction, between the family and in particular the mother, and education' (p.170). Oddly, however, David accuses both Bernstein and Bourdieu of neglecting links with 'socio-economic production'.

Another exception is Delamont (1976, 1984) who documents different intellectual styles among daughters of the intelligentsia and property-owning bourgeoisie in an élite girls' school in Scotland. Delamont suggests that the competing school subcultures parallel the differences between the fractions of the middle class:

> These two groups can be seen as both recapitulating their family styles in their own adolescence, and using the school to prepare for their own adult life styles. Both cliques wanted to pass public exams and enter further education or training, and the school provides a service for both. In addition, it provides a socially exclusive atmosphere in which the future wives of the next generation of Scottish capitalists can meet and form networks, while for the future manipulators of culture, it provides an arena in which they can practise symbolic negotiation with highly qualified staff. (1976, p.41)

Delamont's use of the Bernsteinian framework is also developed elsewhere (Delamont, 1984). Other commentators on gender and education (e.g. Acker, 1981) pay no attention to Bernstein's remarks on the significance of women. It might, of course, be argued that his observations merely recapitulate the one way in which women are partly visible in the sociology of education – as mothers. That is true, but not the whole story. Bernstein's views are underpinned by a sense of the relationship between the gender order and the moral order which is more akin to recent anthropological studies of gender and cosmology (e.g. Ardener, 1975). A concern of this sort is hinted at, albeit cryptically, in one of Bernstein's more recent publications (1981, appendix 2, p.356). The relationship between dominant and dominated, in Bernstein's theory of codes, corresponds to the anthropological distinction between 'dominant' and 'muted' models.

As women become crucial agents in cultural reproduction, mothering thus becomes 'professionalized' in the new middle-class home. Commenting on the role of women in pedagogic innovations leading to 'invisible pedagogy', Bernstein writes 'women transformed maternal caring and preparing into a *scientific* activity' (1973a, *CCC* 3, p.132: emphasis in original). The highly personalized, weakly classified and framed mode of primary socialization is thus demanding of the mother's attention, unlike earlier forms which could be delegated to others (nurse, nanny, governess or tutor). The child's development is closely monitored, and all aspects are incorporated within the surveillance of the professionalized parent. Excellent empirical evidence for this is provided in Cohen's ethnography of 'new' middle-class women on a private housing estate in the south of England. She endorses Bernstein's characterization of the professionalized mother, emphasizing that even in households where 'traditional' sex roles do not pertain, child rearing and pedagogy are the special concern, individually and collectively, of the estate mothers (Cohen, 1981).

This emphasis on the professionalization of parenthood and its significance was hardly a novel component in Bernstein's commentary on the family. As early as 1958 he had written:

> One of the aims of the middle-class family is to produce a child oriented to certain values but individually differentiated within them. The child is born into an environment where he is seen and responded to as an individual; with his own rights, that is, he has a specific social status. This early process of individuation is accomplished by two important factors: the scrupulous observation of the child by the parents so that the very fine stages of development and the emergence of new patterns of behaviour are the object of attention and comment. (1958, *CCC* 1, p.27)

Again, the thematic continuity of Bernstein's thought is readily discernible, although this contention is a major element only in the later papers.

Bernstein also argues that invisible pedagogies are congruent with middle-class concepts of time and space. The weak bounding of temporal and spatial arrangements presupposes a more leisurely and expansive approach to socialization. Again, there are differences within the middle class, and such weak bounding is to be understood as characteristic of the new middle class. Finally, Bernstein suggests that invisible pedagogy is parallel to the mode of social control which is implied by a personalizing domestic environment, where 'control is vested in the process of interpersonal communication' which reflects the elaborated code.

Within the middle class, therefore, there are *two* forms of 'organic solidarity'. That of the old middle class is predicated upon 'individuation', while that of the new middle class reflects 'personalizing' differentiation. Bernstein thus proposes a modification of the underlying Durkheimian model:

> His analysis is based upon the old middle class. He did not foresee, although his conceptual procedures make this possible, a form of organic solidarity based upon weak classification and weak frames; that is, a form of solidarity developed by the new middle class. Durkheim's organic solidarity refers to *individuals* in privatized class relationships; the second form of organic solidarity celebrates the apparent release, not of the individual, but of the person and *new* forms of social control. (1973a, *CCC* 3, p.125, emphases in original)

Here, then, we can see how Bernstein draws some formal links between pedagogy and class differences, in ways which derive quite clearly from his earliest work on primary socialization in the home as well as the subsequent essays on school knowledge.

The relationships are complex in Bernstein's formulation. He suggests, for instance, that the cultural orientations of the new middle class imply a contradiction:

> A deep-rooted ambivalence is the ambience of this group. On the one hand, they stand for variety against inflexibility, expression against repression, the inter-personal against the inter-positional; on the other hand, there is the grim obduracy of the division of labour and of the narrow pathways to its positions of power and prestige. . . . Thus if the new middle class is to repeat its position in the class structure, then appropriate secondary socialization into privileged education becomes crucial. . . . Thus the new middle class take up some

> ambivalent enthusiasm for the invisible pedagogy for the early socialization of the child, but settle for the *visible* pedagogy of the secondary school. (1973a, *CCC* 3, pp.126–7, emphasis in original)

This point is taken up by Delamont (1976) who cites the history of the girls' school she studied. The kindergarten and preparatory departments were established on lines of 'invisible' pedagogy, inspired by the thought of Froebel. On entering the main school's forms at the age of seven, however, the girls encounter visible pedagogy. Further, as Delamont remarks, the daughters of the intelligentsia she interviewed in the school were able to reproduce the vocabularies of motive espoused by people like their parents: 'All were able to reproduce their parents' justifications for transferring them to St. Luke's. These form a fascinating collection of liberal vacillation attempting to reconcile the contradictions Bernstein outlines' (p.39). Punch (1970) produces a telling, if caricatured, portrayal of this middle-class dilemma:

> children crystallize the intellectual's dilemma because there may well emerge an incipient conflict between his ideology and his children's perceived interests. . . . He may, too, have socialized his children out of an orthodox educational environment which can find it hard to accommodate the precocious, outspoken, capricious, imperious, sensitive child of intellectual parents, who have probably transmitted their distaste for uniforms, corporal punishment, compulsory religion, authority and so on, to their progeny. (p.862)

This is certainly congruent with the picture conveyed by Delamont's description of the daughters of the intelligentsia, even in a school well used to catering for them. Relationships between class and pedagogy are therefore by no means simple or homogeneous.

Bernstein's ideas here are certainly not fashionable synonyms for cultural 'deficit', but his model suggests possible discontinuities between the family and the school for some categories of child. The guiding principles of middle-class (especially new middle-class) socialization are broadly homologous with those of 'progressive', invisible pedagogy. The pupil and the parents may thus be equipped with the requisite cultural competence to 'crack' the educational code, while those very competences remain 'invisible' to those excluded from their symbolic domains. The visible pedagogy is at least more readily grasped by the working-class parent, even though its cultural prerequisites may not be mastered:

> From the point of view of working-class parents, the visible pedagogy of the collection code at the primary level is immediately understandable. The basic competencies which it is transmitting of reading, writing, and counting, in an ordered explicit sequence, make sense. . . . However, in the case of the invisible pedagogy, there is possibly a sharp discontinuity. The competencies and their progression disappear, the form of social control may well be at variance with the home. The theory of the invisible pedagogy may not be known by the mother or be perfectly understood. (1973a, *CCC* 3, pp. 138–9)

Such a discontinuity may be sharpened if the parents' own pedagogic 'help' is at odds with, and discouraged or discounted by the school.

Similar remarks are put forward concerning the changing nature of evaluation. Under the auspices of invisible pedagogy the criteria for evaluation and their principles of application are diffuse and invisible themselves. On the other hand, the theory and practice of the pedagogy mean that in principle a very wide range of pupil competencies and behaviours are treated as appropriate for scrutiny and surveillance. This contrasts with the visible, explicit and restricted evaluative grid of the visible pedagogy.

The procedures of evaluation associated with the invisible pedagogy enhance the possibility of teacher control. The invisible pedagogy and its mode of evaluation do not furnish apparently 'objective' criteria for the comparison of progress between pupils: indeed what counts as 'progress' is likely to be much less clear-cut a definition. This is especially likely to lead to distance between the school and the working-class parent, since the pedagogy reflects and reproduces the modes of perception and control characteristic of the middle classes (the new middle class in particular).

The invisible pedagogy, therefore, is in no sense a mode devoid of social control. On the contrary, it provides possibilities for highly pervasive and effective control. It may be all the stronger for being *implicit* and *personal*. It is likely to be realized through diffuse criteria which are not readily visible and accountable. The pedagogue who manages invisible means of transmission is thus furnished with a potent way of defining reality and manipulating the consequences of such reality construction.

There is thus a parallel between modes of pedagogy and control on the one hand and primary socialization in different family types on the other. There is a similar formal analysis to be performed concerning relations of education and production (work). The language of codes is employed to characterize different forms of production in such a way that systemic relations between the two domains may be suggested. This mode of analysis – brief though it is in the first published essays explicitly raising the topic (1977b, *CCC* 3, pp. 174–200) – reminds us that the division of labour and relations of production lie behind all of Bernstein's work.

In the field of production classification refers to relationships between the categories of production; that is, 'the relationships between the various agents, unskilled, skilled, technologists, managers, administrators etc.' (p. 181). Where relations between these categories of actors are strongly bounded, fixed and stable then we can talk of strong classification. Weak classification will correspondingly refer to conditions where there is reduced insulation. Likewise framing is deployed to characterize the regulation of productive activity. Strong framing will be a matter of repetitive, individually performed, strongly paced and explicitly sequenced acts, which Bernstein refers to as *divisive* acts. Weak framing, on the other hand, exists where

> the primary unit of production is relatively co-operative, group based, where there is an opportunity to vary the conditions and perhaps sequencing and pacing, where the outcome is less a fraction of the total object of production but bears a more direct relation to it. (p. 182)

We are thus dealing with relations between agents of production and the realizations of those relations in the social act of production. Bernstein goes on to specify different codes of production based on variations in the relative strength of classification and framing, and to outline formal relations between such production codes and educational codes. This is *not* proposed as a mechanistic form of correspondence, since Bernstein suggests that the allocatory device generates 'contradictions and discrepancies' in relation to:

> (a) the relationships between the distribution of the categories it creates and the distribution of the required categories of the mode of production;
> (b) the relationships *between the categories* it creates and the relationships *between the categories* required by the mode of production;
> (c) the realization of its categories (skills and dispositions) and the expected realizations of the categories of the mode of production. (1977b, pp. 185–6, emphases in original)

In Bernstein's terms these constitute the *systemic* relationships between education and production.

These systemic relations are the material base for education, even though education and production are not in relations of direct correspondence. Indeed, Bernstein explicitly distances himself from Bowles and Gintis (e.g. 1976): 'We agree that the school may well *legitimize* values and attitudes relevant to the mode of production, but this does not mean that these are so internalized as to constitute *specific personalities*' (1977b, pp. 188–9, emphases in original).

There is, therefore, more than a measure of *relative autonomy*: that is, education's relative independence from production. This is itself a function of the strength of boundary or classification between the two domains. In contemporary industrial society, indeed, the appearance of relative autonomy is itself a message (perhaps at the level of meta-communication) of the educational field. Such independence legitimizes educational discourse and practice as trading in a disinterested fashion in 'objective, neutral, altruistic and dedicated' ways. This in turn, Bernstein argues, is dependent upon a strong boundary or separation between those sectors of the middle class who own and manage the means of economic production and those who own and manipulate the means of symbolic or cultural production and reproduction. The indirect relation of education to production Bernstein suggests is the 'fundamental ideological message of the educational system' (1977b, p.190). This has been summarized by Browne (1981) who argues that the role of the school in reproducing and legitimizing the separation of mental and manual labour is of crucial significance in capitalist society. Browne asserts that the distinction within the new middle class identified by Bernstein is 'itself already derived from a division based on the separation of the direct producers from the means of production' (p.460).

In exemplifying mismatches between production codes and education codes, Bernstein comments illuminatingly on the current position of pupils defined as 'less able' in British state schooling. Their most likely occupational fate (provided, of course, they are fortunate enough to enter the world of work at all) is characterized by *strong* classification and framing. That is, in the workplace there will be strong boundaries between classes of agents, and productive categories will be realized in strongly paced and sequenced 'divisive' acts. The repetitive tasks of machine-minding, sorting, packing etc. in an industrial setting with a highly segmented workforce come readily to mind by way of exemplification. This is at odds with the general tenor of schooling they are likely to have received, which Bernstein suggests has moved towards weakened classification and frame. That is, this general shift has been particularly pronounced for schooling at the lowest end of the ability range. Not only does this discrepancy highlight the possibility of disjuncture between school and economic life, but 'Further, the school, rather than equipping the worker with appropriate attitudes and discipline, may indirectly and unwittingly provide a range of countervailing strategies' (1977b, p.187).

Although Bernstein himself does not go on to argue the issue, it is arguable that recent developments in secondary and further education indicate more or less conscious efforts to eliminate this formal discrepancy. The curricula of 'work experience', 'work preparation', 'transition' courses and the like tend to interrupt the pattern of weak classification and framing. The introduction of such curricula is often based upon weak classification – as one might expect. There is a weak boundary between educational work and everyday work or experience; likewise, internal classification is weak and curricula are not sharply delimited. On the other hand, pedagogy is often strongly framed, and is couched in terms of clearly demarcated objectives, tasks, sequencing and pacing. This is certainly a view proposed by Dickinson and Erben (1983), on the basis of their consideration of the work of Claude Grignon: 'We suggest that the combination of weak classification and strong frame is a pedagogy of technicisation' (p. 109). In a parallel paper the same authors argue that the implementation of the MSC's Youth Training Scheme will tend towards weak classification and strong framing (Dickinson and Erben, 1984). This is also argued by Moore (1983) who points out that the new technicist forms of education imply an ideological shift away from control by educationists with an indirect relationship with production to agencies with a more direct relationship. Moore also suggests that this is accompanied by a change from elaborating to restricting orientations to content and pedagogy.

Bernstein's remarks on the relations between education and production are important in illuminating a number of features concerning his general sociology of reproduction and the nature of structuralism. Some critics have claimed to find in him an example of that variety of reasoning which postulates a strict structural relation of *determinism*. It is argued that the notion of 'code' is no more than a mechanism for 'reproduction' as correspondence. Indeed, this view is not confined to hostile critics. Apple (1981, p.6) includes Bernstein among a canon of reproduction theorists of whom he claims:

> Their logic sees the institution as acting only to reproduce a social order. Both the form and content of the formal corpus of school knowledge and the hidden curriculum help create the conditions for the cultural and economic reproduction of class relations in our society.

This is too coarse a characterization and implies too straightforward a process of transmission than Bernstein ever conveyed. Giroux (1981, pp. 10–11) contains a more sophisticated view:

> Power and control in this perspective are embedded in the structuring devices that shape the experiences and consciousness of human beings as they pass through such social sites as

the family, the school, and the workplace. While Bernstein rejects any form of mechanical correspondence among these different social sites, he nevertheless tends to assume that, regardless of the *form* of social control they perpetuate, all of these social spheres share in the reproduction of class control and the maldistribution of power that underlies the existing mode of production. Thus, in the end, Bernstein argues that educational reforms that call for a change in the *form* of social control pose little threat to the class basis of power and will do just as little to effect social change.

Bernstein's emphasis on the different strengths of classification between fields of production and reproduction denies any simple reliance upon a correspondence theory, then. Moreover, 'relative autonomy' is itself recognized as variable in the realization of such classification. It is *not* proposed as an absolute, all-or-nothing principle of a general theory: 'We shall define the relative autonomy of education in terms of the strength of the classification between the category education and the category production' (1977b, p.188). Furthermore, Bernstein does *not* suggest that education operates equally in the production and reproduction of 'social personalities'. This is indicated, if only briefly, in a footnote:

> It is possible that education is relatively more successful in the *constituting* of specific personalities only in the case of high-level agents of reproduction, whereas for manual workers it is rather more *regulative* of the expression of, rather than constituting, the personality. (1977b, *CCC* 3, p.199, n.5; emphases in original)

It would, therefore, be quite wrong to assume that Bernstein's scheme implies that form and content of education somehow impose themselves equally on all pupils, students or agents of reproduction. Indeed, it will be recalled that one of Bernstein's earliest papers in the sociology of the school was explicitly concerned with documenting a variety of ways in which there might be discrepancy between families and schools as socializing agencies (1966a, *CCC* 3, pp.37–53).

In Bernstein's most recent work – some of it unpublished[1] the two major themes of this chapter – pedagogic discourse and the classification of production/reproduction reappear. The starting-point is the collection of theories which underpin and legitimize the 'invisible pedagogy', outlined earlier in the chapter.

Now the interesting thing about the collection of theories and this list of principles is that the former 'form a strange, if not contradictory group' (1973a, *CCC* 3, p.123). They form what Bernstein calls the 'theology of the infant school', and like much theology it is not internally consistent. While the general principles can be derived from the theories, this is achieved by selecting elements and lifting them out of their original theoretical context.

In other words, this 'pedagogic discourse' is constructed out of a double process. Elements are decontextualized from their original location and then recontextualized into a new assemblage. This is a recurrent feature of pedagogic discourse. It is predominantly a secondary domain which, as it were, 'borrows' from other domains and discourses (such as psychology, linguistics and sociology) – though frequently borrowed from in turn in other secondary domains, such as those concerned with health and welfare. The pedagogic discourse so constructed consists of 'the rules regulating the production, distribution, reproduction, inter-relation and change of what counts as legitimate pedagogic texts' (Bernstein, seminars).

As a first approximation, then, we can think of the construction of pedagogic discourse as yet another example of *bricolage*. There are 'primary contextualizing fields', which include the specialized discourses such as the natural sciences, the humanities and the social sciences. They comprise a 'field' which is an arena of *production* of knowledge/discourse. (The use of 'field' here parallels the style and usage of Bourdieu – e.g. 1975.) In contrast, there are fields of *recontextualization* and *reproduction*. Here discursive elements of the primary field are selected, combined and recontextualized. This is a process of several stages, and takes place within highly differentiated fields. The text is re-formed (or 'deformed') when it enters, say, academic teacher-training. It then enters into the shaping and constitution of the teacher's occupational consciousness; in turn the text is itself 'read' and reinterpreted in this context. Then in the pedagogical encounter we have the text as it impinges on classroom practice, and on the consciousness of the pupil.

The different contexts – especially the fields of production, such as the academy, and the fields of reproduction – are normally strongly classified. There are clear institutional differences and symbolic membranes which demarcate and distinguish them. Were it not for such strong classification then we would be much less likely to encounter the extreme processes of decontextualization and recontextualization that we in fact do. Buswell (1980) exemplifies some of the particular processes which contribute to a strong classification between primary and secondary fields. She draws attention to the fact that externally-imposed curriculum 'packages' may contribute to the strength of such boundaries, while de-skilling the classroom teacher (cf. Gleeson, 1978).

In the case of Bernstein himself, for example, the abstraction of his ideas from the primary field of sociological theory and its relocation in varieties of pedagogic discourse exemplifies this. The 'Bernstein' of, say, Labov or Rosen inhabits a discursive space strongly separated from that of post-Durkheimian anthropology. Likewise the 'Bernstein' reproduced in the consciousness of teachers is different again (cf. Gordon, 1978a and b). The pedagogic discourse of teachers, even in what Keddie (1971) refers to as the 'educationalist' context is strongly classified from the primary field. It is the unfortunate fate of many 'influential' authors that their influence is felt only through such secondary recontextualizations: Piaget is an obvious example in the pedagogic domain – even though, as Bernstein notes, he protested that his theories were not directly relevant to pedagogy. The same is true of Bernstein himself, of course.

There is a process, then, whereby from all the possible ideas, authors, traditions and texts, selection and recombination promote a restricted set to be reformulated into pedagogic discourse. This in itself is an act of 'classification', partaking of that 'selective tradition' (Williams, 1965) through which the orthodoxies of taste and academic respectability are constructed and reconstructed. There are, to paraphrase Garfinkel (1967) 'good organizational reasons' for such transformations and deformations. The reproduction of discourse requires such classification and transposition.

At the heart of the 'pedagogic device' is the coding of power whereby 'the thinkable' is discriminated and demarcated, in a fashion which corresponds to the function of 'classification'. In modern, complex societies the contrast between the 'sacred' and the 'profane' is formally paralleled by the classificatory principles emanating from the higher reaches of the education system (cf. Bernstein and Diaz, 1984). The pedagogic device is a mechanism for the *distribution* of the 'thinkable' among different social groups, for the identification of what may be thought simultaneously implies *who* may think it. Social order is thus equivalent to the cosmological order of legitimate categories of consciousness.

In turn, the pedagogic device specifies the 'recontextualizing rules' of pedagogic discourse: in other words, the specialized communication through which the educational process is to be accomplished. Here Bernstein proposes two closely related aspects – *instructional discourse*, and *regulative discourse*. The former specifies how skills or competencies are to be transmitted; the latter specifies how social order, social relations and social identities are to be constructed. The contrast is, of course, reminiscent of the distinction between instrumental and expressive orders which has informed Bernstein's conceptual orderings from the outset (cf. Bernstein, 1985, note B).

Pedagogic discourse is not articulated by the skill and dispositions to be transmitted. Rather, it is a way of recontextualizing or reformulating primary discourse. In that sense it is always secondary, and is itself 'empty'. The pedagogy of science, for instance, is not simply a reflection of scientific discourse. Rather, pedagogic discourse provides a device for the rewriting of 'science' into a series of texts which are arranged according to time (age and developmental stages), which are inscribed with instructional theories, and which distribute competencies according to classificatory principles (such as 'ability' and 'subjects'):

> We have argued that this grammar which produces the internal orderings of pedagogic discourse is not a grammar for specializing a specific discourse, creating its own rules of demarcation and internal order, but a principle of de-locating, re-locating and re-focussing *other* specialized discourses, bringing them into a new relation with each other and introducing a new

> temporal internal ordering. (Bernstein, 1985, emphasis in original)

'Official' pedagogic discourse in modern societies regulates the production, distribution and reproduction of pedagogic texts. It thus sets limits on principles of transmission and realization of pedagogic theory and practice. It specifies the principles of organizational and developmental ordering of both material and discursive resources.

The transformation of texts through these dislocations and relocations does not simply reflect inadequacy or incapacity on the part of interpreters. Bernstein is not just bewailing problems of 'over-simplification' or the mangling of his own contributions. Rather, the focus of interest is primarily on the sociology of knowledge, and the relationship between knowledge creation and knowledge dissemination. To some extent the process of decontextualization and recontextualization, as described by Bernstein, is akin to that discussed by Fleck (1979) and Kuhn (1982) in their accounts of scientific knowledge. They variously identify 'journal science', 'vademecum science', 'textbook science' and 'popular science'. These 'socio-intellectual forms' as Fleck calls them (p. 112) would constitute, in Bernstein's terms, contrasting 'fields' of production and reproduction.

Fleck (p. 119) suggests some of the processes of transformation at work when contents pass from one field to another. For instance:

> The vademecum is . . . not simply the result of either a compilation or a collection of various journal contributions. The former is impossible because such papers often contradict each other. The latter does not yield a closed system, which is the goal of vademecum science. A vademecum is built up from individual contributions through selection and orderly arrangement like a mosaic from many colored stones.

He writes in a similar vein on the domain of 'popular science':

> Here is an artistically attractive, lively, and readable exposition with last, but not least, the apodictic valuation simply to accept or reject a certain point of view. Simplified, lucid, and apodic-

> tic science – these are the most important characteristics of exoteric knowledge. *In place of the specific constraint of thought by any proof, which can be found only with great effort, a vivid picture is created through simplification and valuation.* (pp. 112–13, emphasis in original)

The secondary fields of recontextualization are, of course, domains where primary interest is in *consumption* of texts. As Kuhn says of textbooks:

> Textbooks are, after all, written some time after the discoveries and confirmation procedures whose *outcomes* they record. Furthermore, they are written for purposes of pedagogy. The objective of the textbook is to provide the reader, in the most economical and easily assimilable form, with a statement of what the contemporary scientific community believes it knows and of the principal uses to which that knowledge can be put. Information about how that knowledge was acquired (discovery) and about why it was accepted by the profession (confirmation) would at best be excess baggage. (1982, p. 79)

The process is, as it were, one of myth-creation, much as that described by Lévi-Strauss: the elements are juggled, juxtaposed and ordered in such a way as to reduce or gloss over ambiguity and to resolve contradictions. Such formulations also serve to 'position' the consumers of a discourse, in that they establish a particular relationship between teachers and learners within the intellectual field (again, cf. Bourdieu).

The articulation of texts into pedagogic discourse parallels the coding of curriculum, depending as it does on the selection and recombination of contents into a new contextualization. There are key agents and agencies in this work – who act as gatekeepers, interpreters, codifiers, critics and so on. They are the bards and *bricoleurs* who construct the myths, they are the interpreters of the sacred mysteries to the laity (Aaron to Moses). They people the stage of pedagogic instruction and debate with the heroes and folk-devils of academic legend. Nobody could be more conscious of this phenomenon than Bernstein himself, who has been thoroughly embroiled in pedagogic discourse while remaining an observer of its twists and turns. For him authors such as Lawton

(1968) acted as transmitters and amplifiers of the basic theory, helping to codify and translate it into the popular consciousness of educationalist contexts.

Round such a process of mythopoiesis there arise industries and growth areas of secondary interpretations; exegesis and commentary help to 'fix' the text in the canon of received wisdom. This process feeds off itself, as those secondary domains reaffirm and legitimize the classification within and between fields of production and reproduction. Their work includes the selection of some authors as 'significant' while others are ignored: as Bernstein notes, some texts may be 'sleepers' which are only resuscitated through such recontextualizations. Texts are arranged into hierarchies of worth, schools, traditions, disputations, orthodoxies and deviations. They are glossed with moral and political motives and consequences. The rhetoric and textual arrangement of such secondary texts is a major topic in the sociology of educational knowledge which as yet remains under-explored; Bernstein's recent proposals point us in that direction. (The reader who has persevered this far will be aware that *this* text partakes of that selfsame process.)

To some extent there is a danger of oversimplification in the identification of 'primary' and 'secondary' fields. The distinction is somewhat arbitrary, though it has clear heuristic value. Taken to its logical extreme, the model would take account of the extent to which there is a constant circulation of texts within and between domains of discourse. No one can be assigned absolute priority over the other. In the same way we should beware of assigning special place and privilege to specific texts. The full extension of Bernstein's line of thought would be to adopt the notion of 'intertextuality' (Kristéva, 1980): that is, the recognition that the text is dependent upon, is suffused by, and indeed constituted by prior texts, codes and practices.

Since the 'text' is constructed in the act of reading it, it follows from this point of view that we cannot ever think of a 'pure' text which remains inviolate and incorruptible. In Bernstein's own case, therefore, he was inevitably read in the light of existing modes of thought. His work was assimilated to prior frames of reference and interpretive schemes – on class, race, language, educability, equality and so on. In the course of that 'Bernstein' became part and parcel of those same contexts of interpretation.

This book itself proposes a particular frame of reference for such interpretation, but from this point of view cannot claim simply to have recuperated the 'pure' Bernstein. The ur-text is perhaps a romantic myth, or such is the logic of Bernstein's current position. (For a recent review of 'the dissemination of the text' and 'the intertextualization of context' in the light of post-structuralist critical theory, see Leitch, 1983, chs 5 and 6.)

Such a view does not really undermine the key issue which Bernstein himself seeks to address. That is, the *ideological* nature of such processes of selection and circulation. For he is not simply preoccupied with an exercise in the 'history of ideas', mapping the genesis and development of a particular text and its use in education. The point is, rather, that the circulation of texts and the production of pedagogic discourse – indeed any discourse – is the play of *power*.

In many ways these most recent concerns confirm and extend Bernstein's affinity with French movements of structuralist and post-structuralist thought. Most notably, Foucault's 'archaeology of knowledge' is a key point of reference (e.g. Foucault, 1972). His massive project defies easy classification and summary. Profoundly influenced by the structuralist movement he distances himself from it; he deals with ideas in history while rejecting 'the history of ideas'. In a fashion similar to Lévi-Strauss's adoption of the geologist's image of sedimentation and stratification (1961, pp.60–1; Leach, 1970, pp.17–18). Foucault develops the metaphor of archaeology. Both images convey the desired connotations of *discontinuity*. Foucault's overall work – whether its substantive focus be on medicine, insanity, sexuality or punishment – is concerned with difference, discontinuity and boundary. He is preoccupied with the processes and rules whereby 'discourse' or 'discursive formations' emerge and are constituted.

Some of these 'rules' are analogous to those connoted by Bernstein's classification and framing. Foucault identifies, for instance, 'procedures of exclusion', which intersect and interplay to define what is thinkable and what unthinkable, and so to construct the objects of discourse themselves. There are principles of 'prohibition' – we are not free to speak of anything when, where and how we like – and principles of 'division and rejection', which demarcate areas of discourse which are beyond the pale (such as that of the madman – cf. Foucault, 1967). Within the discourse so delimited there operate principles of 'rarefaction' which generate its internal coherence. They include the work of 'commentary', the attribution of 'authorship', the development of impersonal regimes of 'discipline', 'rituals' and 'societies' of discourse. These procedures and agencies thus articulate 'discourse'. For Foucault these procedures and relations of discursive formations are the exercise of *power*. Power is not, from this perspective, an attribute or possession of an actor or collectivity: it is a relational concept. Moreover, power is dispersed throughout multiple sites and discursive fields. (For a discussion of Foucault on knowledge and power see Sheridan, 1980, esp. pp. 113–63.)

For Bernstein too the exercise of power is refracted through the articulation of discourse, but he insists on a crucial difference between his own position and that of Foucault. For while Foucault writes freely of the play of power, his is not a *sociological* account, in that there is no corresponding treatment of social structure. Power and discourse are strangely disembodied, floating in time and space. On the other hand, one of the things which has consistently distinguished Bernstein's version of structuralism has been an insistence on the fundamental importance of social structure – conceived in terms of the division of labour. Whereas for Foucault the discursive formations and practices obey their own laws of transformation, for Bernstein the distribution and circulation of texts are determined by social relationships. To that extent, therefore, Bernstein's deployment of structuralist notions follows a well-established British tradition, exemplified in anthropology by Mary Douglas and Edmund Leach, and in a slightly different way by David Lodge (e.g. 1977) in critical theory, of the 'domestication' of structuralism.

There is a corresponding difference between Bernstein and Bourdieu. While Bourdieu and Passeron (1977) are preoccupied with the structures of culture and their legitimization, this is conducted at a very general level. In their analyses 'there is very little systematic and specific analysis of the principles whereby a specific discourse is constituted nor of the principles of its transmission' (Diaz, 1983, p. 17).

Bernstein is not a follower of Foucault, then, any more than Foucault is a Bernsteinian. Yet there are clear and important convergences. Foucault's own comments on education are thoroughly reminiscent of Bernstein's. An education system incorporates its rituals of discourse, its disciplines and so on.

> But we know very well that, in its distribution, in what it permits and what it prevents, it follows the lines laid down by social differences, conflicts and struggles. Every educational system is a political means of maintaining or modifying the appropriation of discourses, with the knowledge and power they bring with them. (Foucault, 1971, p.46, cited in Sheridan, 1980, p.127)

These remarks are more or less contemporary with Bernstein's call for sociological inquiry into how a society 'selects, classifies, distributes, transmits and evaluates the educational knowledge it considers to be public', which, he argued, reflects 'both the distribution of power and the principles of social control' (1971b, *CCC* 1, p.202; *CCC* 3, p.85).

Bernstein (1985) argues that the work of (re)producing pedagogic discourse includes the participation of state agencies (cf. Bernstein and Diaz, 1984). Amongst other things, the state may promote Official Pedagogic Discourse, which regulates and sets limits to the realizations of discourse in the various fields of recontextualization and reproduction:

> specialized departments and sub-agencies of the state and local educational authorities, together with their apparatus of researchers, advisers and inspectors;
>
> university departments of education, research institutes and similar organizations;
>
> specialized media of education;
>
> other fields which are not directly devoted to education but which exert influence – directly or indirectly – over recontextualization and reproduction.

As we should expect, Bernstein does not propose direct relations of correspondence and determinism between one field and another – and regulation by the state is in principle no different.

Indeed, he would argue, I believe, that the message of relative autonomy in an educational system rests on fairly strong classification between the state and other fields. (The argument parallels the relations of classification between production and reproduction referred to above and in the previous chapter.)

Hitherto Bernstein has done little more than sketch out the components of an account of pedagogic discourse, but a number of general features are already discernible. First it is in part a reflection of his own biography. It can be asked of any author/text why it has been selected, 'marked' with special significance and entered into circulation. We can trace the timing of such entries into the pedagogic domain, as we can trace the trajectories whereby texts become devalued and withdrawn from circulation. The fate of Bernstein and his texts can be charted in just this way through his appropriation by protagonists of 'left' and 'right', and the adoption of his ideas as tokens in the exchange of pedagogical and ideological dispute.

Secondly, the invocation of 'discourse', broadly congruent with Foucault's perspective, is itself in keeping with the non-humanist stance of much of Bernstein's structuralism – and indeed structuralism in general. Although by no means articulated fully and explicitly, Bernstein's notions of language, discourse and structure imply that social actors and meanings are constituted by the 'codes' rather than the reverse. Discourse analysis, for example, implies a 'non-subjective' notion of 'meaning'. In the same fashion, Bernstein's theory of language suggests that the codes have an autonomous status: it is the code which 'positions' and constitutes the subject, rather than the reverse.

Throughout Bernstein's work, then, 'the subject' is 'decentred' or 'displaced'. As with authors in the French structuralist movement (Lévi-Strauss, Lacan, Foucault, etc.) the subjective consciousness is resolved or dissolved into discursive and linguistic practices. As Derrida (1973, p. 145) has it:

> the subject . . . is inscribed in the language . . . he is a 'function' of the language. He becomes a speaking subject only by conforming his speech . . . to the system of linguistic prescriptions taken as the system of differences.

The 'subject' is thus a matter of signifying practices (Kristéva, 1980): 'the pure act of the *cogito* is empty, and remains to be mediated by the world of signs and the interpretation of those signs' (Ricoeur, 1974). Even the psychoanalyst Lacan rejects any notion of the unitary subject in favour of a non-unitary psyche dispersed through systems of signs (Lacan, 1977a, 1977b). Similarly, whether the substantive focus be language codes, knowledge codes or discursive practices, Bernstein reverses the polarity of a subject-centred discipline. Codes constitute the person, not vice versa; discourse positions the subject. The perspective is thoroughly congruent with the position enunciated by Lévi-Strauss, when he maintains that myths live through persons, rather than persons through myths. It is paralleled by Bourdieu's aphorism that 'culture classifies and classifies the classifiers'.

This tendency in Bernstein's sociology helps to explain the repeated misunderstandings and criticisms with which it has been received. Such misperceptions stemmed from intellectual traditions which privileged 'the speaking subject'. Hence the notion of 'the restricted code' was readily – if inappropriately – assimilated to discourse on personal and moral qualities of the subject.

In dwelling on these things I am perhaps guilty of overstressing one side of Bernstein's work. While insisting that Bernstein's *oeuvre* must be seen as a sustained assault on the same set of themes I have consistently proposed a broadly structuralist framework for an understanding of the sociology but that perspective certainly should not be taken to extremes. I have no intention of suggesting that Bernstein is simply an exponent of more or less fashionable French theories. Over the years he has forged his own theoretical framework. It has important affinities with the French school, with which it shares common roots, and over the years those convergences have been increasingly clear and explicit. Yet it remains distinctively Bernstein's own, and maintains a characteristically British flavour.

In the course of this book I have offered a view of Bernstein which respects the complexity and sophistication that can be found in his sociology. In order to do so I have had to introduce some potentially difficult ideas, though I naturally hope that the reader will not have found the presentation unnecessarily mysterious. The danger in undertaking an introductory essay of this sort is to veer towards an oversimplification which does a grave disservice to the topic and to the reader. There is no sense in which this book could ever claim to be a 'definitive' study. The full complexities of Bernstein's thought and its relationship with other theoretical positions will continue to demand exploration. Researchers will continue to find illumination in the deployment of his concepts in many fields of sociological enquiry. Moreover, Bernstein's project continues. His most recent work awaits wide dissemination, and I have barely done more than allude to it here: paradoxically, but fittingly, this final chapter has been no more than a brief introduction.

Note

1 This work is just starting to see the light of day (Bernstein and Diaz, 1984; Bernstein, 1985); it has been the subject matter of seminars and guest lectures, such as the unpublished text of a presentation at Lund University, Sweden, on 'The circulation of pedagogic texts', and is available in its most developed form to date in the work of graduate students (e.g. Cox Donoso, 1984; Diaz, 1983; Moore, 1983). See also Pedro (1981) and Tyler (1984): the latter came to my attention too late in the drafting of this book for full justice to have been done to it.

Bibliographical note and bibliography of Bernstein's publications

The following bibliography of Bernstein's works lists those papers referred to in the text of the book, and others. Many of Bernstein's papers have been reprinted and anthologized – some repeatedly. I have not attempted to list all the reprintings, but have indicated some of the most readily available sources.

The referencing is by no means straightforward. Bernstein himself has edited three volumes of collected papers under the general title *Class, Codes and Control*. Volumes 1 and 3 each have appeared in more than one edition. The details are:

Class, Codes and Control, Volume 1: Theoretical Studies towards a Sociology of Language, London, Routledge & Kegan Paul, 1971.

Class, Codes and Control, Volume 1, revised paperback edition, St Albans, Paladin, 1973.

Class, Codes and Control, Volume 1, 2nd revised edition, London, Routledge & Kegan Paul, 1974.

Class, Codes and Control, Volume 2: Applied Studies towards a Sociology of Language, London, Routledge & Kegan Paul, 1973.

Class, Codes and Control, Volume 3: Towards a Theory of Educational Transmissions, London, Routledge & Kegan Paul, 1975.

Class, Codes and Control, Volume 3, 2nd revised edition, London, Routledge & Kegan Paul, 1977.

In the text I have referred to the original publication, and provided reference to the location in the *Class, Codes and Control* (*CCC*) volumes. In all cases reference is made to the latest edition. The key paper 'On the classification and framing of educational knowledge' is reprinted in both volume 1 and volume 3; I have provided page references to both sources.

Monographs in the series 'Primary Socialization, Language and Education', under the general editorship of Bernstein, are also listed. They report the empirical work undertaken by Bernstein and his colleagues in the Sociological Research Unit.

A selective, annotated bibliography of work relating to Bernstein will be made available as a working paper of the Social Research Unit, University College, Cardiff. The preparation of that resource has been made possible by the award of a personal grant from the British Academy.

Bernstein's publications

1958 'Some sociological determinants of perception', *British Journal of Sociology*, 9, (1), 159–74.
In *Class, Codes and Control*, 1, 23–41.

1959a 'A public language: some sociological implications of a linguistic form', *British Journal of Sociology*, 10, (4), 311–26.
In *Class, Codes and Control*, 1, 42–60.

1959b 'Soziokulturelle Determinanten des Lernens', *Koelner Zeitschrift für Soziologie und Sozial Psychologie*, 4, (1), 52–79. (Special issue, edited by P. Heintz, on the Sociology of the School.)

1960a 'Language and social class', *British Journal of Sociology*, 11, (3), 271–6.
In *Class, Codes and Control*, 1, 61–7.

1960b 'A review of *The Lore and Language of Schoolchildren*, by I. Opie, and P. Opie', *British Journal of Sociology*, 11, (2), 178–81.
In *Class, Codes and Control*, 1, 71–5.

1961a 'Aspects of language and learning in the genesis of the social process', *Journal of Child Psychology and Psychiatry*, 1, (4), 313–24.
In D. Hymes (ed.) *Language in Culture and Society: A Reader in Linguistics and Anthropology*, New York, Harper & Row, 1964.

1961b 'Social structure, language and learning', *Educational Research*, 3, (3), 163–76.
In J. P. de Cecco (ed.) *The Psychology of Language, Thought and Instruction*, New York, Holt, Rinehart & Winston, 1967.
In A. H. Passow, M. Goldberg and A. J. Tannenbaum (eds) *Education of the Disadvantaged*, New York, Holt, Rinehart & Winston, 1967.

1961c 'Social class and linguistic development: a theory of social learning', in A. H. Halsey, J. Floud and C. A. Anderson (eds) *Education, Economy and Society*, London, Collier-Macmillan.

1962a 'Linguistic codes, hesitation phenomena and intelligence', *Language and Speech*, 5, (1), 31–46.
In *Class, Codes and Control*, 1, 76–94.

1962b 'Social class, linguistic codes and grammatical elements', *Language and Speech*, 5, (4), 221–40.
In *Class, Codes and Control*, 1, 95–117.

1964a 'Elaborated and restricted codes: their social origins and some consequences', in J. J. Gumperz and D. Hymes (eds) *The Ethnography of Communication, American Anthropologist*, 66, (6), part 2, special issue, 55–69.

1964b 'Social class, speech systems and psychotherapy', *British Journal of Sociology*, 15, (1), 54–64.

1965 'A socio-linguistic approach to social learning', in J. Gould (ed.) *Penguin Survey of the Social Sciences*, Harmondsworth, Penguin.
In *Class, Codes and Control*, 1, 118–39.

1966a 'Sources of consensus and disaffection in education', *Journal of the Association of Assistant Mistresses*, 17, (1), 4–11.
In *Class, Codes and Control*, 3, 37–53.

1966b 'The role of speech in the development and transmission of culture', lecture delivered to the Bank Street Fiftieth Anniversary Symposium.
In G. L. Klopf and W. A. Holman (eds) *Perspectives on Learning*, New York, Mental Health Materials Center, Inc., 1967.

1967a 'Open schools – open society?', *New Society*, 14 September, 351–3.
In *Class, Codes and Control*, 3, 67–75.

1967b 'Elaborated and restricted codes: an outline', in S. Lieberson (ed.) *Explorations in Sociolinguistics*, special issue of *Sociological Inquiry*, 36, (2), 254–61.
In *International Journal of American Linguists*, 33, (2), 126–33.

1970a 'A critique of the concept of compensatory education', in D. Rubinstein and C. Stoneman (eds) *Education for Democracy*, Harmondsworth, Penguin.
In C. B. Cazden, V. P. John and D. Hymes (eds) *Functions of Language in the Classroom*, New York, Teachers College Press, 1972.
In *Class, Codes and Control*, 1, 190–201.

1970b 'Education cannot compensate for society', *New Society*, 26 February, 344–7.
In Open University Reader, *School and Society*, London, Routledge & Kegan Paul, 1971.
In Open University Reader, *Language in Education*, London, Routledge & Kegan Paul, 1972.
In J. Raynor and H. Harden (eds) *Equality and City Schools: Readings in Urban Education*, 2, London, Routledge & Kegan Paul, 1973.

1971a 'A socio-linguistic approach to socialization: with some reference to educability', in D. Hymes and J. Gumperz (eds) *Directions in Sociolinguistics*, New York, Holt, Rinehart & Winston, 1972.
In *Class, Codes and Control*, 1, 143–69.
1971b 'On the classification and framing of educational knowledge', in M. F. D. Young (ed.) *Knowledge and Control*, London, Collier-Macmillan.
In *Class, Codes and Control*, 1, 202–30.
In *Class, Codes and Control*, 3, 85–115.
In E. Hopper (ed.) *Readings in the Theory of Educational Systems*, London, Hutchinson, 1971.
In R. Brown (ed.) *Knowledge, Education and Cultural Change*, London, Tavistock, 1973.
1971c 'Social class, language and socialization', in S. A. Abramson *et al.* (eds) *Current Trends in Linguistics*, 12, Amsterdam, Mouton.
In *Class, Codes and Control*, 1, 170–89.
In Open University Reader, *Language in Education*, London, Routledge & Kegan Paul, 1972.
In P. P. Giglioli (ed.) *Language and Social Context*, Harmondsworth, Penguin.
In J. Karabel and A. H. Halsey (eds) *Power and Ideology in Education*, New York, Oxford University Press, 1977.
1972 'The sociology of education: a brief account', The Open University, Unit 17 of School and Society, Milton Keynes, The Open University, 95–109.
In *Class, Codes and Control*, 3, 157–73.
1973a 'Class and pedagogies: visible and invisible', Paris, OECD.
In *Educational Studies*, 1, (1), 1975, 23–41.
In *Class, Codes and Control*, 3, 116–56. (Revised version.)
In J. Karabel and A. H. Halsey (eds) *Power and Ideology in Education*, New York, Oxford University Press, 1977. (Revised version.)
1973b 'A brief account of the theory of codes', Open University course, Language and Learning, Block 3, Milton Keynes, The Open University.
In *Class, Codes and Control*, 1, 237–57 (incorporated as 'Postscript').
1974a 'Introduction', *Class, Codes and Control*, 1, 2nd edn.
1974b 'Sociology and the sociology of education: a brief account', in J. Rex (ed.) *Approaches to Sociology: An Introduction to Major Trends in British Sociology*, London, Routledge & Kegan Paul.
1975 'On the curriculum', *Class, Codes and Control*, 3, 174–84.
1977a 'Introduction', *Class, Codes and Control*, 3, 2nd edn.
1977b 'Aspects of the relations between education and production', *Class, Codes and Control*, 3, 174–200.

1981 'Codes, modalities and the process of cultural reproduction – a model', *Language in Society*, 10, (3), 327–63.
In M. Apple (ed.) *Social and Cultural Reproduction*, London, Routledge & Kegan Paul.
(These are revised versions of *Pedagogical Bulletin*, no. 7, Department of Education, University of Lund, Sweden, 1980.)

1985 'On pedagogic discourse', in J. Richardson (ed.) *Handbook of Theory and Research in the Sociology of Education*, Westport, Conn., Greenwood Press.

Jointly authored

1965 —— and J. Cook, 'Coding grid: theory and operation' and 'Patterns of maternal and child control', chs 2 and 5 in J. Cook-Gumperz, *Social Control and Socialization*, London, Routledge & Kegan Paul, 1973.

1966 ——, J. Elvin and R. Peters, 'Ritual in education', *Philosophical Transactions of the Royal Society*, series B, 251, (772).
In *Class, Codes and Control*, 3, 54–66.

1967 —— and D. Young, 'Social class differences in conceptions of the uses of toys', *Sociology*, 1, (2), pp. 131–40.
In *Class, Codes and Control*, 2, 13–23.

1969 —— and B. Davies, 'Some sociological comments on Plowden', in R. S. Peters (ed.) *Perspectives on Plowden*, London, Routledge & Kegan Paul.

1969 —— and D. Henderson, 'Social class differences in the relevance of language to socialization', *Sociology*, 3, (1), 1–20.

1970 —— and W. Brandis, 'Social class differences in communication and control', in W. Brandis and D. Henderson, *Social Class, Language and Communication*, London, Routledge & Kegan Paul.

1984 (with M. Diaz) 'Towards a theory of pedagogic discourse', *Collected Original Reports in Education* (microfiche), 8, (3).

Monographs in the SRU 'Primary Socialization, Language and Education' series (all published by Routledge & Kegan Paul).

D. S. Adlam (with the assistance of G. Turner and L. Lineker) (1977) *Code in Context*.

W. Brandis and B. Bernstein (1974) *Selection and Control*.

W. Brandis and D. Henderson (1970) *Social Class, Language and Communication*.

J. Cook-Gumperz (1973) *Social Control and Socialization*.

D. M. Gahagan and G. A. Gahagan (1970) *Talk Reform*.

P. R. Hawkins (1977) *Social Class, the Nominal Group and Verbal Strategies.*
W. P. Robinson and S. D. A. Rackstraw (1972) *A. Question of Answers* (2 vols).
G. J. Turner and B. A. Mohan (1970) *A Linguistic Description and Computer Program for Children's Speech.*

General bibliography

Acker, S. (1981) 'No-woman's-land: British sociology of education 1960–1976', *Sociological Review*, 29, (1), 77–104.

Adlam, D. (1977) 'Introduction', in D. Adlam, *Code in Context*, London, Routledge & Kegan Paul.

—— and G. J. Turner (1977) 'Code in context' in D. Adlam, *Code in Context*, London, Routledge & Kegan Paul.

Allan, G. (1977) 'Class variation in friendship patterns', *British Journal of Sociology*, 28, (3), 389–93.

Anderson, P. (1969) 'Components of the national culture', in R. Blackburn and A. Cockburn (eds) *Student Power*, Harmondsworth, Penguin.

Apple, M. (1981) 'The other side of the hidden curriculum: correspondence theories and the labor process', *Interchange*, 11, (3), 5–22.

Ardener, E. (1971) 'Introduction: social anthropology and language', in E. Ardener (ed.) *Social Anthropology and Language*, London, Tavistock.

Ardener, S. (ed.) (1975) *Perceiving Women*, London, Malaby.

Armstrong, D. (1980) 'Health care and the structure of medical education', in H. Noack (ed.) *Medical Education and Primary Health Care*, London, Croom Helm.

Atkinson, M., D. Kilby and I. Roca (1982) *Foundations of General Linguistics*, London, George Allen & Unwin.

Atkinson, P. (1977) 'Professional segmentation and students' experience in a Scottish medical school', *Scottish Journal of Sociology*, 2, (1), 71–85.

—— (1981a) 'Bernstein's structuralism', *Educational Analysis*, 3, (1), 85–96.

—— (1981b) *The Clinical Experience: The Construction and Reconstruction of Medical Reality*, Farnborough, Gower.

—— (1983) 'The reproduction of the professional community', in R. Dingwall and P. Lewis (eds) *The Sociology of the Professions: Doctors, Lawyers and Others*, London, Macmillan.

—— and S. Delamont (1977) 'Mock-ups and cock-ups: the stage-management of guided discovery instruction', in P. Woods and M. Hammersley (eds) *School Experience*, London, Croom Helm.

Barnes, D. (1971) 'Bernstein in the classroom', *Times Educational Supplement*, 19 November, 4.

Barthes, R. (1967) *Elements of Semiology*, London, Cape.

Bateson, G. (1972) *Steps to an Ecology of Mind*, New York, Ballantine.

Belsey, C. (1982) 'Re-reading the great tradition', in P. Widdowson (ed.) *Re-Reading English*, London, Methuen.

Bereiter, C. and S. Engelmann (1966) *Teaching Disadvantaged Children in the Preschool*, Englewood Cliffs, NJ, Prentice-Hall.

Berger, P. and T. Luckmann (1967) *The Social Construction of Reality*, London, Allen Lane.

Bernbaum, G. (1977) *Knowledge and Ideology in the Sociology of Education*, London, Macmillan.

Bertram, H. (1977) 'Social structure and intelligence: old topic, new response', *Koelner Zeitschrift für Soziologie und Sozial Psychologie*, 29, (3), 461–86.

Bisseret, N. (1975) 'Social class and language: beyond privilege/handicap problematics', *Homme et la Société*, 37, (3), 247–70.

—— (1979) *Education, Class Language and Ideology*, London, Routledge & Kegan Paul.

Bloor, D. (1982) 'Polyhedra and the abominations of Leviticus: cognitive styles in mathematics', in M. Douglas (ed.) *Essays in the Sociology of Perception*, London, Routledge & Kegan Paul.

Bokszanski, Z. (1978) 'The personal barriers of cultural growth and the educational systems', paper presented at the 9th World Congress of Sociology, Uppsala.

Borzym, I. (1981) 'The family value system and scholastic achievement of school-children differing in ability level', *Polish Psychological Bulletin*, 12, (4), 201–11.

Bourdieu, P. (1973) 'Cultural reproduction and social reproduction', in R. Brown (ed.) *Knowledge, Education and Cultural Change*, London, Tavistock.

—— (1974) 'The school as a conservative force: scholastic and cultural inequalities', in J. Eggleston (ed.) *Contemporary Research in the Sociology of Education*, London, Methuen.

—— (1975) 'The specificity of the scientific field and the social conditions of the progress of reason', *Social Science Information*, 14, (5), 19–47.

—— and J-C. Passeron (1977) *Reproduction in Education, Society and Culture*, London, Sage.

—— and —— (1979) *The Inheritors: French Students and their Relation to Culture*, Chicago, University of Chicago Press.

Bowles, S. and H. Gintis (1976) *Schooling in Capitalist America*, London, Routledge & Kegan Paul.

Broughton, J. M. (1981a) 'Piaget's structural developmental-psychology 4: knowledge without a self and without history', *Human Development*, 24, (5), 320–46.

—— (1981b) 'Piaget's structural developmental-psychology 5: ideology-critique and the possibility of a critical developmental theory', *Human Development*, 24, (6), 382–411.

Brown, R. and A. Gilman (1960) 'The pronouns of solidarity and power' in T. Sebeok (ed.) *Style in Language*, Cambridge, Mass., MIT Press.

Browne, K. (1981) 'Schooling, capitalism and the mental–manual division of labour', *Sociological Review*, 29, (3), 445–73.

Brunner, J. J. (1978) 'The experiences of social control', *Revista Mexicana de Sociologia*, 40, additional number, 233–51.

Burns, T. and G. M. Stalker (1961) *The Management of Innovation*, London, Tavistock.

Buswell, C. (1980) 'Pedagogic change and social change', *British Journal of Sociology of Education*, 1, (3), 293–306.

Cais, J. (1982) 'Cultural heritage, socialization and verbal behavior: formal and informal speech of middle- and lower-class Israeli girls', paper presented at the 10th World Congress of Sociology, Mexico City.

Cazden, C. B. (1970) 'The situation: a neglected source of social class differences in language use', *Journal of Social Issues*, 26, (2), 35–60.

Cecco, J. P. de (ed.) (1967) *The Psychology of Language, Thought and Instruction*, New York, Holt, Rinehart & Winston.

Cherkaoui, M. (1974) 'Class structure, linguistic performance and types of socialization: Bernstein and his school', *Revue Française de Sociologie*, 15, (4), 585–99.

—— (1977) 'Basil Bernstein and Emile Durkheim: two theories of change in educational systems', *Harvard Educational Review*, 47, (4), 556–64.

—— (1978) 'Social systems and educational learning: political stakes in the distribution of knowledge according to Durkheim', *Revue Française de Science Politique*, 28, (2), 313–48.

Coates, R., H. Rosen and C. Sanders (1982) 'Language for life', University of Sussex Education Area, Occasional Paper (10).

Cohen, G. (1981) 'Culture and educational achievement', *Harvard Educational Review*, 51, (2), 270–85.

Colditz, G. A. and M. Sheehan (1982) 'The impact of instructional style on the development of professional characteristics', *Medical Education*, 16, (2), 127–32.

Cook-Gumperz, J. (1973) *Social Control and Socialization*, London, Routledge & Kegan Paul.

Cooper, B. (1976) 'Bernstein's codes: a classroom study', University of Sussex Education Area, Occasional Paper (6).

Cooper, D. E. (1984) 'Labov, Larry and Charles', *Oxford Review of Education*, 10, (2), 177–92.

Corner, J. (1980) 'Codes and cultural analysis', *Media, Culture and Society*, 2, (1), 73–86.

Coulthard, M. (1969) 'A discussion of restricted and elaborated codes', *Educational Review*, 22, 38–50.

Cox Donoso, C. (1984) 'Continuity, conflict and change in state education in Chile: a study of pedagogic projects of the Christian Democrat and Popular Unity Parties', unpublished PhD Thesis, University of London Institute of Education.

Creber, P. (1972) *Lost for Words*, Harmondsworth, Penguin.

Culler, J. (1975) *Structuralist Poetics*, London, Routledge & Kegan Paul.

—— (1976) *Saussure*, London, Fontana.

David, M. (1978) 'The family-education couple: towards an analysis of the William Tyndale dispute', in G. Littlejohn, B. Smart, J. Wakeford and N. Yuval-Davis (eds) *Power and the State*, London, Croom Helm.

Davies, B. (1976) *Social Control and Education*, London, Methuen.

Davies, C. (1980) 'Curriculum structures and institutions: the case of nursing in Britain and the USA', paper presented to the BSA Medical Sociology Group annual conference, University of Warwick.

Dearden, R. F., P. Hirst and R. S. Peters (eds) (1972) *Education and the Development of Reason*, London, Routledge & Kegan Paul.

Delamont, S. (1976) 'The girls most likely to: cultural reproduction and Scottish elites', *Scottish Journal of Sociology*, 1, (1), 29–43.

—— (1983) *Interaction in the Classroom*, 2nd edn, London, Methuen.

—— (1984) 'Debs, dollies, swots and weeds', in G. Walford (ed.) *British Public Schools: Policy and Practice*, Lewes, Falmer.

Dennis, N., F. Henriques and C. Slaughter (1956) *Coal is Our Life*, London, Eyre & Spottiswoode.

Derrida, J. (1973) 'Difference', in *Speech and Phenomena and Other Essays on Husserl's Theory of Signs*, Evanston, Ill., Northwestern University Press.

Diaz, M. (1983) 'A model of pedagogic discourse with special application to the Colombian primary level of education', unpublished Ph.D. Thesis, University of London Institute of Education.

Dickinson, H. and M. Erben (1983) 'The "technicisation" of morality and culture: a consideration of the work of Claude Grignon and its relevance to further education in Britain', in D. Gleeson (ed.) *Youth Training and the Search for Work*, London, Routledge & Kegan Paul.

—— and —— (1984) '"Moral positioning" and occupational socialization in the training of hairdressers, secretaries and caterers', *Journal of Moral Education*, 13, (1), 49–55.

Dimaggio, P. (1982a) 'Cultural entrepreneurship in 19th century Boston: the creation of an organizational base for high culture in America', *Media, Culture and Society*, 4, (1), 33–50.

—— (1982b) 'Cultural entrepreneurship in 19th century Boston 2: the classification and framing of American art', *Media, Culture and Society*, 4, (4), 303–22.

—— and M. Useem (1978) 'Cultural property and public policy: emerging tensions in government support for arts', *Social Research*, 45, (2), 356–89.

Dittmar, N. (1976) *Sociolinguistics: A Critical Survey of Theory and Application*, London, Edward Arnold.

Douglas, M. (1966) *Purity and Danger*, London, Routledge & Kegan Paul.

—— (1968) 'Pollution', *International Encyclopedia of the Social Sciences*, XII, 336–41, New York, Crowell Collier & Macmillan Inc.

—— (1970) *Natural Symbols*, London, Barrie & Rockiff.

—— (1978) 'Cultural bias', London, Royal Anthropological Institute Occasional Paper (35).

—— (1981) 'Good taste: review of Pierre Bourdieu, *La Distinction*', *Times Literary Supplement*, 13 February, 163–69.

—— (ed.) (1982) *Essays in the Sociology of Perception*, London, Routledge and Kegan Paul.

Dundes, A. J. Leach and B. Özkök (1972) 'The strategy of Turkish boys' verbal dueling', in J. Gumperz and D. Hymes (eds) *Directions in Sociolinguistics: The Ethnography of Communication*, New York, Holt, Rinehart & Winston.

Durkheim, E. and M. Mauss (1963) *Primitive Classification*, London, Cohen & West.

Easthope, G. (1976) 'Religious war in Northern Ireland', *Sociology*, 10, (3), 427–50.

Ebel, H. (1972) 'The situation of educational sociology in the Federal Republic of Germany', *International Review of Education*, 18, (1), 108–12.

Edge, D. O. (1973) 'Technological metaphor', in D. O. Edge and J. N. Wolfe (eds) *Meaning and Control: Essays in Social Aspects of Science and Technology*, London, Tavistock.

Edwards, A. D. (1976a) 'Speech codes and speech variants: social class and task differences in children's speech', *Journal of Child Language*, 3, (1), 247–65.

—— (1976b) *Language in Culture and Class,* London, Heinemann.

—— (1980) 'Perspectives on classroom language', *Educational Analysis*, 2, (2), 31–46.

—— (1981) 'Analysing classroom talk', in P. French and M. Maclure (eds) *Adult–Child Conversation*, London, Croom Helm.

—— and V. J. Furlong (1978) *The Language of Teaching*, London, Heinemann.

Elchardus, M. (1981) 'Class structuration and achievement', *Sociological Review*, 29, (3), 413–44.

Eldridge, J. (1980) *Recent British Sociology*, London, Macmillan.

Erben, M. and H. Dickinson (1981) 'Aspects of technical education in France: a consideration of the work of Claude Grignon and its relevance in further education in Britain', *Proceedings of the Standing Conference on the Sociology of Further Education*, Coombe Lodge, Blagdon.

Esperet, B. (1976) 'Language, environment and intelligence: concepts developed by Bernstein, B.', *Bulletin de Psychologie*, 29, (1–3), 10–35.

Evans, G. T. and M. E. Poole (1975) 'Relationships between verbal and nonverbal abilities for migrant children and Australian children of low socio-economic status – similarities and contrasts', *Australian Journal of Education*, 19, (3), 209–30.

Faris, R. E. (1970) *Chicago Sociology 1920–1932*, Chicago, University of Chicago Press.

Fermor, P. L. (1958) *Mani: Travels in the Peloponnese*, London, John Murray.

Firth, J. R. (1934) 'Linguistics and the functional point of view', *English Studies*, 16, (1), 18–24.

Fleck, L. (1979) *Genesis and Development of a Scientific Fact*, Chicago, University of Chicago Press.

Foucault, M. (1967) *Madness and Civilization*, London, Tavistock.

—— (1971) *L'Ordre du Discours*, Paris, Gallimard.

—— (1972) *The Archaeology of Knowledge*, London, Tavistock.

—— (1973) *The Birth of the Clinic*, London, Tavistock.

Fowler, R. (1977) *Linguistics and the Novel*, London, Methuen.

Frake, C. (1977) 'Plying frames can be dangerous; some reflections on methodology in cognitive anthropology', *Quarterly Newsletter of the Institute for Comparative Human Cognition*, (1), 1–7.

Fries, C. C. (1940) *American English Grammar*, New York, Appleton-Century-Crofts.

Gardner, H. (1976) *The Quest for Mind: Piaget, Lévi-Strauss and the Structuralist Movement*, London, Quartet Books.

Garfinkel, H. (1967) *Studies in Ethnomethodology*, Engelwood Cliffs, NJ, Prentice-Hall.

Gibson, R. (1984) *Structuralism and Education*, London, Hodder & Stoughton.

Giddens, A. (1980) *The Class Structure of the Advanced Societies*, 2nd edn, London, Hutchinson.

Gilmore, P. (1981) 'Spelling "Mississippi": recontextualizing a literacy-related speech event', paper presented at the Second Annual University of Pennsylvania Ethnography in Education Research Forum, Philadelphia.

Giroux, H. (1981) 'Hegemony, resistance, and the paradox of educational reform', *Interchange*, 12, (2–3), 3–26.

Gleeson, D. (1978) 'Curriculum development and social change: towards a reappraisal of teacher action', *Journal of Further and Higher Education*, 2, (1), 41–51.

Goffman, E. (1951) 'Symbols of class status', *British Journal of Sociology*, 2, (4), 294–304.

—— (1974) *Frame Analysis*, Harmondsworth, Penguin.

Goldthorpe, J. H. and P. Bevan (1977) 'The study of social stratification in Great Britain, 1946–1976', *Social Science Information*, 16, (3–4), 279–334.

Gonos, G. (1977) ' "Situation" versus "frame": the "interactionist" and the "structuralist" analyses of everyday life', *American Sociological Review*, 42, (6), 854–67.

Goodson, I. (1981) 'Becoming an academic subject – patterns of explanation and evolution', *British Journal of Sociology of Education*, 2, (2), 163–80.

—— (1983) 'Defining and defending the subject: geography versus environmental studies', in M. Hammersley and A. Hargreaves (eds) *Curriculum Practice: Some Sociological Case Studies*, Lewes, Falmer.

Gordon, J. C. B. (1976a) 'An examination of Bernstein's theory of restricted and elaborated codes', University of East Anglia Papers in Linguistics, (2), 1–21.

—— (1976b) 'Concepts of verbal deficit in Bernstein's writings on language and social class', *Nottingham Linguistic Circular*, 5, (2), 31–8.

—— (1977) 'Linguistics and the concept of verbal deficit', *Nottingham Linguistic Circular*, 6, (2), 51–9.

—— (1978a) 'Folk-linguistics and the essence of verbal deficit theories', University of East Anglia Papers in Linguistics, (7), 11–20.

—— (1978b) 'The reception of Bernstein's sociolinguistic theory among primary school teachers', University of East Anglia Papers in Linguistics, supplement no. 1.

—— (1981) *Verbal Deficit*, London, Croom Helm.

Grimshaw, A. D. (1976) 'Polity, class, school, and talk: the sociology of Basil Bernstein', *Theory and Society*, 3, (4), 553–72.

Grinberglewin, Z. (1979) 'Restricted verbal codes; an attempt at modification based on the production of alternatives and observation of solutions', *Arquivos Brasileiros de Psicologia*, (3), 121–60.

Gumperz, J. (1977) 'Sociocultural knowledge in conversational inference', in M. Savile-Troike (ed.) *Linguistics and Anthropology*, Georgetown University Round Table on Languages and Linguistics, Washington, DC, Georgetown University Press.

—— (1982) *Discourse Strategies*, Cambridge, Cambridge University Press.

Hagen, A. (1976) 'Sociolinguistics and native language instruction 2; some language pedagogy aspects', *Levende Talen*, 319, 347–63.

Halliday, M. A. K. (1973) *Explorations in the Functions of Language*, London, Edward Arnold.

—— (1975) *Learning How to Mean*, London, Edward Arnold.

—— (1978) *Language as Social Semiotic*, London, Edward Arnold.

Halsey, A. H. (1978) *Change in British Society*, Oxford, Clarendon Press.

—— (1982) 'Professionals and provincials: the British post-war sociologists', *European Journal of Sociology*, 23, (1), 150–75.

Hammersley, M. (1984) 'Some reflections upon the macro–micro problem in the sociology of education', *Sociological Review*, 32, (2), 316–24.

Hannerz, U. (1969) *Soulside: Inquiries into Ghetto Culture and Community*, New York, Columbia University Press.

Hanson, D. (1965) 'Personal and positional influences in informal groups', *Social Forces*, 44, (2), 202–10.

Harris, W. F. (1978) 'Government without newspapers', paper presented at the 9th World Congress of Sociology, Uppsala.

Harrison, J. (1971) 'Literature and the language really used by men', *College English*, 32, (6), 640–51.

Harrison, J. A., H. Strauss and R. Glaubman (1981) 'Who benefits from the open classroom: the interaction of social background with class setting', *Journal of Educational Research*, 75, (2), 87–94.

Hartig, M. (1977) 'Language barriers', *Linguistik und Didaktik*, 8, (32), 337–41.

Hasan, R. (1968) 'Grammatical cohesion in spoken and written English', part 1, Nuffield Programme in Linguistics and English Teaching, paper no. 7, London, Longmans.

Hawkes, T. (1977) *Structuralism and Semiotics*, London, Methuen.

Hawkins, P. (1969) 'Social class, the nominal group and reference', *Language and Speech*, 12, (2), 125–55. Reprinted in *CCC* 2 (1972).

—— (1977) *Social Class, the Nominal Group and Verbal Strategies*, London, Routledge & Kegan Paul.

Henson, H. (1974) *British Social Anthropologists and Language: A History of Separate Development*, Oxford, Clarendon Press.

Hess-Luttich, E. W. B. (1974) 'Language learning and social values: two concepts of linguistic socialization and their sociological implications', *The Incorporated Linguist*, 13, (4), 106–9.

Hickson, D. J. (1966–7) 'A convergence in organization theory', *Administrative Science Quarterly*, 11, (2), 224–37.

Hill, C. A. and H. Varenne (1981) 'Family language and education: the sociolinguistic model of restricted and elaborated codes', *Social Science Information*, 20, (1), 187–228.

Hirst, P. H. (1974) *Knowledge and the Curriculum*, London, Routledge & Kegan Paul.

Hodgeson, J. T. (1974) 'Changes in English teaching: institutionalization, transmission and ideology', unpublished PhD Thesis, University of London Institute of Education.

Hoggart, R. (1957) *The Uses of Literacy*, London, Chatto & Windus. (Paperback edn, 1958, Harmondsworth, Penguin.)

Holland, J. (1981) 'Social class and changes in orientation to meaning', *Sociology*, 15, (1), 1–18.

Holub, R. C. (1984) *Reception Theory*, London, Methuen.

Hymes, D. (1977) *Foundations of Sociolinguistics: An Ethnographic Approach*, London, Tavistock.

Jackson, B. (1968) *Working Class Community*, Harmondsworth, Penguin.

Jackson, L. A. (1974) 'The myth of elaborated and restricted code', *Higher Education Review*, 6, (2), 65–81.

Jacobsen, B. (1981) 'Collection type and integrated type curricula in systems of higher education: an empirical and theoretical study', *Acta Sociologica*, 24, (1–2), 25–41.

Johnston, K. (1978) 'Dangerous knowledge: a case study in the social control of knowledge', *Australian and New Zealand Journal of Sociology*, 14, (2), 104–12.

Kapferer, J. (1981) 'Socialization and the symbolic order of the school', *Anthropology and Education Quarterly*, 12, (4), 258–74.

Karabel, J. and A. H. Halsey (eds) (1977) *Power and Ideology in Education*, New York, Oxford University Press.

Keddie, N. (1971) 'Classroom knowledge', in M. F. D. Young (ed.) *Knowledge and Control*, London, Collier-Macmillan.

King, R. (1971) 'Unequal access in education – sex and social class', *Social and Economic Administration*, 5, (3), 167–74.

—— (1976) 'Bernstein's sociology of the school: some propositions tested', *British Journal of Sociology*, 27, (4), 430–43.

—— (1979) 'The search for the "invisible" pedagogy', *Sociology*, 13, (3), 445–58.

—— (1980) 'Weberian perspectives and the study of education', *British Journal of Sociology of Education*, 1, (1), 7–23.

—— (1981a) 'Bernstein's sociology of the school – a further testing', *British Journal of Sociology*, 32, (2), 259–65.

—— (1981b) 'Secondary schools: some changes of a decade', *Educational Research*, 23, (3), 173–6.

—— (1982) 'Organizational change in secondary schools: an action approach', *British Journal of Sociology of Education*, 3, (1), 3–18.

—— (1983) *The Sociology of School Organization*, London, Methuen.

Kirk, G. S. (1965) *Homer and the Epic*, Cambridge, Cambridge University Press.

Klann, G. (1975) *Aspects and Problems of the Linguistic Analysis of Language Usage Within Specific Social Levels*, Studies and Reports no. 31, Berlin, Max Planck Institute.

Klopf, G. J. and W. A. Hohman (eds) (1967) *Perspectives on Learning*, New York, Mental Health Materials Center, Inc.

Kloskowska, A. (1973) 'The cultural determination of attitudes', *Polish Sociological Bulletin*, 27–8, (1–2), 5–17.

Knorr-Cetina, K. and A. V. Cicourel (eds) (1981) *Advances in Social Theory and Methodology: Toward an Integration of Micro- and Macro-Sociologies*, London, Routledge & Kegan Paul.

Kochman, T. (ed.) (1972) *Rappin' and Stylin' Out: Communication in Urban Black America*, Urbana, Ill., University of Illinois Press.

Kristéva, J. (1980) *Desire in Language*, New York, Columbia University Press.

Kuhn, T. S. (1970) *The Structure of Scientific Revolutions*, 2nd edn, Chicago, University of Chicago Press.

—— (1982) 'The function of measurement in modern physical science', in B. Barnes and D. Edge (eds) *Science in Context*, Milton Keynes, Open University Press.

Kurzweil, E. (1980) *The Age of Structuralism: Levi-Strauss to Foucault*, New York, Columbia University Press.

Labov, W. (1966) *The Social Stratification of English in New York City*, Washington, D.C., Center for Applied Linguistics.

Labov, W. (1972a) 'The logic of nonstandard English', in P. P. Giglioli (ed.) *Language and Social Context*, Harmondsworth, Penguin.

—— (1972b) 'Rules for ritual insults', in D. Sudnow (ed.) *Studies in Social Interaction*, New York, Free Press.

—— (1978) 'Crossing the gulf between sociology and linguistics', *American Sociologist*, 13, (2), 93–103.

—— (1982) 'Competing value systems in the inner-city schools', in P. Gilmore and A. A. Glatthorn (eds) *Children In and Out of School: Ethnography and Education*, Washington, D.C., Center for Applied Linguistics.

—— and D. Fanshel (1977) *Therapeutic Discourse: Psychotherapy as Conversation*, New York, Academic Press.

Lacan, J. (1977a) *Ecrits*, London, Tavistock.

—— (1977b) *The Four Fundamental Concepts of Psychoanalysis*, Harmondsworth, Penguin.

Lawford, P. (1976) 'Conservative empiricism in literary theory: a scrutiny of the work of F. R. Leavis', part 1, *Red Letters*, (1), 12–15, part 2, *Red Letters*, (2), 9–11.

Lawton, D. (1968) *Social Class, Language and Education*, London, Routledge & Kegan Paul.

Leach, E. R. (1970) *Lévi-Strauss*, London, Fontana.

—— (1976) *Culture and Communication: The Logic by Which Symbols are Connected*, Cambridge, Cambridge University Press.

Leavis, F. R. (1962) *The Great Tradition*, Harmondsworth, Penguin.

Leitch, V. B. (1983) *Deconstructive Criticism: An Advanced Introduction*, London, Hutchinson.

Lemert, C. C. (ed.) (1981) *French Sociology: Rupture and Renewal Since 1968*, New York, Columbia University Press.

Levi-Strauss, C. (1961) *World on the Wane*, London, Hutchinson.

—— (1966) *The Savage Mind*, London, Weidenfeld & Nicolson.

Lineker, L. (1977) 'The instructional context', in D. Adlam, *Code in Context*, London, Routledge & Kegan Paul.

Lodge, D. (1977) *The Modes of Modern Writing*, London, Edward Arnold.

Lofland, L. (1975) 'The "thereness" of women; a selective review of urban sociology', in M. Millman and R. M. Kanter (eds) *Another Voice: Feminist Perspectives on Social Life and Social Science*, New York, Anchor Books.

Loizos, P. (1981) *The Heart Grown Bitter*, Cambridge, Cambridge University Press.

Lumby, M. E. (1976) 'Code-switching and sexual orientation: a test of Bernstein's sociolinguistic theory', *Journal of Homosexuality*, 1, (4), 383–99.

Lyons, J. (1968) *Introduction to Theoretical Linguistics*, Cambridge, Cambridge University Press.

MacCabe, C. (1981) 'On discourse', in C. MacCabe (ed.) *The Talking Cure*, London, Macmillan.

MacDonald, M. (1977) *The Curriculum and Cultural Reproduction*, Unit 18, Open University course E202, Schooling and Society, Milton Keynes, The Open University Press.

Macksey, R. and E. Donato (eds) (1972) *The Structuralist Controversy: The Languages of Criticism and the Sciences of Man*, Baltimore, Johns Hopkins University Press.

Malinowski, B. (1923) 'The problem of meaning in primitive languages', supplement to C. K. Ogden and A. I. Richards, *The Meaning of Meaning*, London, Kegan Paul, Trench, Trubner & Co.

Manning, P. K. (1980) 'Goffman's framing order: style as structure', in

J. Ditton (ed.) *The View from Goffman*, London, Macmillan.

—— (1982) 'Structuralism and the sociology of knowledge', *Knowledge – Creation, Diffusion, Utilization*, 4, (1), 51–72.

Marcellesi, C. (1976) 'Theoretical and methodological problems', *Langue Française*, 32, 8–28.

Marody, M. (1981) 'Language and commonsense knowledge in the explanation of human behaviour', *Polish Sociological Bulletin*, (1), 21–36.

Mead, G. H. (1934) *Mind, Self and Society*, Chicago, University of Chicago Press.

Mead, M. (1937) 'Public opinion mechanisms among primitive peoples', *Public Opinion Quarterly*, 1, 5–16.

Medlicott, P. (1975) 'Language and class', *New Society*, 5 June, 575–6.

Meltzer, J. D. (1978) 'A semiotic approach to suitability for psychotherapy', *Psychiatry*, 41, (4), 360–76.

Miller, D. L. (1973) *George Herbert Mead: Self, Language and the World*, Austin, University of Texas Press.

Moore, R. (1983) 'Education and production: a generative model', unpublished PhD Thesis, University of London Institute of Education.

Mulhern, F. (1979) *The Moment of Scrutiny*, London, New Left Books.

Nafstad, H. E. (1977) *Co-operation between parents, pre-school and the community: local communities and the social and educational value of pre-school*, Strasbourg, Council of Europe, Committee for General and Technical Education.

—— and R. M. Blakar (1975) 'Social class, language and compensatory education in preschool age', *Nordisk Psykologi*, 27, (3), 145–59.

Nakano, Y. (1974) 'Social class and language', *Journal of Educational Sociology* (Japan), 29, 146–60.

Ong, W. J. (1982) *Orality and Literacy: The Technologizing of the Word*, London, Methuen.

Opie, P. and I. Opie (1959) *The Lore and Language of Schoolchildren*, London, Oxford University Press.

Ostrander, D. (1982) 'One- and two-dimensional models of the distribution of beliefs', in M. Douglas (ed.) *Essays in the Sociology of Perception*, London, Routledge & Kegan Paul.

Pap, M. and C. Pleh (1972) 'Language and social class' *Szociologica*, (2), 211–34.

—— and —— (1974) 'Social class differences in the speech of six year old Hungarian children', *Sociology*, 8, (2), 267–75.

Parry, M. (1971) *The Making of Homeric Verse: The Collected Papers of Milman Parry*, ed. A. Parry, Oxford, Clarendon Press.

Parsons, G. (1979) 'Set books and static curricula', *Journal of Curriculum Studies*, 11, 338–40.

—— (1981) 'English literature, relevance and the "Great Tradition"', *Education for Development*, 6, (3), 31–41.

Pearce, J. J. (1972) 'Diversity in written English', in P. S. Doughty, J. J. Pearce and G. M. Thornton, *Exploring Language*, London, Edward Arnold.

Pêcheux, M. (1982) *Language, Semantics and Ideology: Stating the Obvious*, London, Macmillan.

Pedro, E. (1981) *Social Stratification and Classroom Discourse: A Sociolinguistic Analysis of Classrooms*, Stockholm, Gleerup.

Peleg, R. and C. Adler (1977) 'Compensatory education in Israel: conceptions, attitudes and trends', *American Psychologist*, 32, (11), 945–58.

Pfeiffer, H. (1982) 'On the connection between organization of knowledge and pedagogic organization in teaching processes', *Zeitschrift für Paedagogik*, 28, (4), 577–89.

Piaget, J. (1971) *Structuralism*, London, Routledge & Kegan Paul.

Poole, M. E. (1976) *Social Class and Language Utilization at the Tertiary Level*, Brisbane, University of Queensland Press.

—— (1977) 'Language', in F. J. Hunt (ed.) *Socialization in Australia*, Sydney, Angus & Robertson.

—— (1978a) 'Social class and sex contrasts in verbal processing styles', *British Journal of Educational Psychology*, 48, February, 47–61.

—— (1978b) 'Exploration of relationship inherent in linguistic, cognitive and verbal processing domains', *Psychological Reports*, 43, (2), 639–47.

—— (1979a) 'Social class and linguistic coding', *Language and Speech*, 22, (1), 49–67.

—— (1979b) 'Elaboration of linguistic code and verbal processing strategies – interdomain analyses', *Psychological Reports*, 45, (1), 283–96.

Punch, M. (1970) 'Who is the intellectual when he's at home?', *New Society*, 12 November, 859–62.

Quasthoff, U. (1975) 'Sociology plus linguistics do not equal sociolinguistics', *Linguistiche Berichte*, 37, June, 58–67.

Renault, M. (1978) *The Praise Singer*, London, John Murray.

Ricoeur, P. (1974) 'The question of the subject', in *The Conflict of Interpretations*, Evanston, Ill., Northwestern University Press.

Robinson, P. (1981) 'Whatever happened to educability?', *Educational Analysis*, 3, (1), 37–46.

Robinson, W. P. (1965) 'The elaborated code in working class language', *Language and Speech*, 8, (4), 243–52.

—— (1978) *Language Management in Education: The Australian Context*, Sydney, George Allen & Unwin.

Rock, P. (1979) *The Making of Symbolic Interactionism*, London, Macmillan.

. Rogers, S. (1976) 'The language of children and adolescents and the language of schooling', in S. Rogers (ed.) *They Don't Speak Our Language*, London, Edward Arnold.

Rosen, H. (1973) 'Language and class: a critical look at the theories of Basil Bernstein', Bristol, Falling Wall Press.

St John-Brooks, C. (1983) 'English: a curriculum for personal development?', in M. Hammersley and A. Hargreaves (eds) *Curriculum Practice: Some Sociological Case Studies*, Lewes, Falmer.

Sarup, M. (1983) *Marxism/Structuralism/Education*, Lewes, Falmer.

Saussure, F. de (1960) *Course in General Linguistics*, London, Peter Owen.

. Schatzman, L. and A. L. Strauss (1955) 'Social class and modes of communication', *American Journal of Sociology*, 60, (4), 329–38.

Schlumbohm, J. (1979) 'Street and family: collective and individualizing modes of socialization in the lower and upper bourgeoisie in Germany about 1800', *Zeitschrift für Paedogogik*, 5, 697–726.

Schmidt, R. W., H. Lamm and G. Trommsdorff (1978) 'Social class and sex as determinants of future orientation (time perspective) in adults', *European Journal of Social Psychology*, 8, (1), 71–90.

Schutz, A. (1972) *The Phenomenology of the Social World*, London, Heinemann.

Shapin, S. (1975) 'Phrenological knowledge and social structure of early 19th century Edinburgh', *Annals of Science*, 32, (3), 219–43.

—— and B. Barnes (1977) 'Science, nature and control: interpreting Mechanics' Institutes', *Social Studies of Science*, 7, (1), 31–74.

Sharp, R. and A. G. Green (1975) *Education and Social Control*, London, Routledge & Kegan Paul.

Shaw, C. F. and H. R. McKay (1942) *Juvenile Delinquency and Urban Areas*, Chicago, Ill., University of Chicago Behavioral Research Fund Monograph.

Sheridan, A. (1980) *Michel Foucault: The Will to Truth*, London, Tavistock.

Silverman, D. and B. Torode (1980) *The Material Word: Some Theories of Language and its Limits*, London, Routledge & Kegan Paul.

Simmonds, A. P. (1978) *Karl Mannheim's Sociology of Knowledge*, Oxford, Clarendon Press.

Simon, B. (1981) 'The primary school revolution: myth or reality?', in B. Simon and J. Willcocks (eds) *Research and Practice in the Primary Classroom*, London, Routledge & Kegan Paul.

Sleigh, H. (1975) 'Learning to paint: a case study of a school of fine art', unpublished Ph.D. Thesis, University of London.

Steedman, M. J. (1982) 'A generative grammar for jazz chord sequences', unpublished paper, Department of Psychology, University of Warwick.

Strachan, P. (1979) 'Literature as manipulation: towards a social application of literary studies', *British Journal of Aesthetics*, 19, (4), 342–51.

Strauss, A. L. (1978) 'A social world perspective', in N. K. Denzin (ed.) *Studies in Symbolic Interaction Volume I*, Greenwich, Conn., JAI Press.

Stubbs, M. (1983) *Language, Schools and Classrooms*, 2nd edn, London, Methuen.

Sturrock, J. (ed.) (1979) *Structuralism and Since*, London, Oxford University Press.

Tannen, D. (1979) 'What's in a frame? Surface evidence for underlying expectations', in R. O. Freedle (ed.) *New Directions in Discourse Processing*, Norwood, NJ, Ablex.

Thompson, K. (1982) *Emile Durkheim*, Chichester, Ellis Horwood, and London, Tavistock.

Thrasher, F. M. (1927) *The Gang*, Chicago, University of Chicago Press.

Tiryakian, E. A. (1978) 'Emile Durkheim', in T. Bottomore and R. Nisbet (eds) *A History of Sociological Analysis*, London, Heinemann.

Tough, J. (1977) *The Development of Meaning*, London, George Allen & Unwin.

Trudgill, P. (1975) *Accent, Dialect and the School*, London, Edward Arnold.

Turner, G. J. (1973) 'Social class and children's language of control at age five and age seven', in B. Bernstein (ed.) *Class, Codes and Control*, 2, London, Routledge & Kegan Paul.

Turner, R. H. (1961) 'Modes of social ascent through education: sponsored and contest mobility', in A. H. Halsey, J. Floud and C. A. Anderson (eds) *Education, Economy and Society*, London, Collier-Macmillan.

Tyler, W. B. (1984) 'Organizations, factors and codes: a methodological inquiry into Bernstein's theory of educational transmissions', unpublished Ph.D. Thesis, University of Kent.

Van den Broek, J. (1977) 'Class differences in syntactic complexity in the Flemish town of Maaseik', *Language in Society*, 6, (2), 149–81.

Van der Gucht, Cl-M. (1980) 'Cultural and linguistic segregation of pupils of dominated social classes in the school system and its psychological and emotional consequences', *Recherches Sociologiques*, 11, (2), 179–94.

Van Gennep, A. (1960) *The Rites of Passage*, London, Routledge & Kegan Paul.

Walker, M. (1983) 'Control and consciousness in the college', *British Educational Research Journal*, 9, (2), 129–40.

Warner, W. L., W. C. Bailey *et al.* (1944) *Democracy in Jonesville*, New York, Harper.

Webb, C. (1981) 'Classification and framing: a sociological analysis of task-centred nursing and the nursing process', *Journal of Advanced Nursing*, 6, (5), 369–76.

Weeks, D. R. (1973) 'Organization theory – some themes and distinctions', in G. Salaman and K. Thompson (eds) *People and Organizations*, London, Longman.

Weller, L. and S. Levi (1981) 'Social class, IQ, self-concept and teachers' evaluations in Israel', *Adolescence*, 16, (63), 569–76.

Whorf, B. L. (1956) *Language, Thought and Reality*, New York, Wiley.

Whyte, W. F. (1943) *Street Corner Society*, Chicago, University of Chicago Press.

Widdowson, J. (1976) 'The language of the child culture: pattern and tradition in language acquisition and socialization', in S. Rogers (ed.) *They Don't Speak Our Language*, London, Edward Arnold.

Wilde, C. B. (1982) 'Matter and spirit as natural symbols in 18th century British natural philosophy', *British Journal for the History of Science*, 15, (50), 99–131.

Williams, R. (1965) *The Long Revolution*, Harmondsworth, Penguin.

Willis, P. (1977) *Learning to Labour: How Working Class Kids Get Working Class Jobs*, Farnborough, Saxon House.

Winter, R. J. E. (1973) 'An account of an experiment concerning the Whorfian hypothesis, with an explanation and illustration of the use of a coding grid as a method of analysis', unpublished MA Thesis, University of London, Institute of Education.

Wirth, L. (1929) *Community Life and Social Policy*, Chicago, University of Chicago Press.

—— (1956) *The Ghetto*, Chicago, University of Chicago Press.

Young, G. M. (1982) 'The elaborated code: a new formulation within a functional framework', *Language and Speech*, 25, (1), 81–93.

—— (1983) 'A systemic model of the elaborated code', *Language and Speech*, 26, (2), 171–90.

Young, M. F. D. (ed.) (1971) *Knowledge and Control*, London, Collier-Macmillan.

Young, R. E. (1980) 'The controlling curriculum and the practical ideology of teachers', *Australian and New Zealand Journal of Sociology*, 16, (2), 62–70.

—— (1983) 'A school communication deficit hypothesis of educational disadvantage', *Australian Journal of Education*, 27, (1), 3–16.

Zijderfeld, A. C. (1979) *On Clichés: The Supersedure of Meaning by Function in Modernity*, London, Routledge & Kegan Paul.

Zorbaugh, W. H. (1944) *The Gold Coast and the Slum*, Chicago, University of Chicago Press.

Index